Understanding Business

Series Editor: Richard Barker

People and Decisions

Understanding Business
Series Editor: Richard Barker

Titles in the series:

Understanding Business

People and Decisions

Norman Worrall

 Longman

LONGMAN GROUP UK LIMITED
Longman House,
Burnt Mill, Harlow, Essex CM20 2JE, England
and Associated Companies throughout the world.

First published in 1980
Fifth impression 1988

Set in 10 on 12 Plantin (110)

Produced by Longman Group (FE) Ltd
Printed in Hong Kong

ISBN 0-582-35540-0

Contents

Acknowledgements

We are grateful to the following for permission to reproduce copyright material:

Michael Bewes for the item on Associated Brewers Ltd which appears in Chapter 7; British Association for Commercial and Industrial Education and the author for 'The Selection Interview – A Systematic Approach' from *Interviewing in Twenty-Six Steps* by John S. Gough; The Guardian for an article 'The Times Are Out Of Joint' by P. Brogan from *The Guardian*, 4th February, 1979; Management Today for an article 'The Tale of One Foreman' by P. Sills from *Management Today* March 1972; The author, Mr H. F. Nosebag, for his letter which appeared in *The Guardian*, August 1978; *Harvard Business Review* for Fig. 2.3, the exhibit from 'Who are your motivated workers' by M. Scott Myers (January–February 1964). Copyright © 1964 by the President and Fellows of Harvard College; all rights reserved; Addison-Wesley Publishing Company for Fig. 13.3, T. R. Sarbin 'Role theory' in Gardiner Lindzey *Handbook of Social Psychology* Volume I, Addison-Wesley, based on Sarbin and Hardyk 'Contributions to role-taking theory', 1953.

Introduction to the Series

This series produces a new approach to the teaching of business. It is suitable for young managers, students and academic sixth-formers. It has been developed over the last decade to give understanding of the nature and purpose of business activity, whilst also stimulating the minds of the more academically gifted members of society.

The material provides for an analytical understanding of people's problems and behaviour within organisations. The texts discuss the nature of problems, and explore concepts and principles which may be employed to aid their solution. Test materials have been selected from industrial and commercial organisations; from the private and public sector; from non-profit-making institutions. The material is as much to provide general understanding about industrial society and the workings of organisations, as it is to help those who are already engaged in their business or professional career.

The approach of decision-making has been used to draw together ideas, and produce significant elements of reality; the approach gives purpose and challenge to the reader. Any organisation is striving towards more or less closely defined objectives by deciding how to carry out, and control, its activities within constantly changing conditions. The programme looks carefully at these processes of decision-making; it provides the student with an understanding of their overall nature. Ideas from the four functional areas of human behaviour, quantitative data, accounting and the economic environment are drawn together within a decision-making framework; the approach is then applied to different areas of business activity, particularly to those of finance, marketing and production.

This series of eight books has been designed to meet the needs of students (and their lecturers/teachers) studying the business world. The up-to-date materials within each book provide many ideas and activities from which the teacher can choose. Lecturers on management courses may use the books to introduce analytical concepts to practitioners; tertiary management courses may use them as a first text and as a source of well-tried and up-to-date cases; BEC and 'A' Level students may use the books as complete courses.

To meet these different needs, each book in the series has been designed to stand either as a part of the whole, or complete in its own right.

All books have the same chapter format:

a chapter objective and synopsis so that the purpose and pattern are clear;

a factual/explanatory text with case examples where applicable;

a participative work section to provide materials for learning, application and discussion.

The participative sections are an integral part of the whole text and allow students to gain understanding by doing. They are usually divided into three parts. Firstly, some simple revision questions to enable the students to check their own basic understanding. Secondly, a series of exercises and case problems to test their application and to increase their knowledge of the area. Thirdly, a set of essay questions.

There is a teachers' booklet accompanying each student text which introduces the topic area, clarifies possible objectives, suggests approaches to the selected materials and adds additional ideas. The teachers' booklets also provide solutions, where appropriate, to the participative work sections.

The philosophy, approach and materials have been forged in discussion with businessmen, lecturers and teachers. Trial and error has refined much of the text and most of the participative work. The whole venture has been co-ordinated by the Cambridge Business Studies Project Trust. Initial work developed from a link between the Wolfson Foundation, Marlborough College and Shell International Ltd. Trustees for the Project include Professor John Dancy, Sir Michael Clapham and Sir Nicholas Goodison; much early guidance was also given by Professor Sir Austin Robinson.

The series can be used as the basis for an 'A' Level examination run by the Cambridge Local Examinations Syndicate and established in 1967. The examination syllabus and objectives are in line with the materials in these texts.

Richard Barker
Series Editor

Preface

Organisations do not make decisions, only the people within them. This book claims to be unusual in developing a dual perspective on the decision-making process – from the viewpoint of the individual and of the organisation.

The opening chapters are used to establish the nature of this individual, while the following chapters go on to show how he is the building block of increasingly larger structures from work groups to organisations. The remaining chapters focus more explicitly on the dynamics of decision-making in both individuals and in groups. It is not necessary to read the chapters in the written order, except that Chapter 1 is desirable pre-reading for some later in the book. In addition to the usual synopsis at the start of each chapter, the first diagram illustrates the plan of the chapter and readers should find it helpful to study this before reading the text.

I have tried to engage the reader's interest regardless of whether the person is a sixth-former, a diploma or certificate student, or an undergraduate. Problems of exposition concerned me for some time, but pleasure followed the pain. I hope some of this pleasure is communicated to the reader. To give one example of a problem, the world of business and management is nowadays increasingly as much a female as a male domain. Yet to hedge every gender word in the form of him/her, himself/herself and so on is ruinous of style and not at all helpful to the reader. Accordingly, 'him' and suchlike words are to be regarded as generic and not interpreted in the rather dated sense of 'only males'.

Apart from supplying me with much raw material to work on, Richard Barker has been a constant support throughout the whole operation, encouraging or cajoling as appropriate. Rita Anderson introduced me to the project and was very helpful in the early stages. Finally, a grateful salute to my family, Chrysoula, Adrian and Alexis whom I now see more often.

Norman Worrall
Institute of Education
University of London

Chapter 1

The Decision-Making Environment

Synopsis: *The opening section is concerned with catching the flavour of the range of decisions encountered in our daily lives, as well as raising one or two questions that make us stop and think what a decision really is. The second section introduces a general decision model that will be used throughout the rest of the book: only an outline is given since it is the purpose of subsequent chapters to develop the basic model. The decision maker is viewed essentially as a 'human processor' whose limitations are determined by a combination of his own psychological make-up and by factors operating in the world outside. In the final section, we emphasise that the decision environment is one of change: decisions evolve over time, the constraints that operate vary with time, and the very significance of a decision is affected by whether one is involved in it now or viewing it as something in the past or in the future.*

Plan of the chapter: *This is illustrated in Fig. 1.1.*

1.1 Decisions Great and Small

In a single day any ordinary person may decide to skip breakfast, to leave the car and take the train, to bring some work home, to shave or not to shave – indeed any number of low-level, simple, even trivial decisions which he hardly pauses to think about. Most of the unmemorable aspects of our daily lives are brought into being by such simple decisions. They get us up in the morning, from home to work and through the evening into bed, in pretty much the same way as we started. We can characterise them as simple or low-level because: (a) the outcomes (e.g. going by train rather than by car) of our choices are unlikely to have any serious bearing on the subsequent

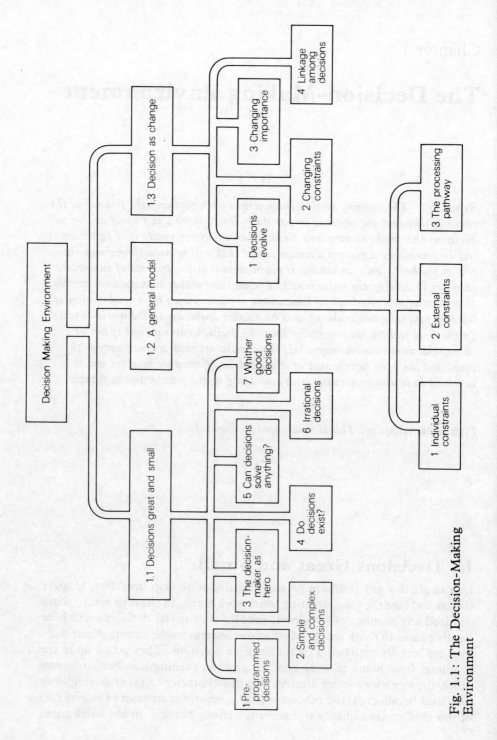

Fig. 1.1: The Decision-Making Environment

lives of ourselves or anybody else; (b) the range of choices for practical purposes is small – either tea or coffee; the green dress or the black one; going to the cinema or watching television; (c) there is little or no **risk** associated with the decision – if you ask for tea in the restaurant you know you will get it, and even if by some fluke you do not it will hardly be a personal disaster; (d) you have ample information to make a 'best' choice, i.e. you know what you want, what is available, and you choose accordingly (e.g. from a restaurant menu).

However, embedded in this humdrum complex of low-order decision making which recurs day in day out there are for most people a number of events far more worthy of the name 'decision'. Deciding whether to go to see the doctor, where to invest a sum of money, whether to get married, what to do about a difficult work situation. These are examples of decision situations where several choices *are* possible, where there *is* uncertainty associated with any choice, where all the information may not be available, and where the fortunes of others beside yourself may be significantly affected by the outcome.

Very important people are faced with decision situations which would alarm ordinary mortals. Should I close the factory? Should I dismiss the ambassador? Should I raise the bank rate? Should I declare war ... ? Of course the sheer range of these examples approaches the absurd, but strictly they all represent cases of a person being faced with two or more possible choices and opting for one of them. In this book we shall generally steer away from the trivial end of the decision-making continuum and focus on situations where real issues are involved. We will discover that real decision making is distinctly lacking in the neat and tidy. However, most of the people pull through for most of the time, even though this can be put down to the happy failings of the competition or a lucky turn of events as often as to their own skills.

1.1.1 **Pre-programmed Decisions**

a. Reflexes

Reflex actions such as putting up a hand to protect the face are automatic and require no thinking. Such reflex 'decisions' are pre-programmed before we are even born. If fact it would seem odd to say that because a man was falling over he 'decided' to throw out his hands to steady himself. Protective behaviours such as this are built into our repertoire without any need for thinking or making decisions at the time they are needed.

b. Habits

Another case of decisions being ready programmed can be found in personal habits. It may be our habit to take cereal for breakfast, to walk home through the park, always to go for the same seat on the bus or train, and so on. In such cases, decisions made once or twice in the past had satisfactory outcomes and are simply repeated. Such habits release us from the exhausting prospect of having to make a decision before we ever move a finger or utter a word. In so doing they also release us from humdrum routine, allowing us to concentrate on the more interesting aspects of daily life. It is when habits are applied to major decisions that they can be dangerous, since decision environments change even though habits may not. One of the reasons why change is so painful to many people (changing one's job or even, for example, going on holiday to a different country) is that hundreds of comfortably established habits are immediately transformed into new decisions that have to be taken.

c. Skills

Skills such as reading a book or driving a car *are* characterised in the early stages by a series of difficult decisions about what to do now, or next. But once we are well practised, whether in technical skills such as typing or in social skills such as meeting people or chatting at parties, there is no conscious deciding about anything – we just do it automatically. The early stages of learning a skill are, as it were, 'writing a programme' which is modified ('debugged') by later testing and is eventually executed fluently. In a real sense, the deciding has already been done long ago, and different 'subroutines' have been prepared to handle eventualities that may arise. Thus highly skilled behaviour can be regarded as being pre-programmed so as to minimise the need for on-the-spot decision making.

1.1.2 Simple and Complex Decisions

A distinction between trivial and significant (or simple and complex) decision making can be misleading. In particular we can make the mistake of thinking certain decisions are simple when they are not at all. Take the example of choosing a holiday: let us say you turn through the brochure and informally work out some list of priorities such as good food/private bath/close to sea/ some nightlife, and so on, and make your choice accordingly. But how often are you surprised or disappointed when you actually get to your hotel? One major reason is that holiday brochures are notoriously distorted sources of information. Even if they were not, it would be impossible to answer the question, 'Will *I* like the Hotel Esplanade?' with certainty until you are there. This is because the brochure is unlikely to have told you to watch out for the grumpy waiter on the table near the window (incomplete information) and even if it had done, the new restaurant manager could well have sorted out things by the time you got there (out-of-date information). Usually in holiday planning we accept that some **uncertainty** concerning hotels is unavoidable, or that a high risk of bad weather is acceptable if low-season fares are attractive. In other words, we generally operate *as though* decisions were relatively simple, and this allows us to get by most of the time. Certainly, if we were to worry about all the catastrophes that might befall us we would hardly be able to decide anything at all.

1.1.3 **The Decision Maker as Hero**

There is a romantic view of the top 'decision maker' as *the* person in business, government or whatever sphere of life who determines the destinies of others. But this is unrealistic for several reasons. First, although generals may appear to command armies, ministers to rule their departments, and chairmen to run their companies, it is true to say that the bulk of the decision making is done by advisers who select information and feed it to the top man, then show him the consequences (in their estimation) of acting this way or that. Newspaper interpretations play up the individual heroic aspect but, although it is true that decision makers can be autocratic and even reckless, the constraints preventing their being so are great and usually make for a short career.

1.1.4 **Do Decisions Exist?**

Not always. In the first place, decisions are not necessarily identifiable or discrete events but rather gradual shifts in direction of behaviour or even of thinking. A change in marketing policy may be impossible to pin down to any decision or even sequence of decisions, being rather a gradual adjustment to the winds of change from one year to the next. The 'decision' here has been implicit rather than explicit. To take a different example, you might 'decide' that the government at the time was wrong to nationalise the railways, or that any future government would be ill-advised to introduce import tariffs. Neither of these decisions requires you to *do* anything, even though you have surely examined the available information and come to a conclusion. Perhaps the most important sense in which decisions do not 'exist' is when people do something rash or unexpected and it is impossible for us to understand how they could possibly do it. When the company secretary absconds with the funds we infer that he must have been under some sort of stress or that he was temporarily of unsound mind. This only means that we do not *understand* his decision – since it clearly was one. Continuing the criminal theme, it is interesting that the distinction among cases of manslaughter, homicide and murder hangs essentially on the strength of the *recognisable* decision component in the act of killing that took place.

1.1.5 **Can Decisions Solve Anything?**

The classical view of a decision situation is one of some burgeoning crisis leading to a decision whose outcome results in a return to equilibrium. Actually it is hard – impossible even – to think of a significant real-life decision that has ever resolved anything in any final sense. If you have department heads baying at you for more funds, whatever solution you come up with will only change the variables in the situation when you have to make the decision next time. Any single decision is usually something which opens the gate to more subtle or more complex decision situations. Planners and politicians learn to live with the fact that problem resolution in any absolute sense is rare: they learn to tack and trim with the prevailing winds knowing that temporary or partial resolution is all that can be expected.

1.1.6 Irrational Decisions

Could anything make less sense than the aforementioned case of the company secretary who absconded with the funds? What about the respectable, middle-aged executive who leaves his loving family and moves in with an actress? The man in the street may well shake his head in disbelief, but the fact is that such decisions perceived by outsiders as quite irrational can nevertheless be perfectly rational to the person concerned. People centrally involved in decisions typically have access to quite different kinds and amounts of information relative to observers in the wings. Being told to take on more staff when order books are nearly empty may seem total madness to the section supervisor who cannot see this as only one component of a decision jigsaw in which management and unions are trading concessions. Any piece of a jigsaw looks odd by itself on the table, but in its proper context can look superbly correct.

Thus lack of perspective and restricted information can make certain decisions appear irrational and at the same time provide useful fodder for newspaper columnists in their interpretations of the political business scene. Of course, other decisions *persist* in appearing irrational even after the 'full facts' are known; in such cases we may aver that the full facts are not really known at all. Once we understand that the real reason for the chairman deciding to open a new factory was to court favour with a particular government minister for his own personal gain, then the decision becomes in some sense a rational one. In fact we shall repeatedly discover throughout this book that while man may not be objectively rational all or even most of the time, he at least maintains a kind of consistency in line with his own perception of changing situations; that is, he follows a kind of personal or **subjective rationality.**

Take the case of a production manager caught out by a machine breakdown outside the scope of his maintenance staff. He spends the best part of the day phoning possible suppliers of the rogue component. His first quotation is £700, but he defers commitment, feeling he can do better. Two later contacts quote him £800 and £900: he has missed his lunch and is tired but tries to make contact again with the initial £700 supplier. Apparently they have closed for Friday, but going for second best he manages to get in touch with the £800 supplier who confirms the quotation but cannot deliver during the weekend. He is kicking himself for not accepting the £700 supplier who was also guaranteeing 24-hour delivery. However, the £900 supplier is now on the line, and he has to decide, tired and hungry man that he is, whether he really wants production on Monday. Whatever decision he takes now he may well regret on Monday when he is neither tired nor hungry and has to draft a sheepish explanatory memorandum to the finance officer. A spectator might regard our production manager's decision as poor or even irrational. Yet with knowledge of the constraints that prevail we can recognise a clear subjective rationality in the way our manager handled a decision situation which was changing all the time.

1.1.7 **Whither Good Decisions?**

Most galling of all, a good decision does not necessarily lead to a good outcome. Because of shifting constraints in the decision situation what was a good decision today may be a bad decision next year when the time for implementation comes and there is a slump in world prices or some foreign government requisitions your new factory. If there were no uncertainty about the future then of course every good decision *would* lead to a good outcome. Uncertainty about people and about events is the bugbear of real-life decisions, but it is at the same time the single factor which makes the study of decision making as fascinating as it is.

1.2 **A General Model**

Throughout this book we will be emphasising the importance of the *changing* nature of the decision environment. But in order to have time to look at the finer-grain details we have to press 'frame hold', as it were, on the cine projector and examine a single frame. Figure 1.2 is meant to represent just such a 'single-frame' view of the decision process. This diagram will be constantly referred to throughout the book as our *general decision* **model**. It is general in the sense that it includes most of the bits and pieces most people would want to see there, and also in the sense that it is adaptable to suit the wide range of decision examples dealt with in this book.

In the following sections we shall talk through the major structural aspects of the model and then go on to elaborate by example more precisely how the structure works. A clock is only a static 'model' of interlocking wheels and cogs until someone turns a key or presses a switch, whereupon the structure starts to work. Our decision model has to work as well, at least figuratively, in the sense that we have to be able to see how some problem input can pass through the various stages in the model and give rise to an emergent decision.

Note that what follows is only a skeleton discussion of the general decision model in order that early chapters will fit into place as you read them. Full discussion of the model then follows in subsequent chapters.

1.2.1 **Individual Constraints**

The diagram (Fig. 1.2) is essentially made up of two boxes, one labelled 'Individual Constraints' and the other 'External Constraints', which are 'squeezing' a centre circle in which we find represented the three major steps involved in human information processing: **perceiving**, analysing and deciding. In the 'Individual Constraints' box we find listed essentially the person's psychological make-up, which determines, limits, or indeed constrains, the kind of decisions he can take. For example, is his *intelligence* such that he can retain an array of information and attach proper importance to each item?

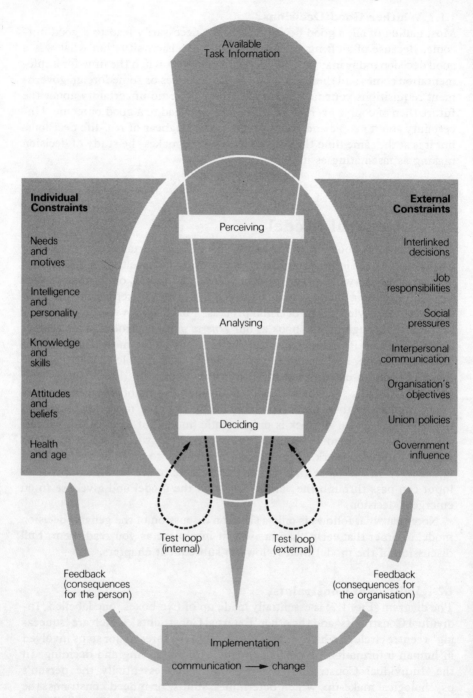

Fig. 1.2: General Model of the Human Decision Maker

In his *personality*, is he prone to emotional outbursts or risky gambles, or is he slow and conscientious, or what? Are his *needs and motives* such that there will be no conflict between what is best for his organisation and what is best in terms of his own career? Has experience given him an appropriate *skill and knowledge* level for the problem in hand? Are his basic **attitudes** to the task satisfactory, or does he regard the job as beneath him or outside his remit? And last but not least of the individual constraints, is he up to par in *health*, including *resistance to stress*? (People suffering from alcoholism, jet lag or even humble toothache make less than efficient decision makers.)

We will shortly be developing this first outline of 'psychological' constraints affecting decision-making efficiency, but no doubt it is already apparent to you that people are going to differ in respect of how intelligent, how skilled, how highly motivated and so on they are with respect to a given task. It is these individual differences which are crucial in understanding why we have good and bad decision makers, and which accordingly constitute the subject of our opening chapters.

1.2.2 External Constraints

The box on the right of Fig. 1.2 labelled 'External Constraints' concerns those factors over which the person has relatively little or no control but which to varying degrees will nevertheless influence the decision. For example, parallel wage-claim discussions involving *interlocked decisions* may be taking place in other divisions, and your settlement must not be out of line. Again, the definition of your *job role* and its attendant responsibilities will define how specific or far reaching your problem analysis and decision is allowed to be. *Social pressures* from colleagues, advisers, even from family, may bend your judgement. The fact that you like Mr Brown but not Mr Green will facilitate **interpersonal communication** with the former, but cut you off from the valuable expertise of the latter. *Organisational objectives* may or may not be compatible with your own attitudes and beliefs; *union or CBI directives* may upset a solution perfectly acceptable to both labour and management in your firm; *government influence* either through the law or through ministerial pressure may be affecting the cost–benefit calculations of decisions relating to particular products or particular locations or particular expansion policies. You may be able to think of other constraints not listed. We could also have noted, for example, the constraints imposed by the level of scientific and technological knowledge available at the time the decision has to be taken.

1.2.3 The Processing Pathway

So much for the different kinds of constraints that act on the decision-making process in the centre of the model. Let us now focus on this central process – that is on the information processing itself.

a. Perceiving Stage

Imagine you are at a meeting and a voice asks for your views. This is a decision situation since you have to decide whether you wish to contribute and if so whether to agree or disagree with previous contributors. You have quite an array of information available. Your data are in front of you; across the table is the smile of anticipation from the last speaker; there are also the nods or averted eyes of other members of the committee, and somebody whispers a remark into your ear, but you don't catch all of it. All this and more besides, like the remnant of the tea break in your mouth, the smell of tobacco fug in the room, the sound of doors slamming down the corridor and traffic outside the window, are all bits of information that are available to be picked up at this chosen point in time. Since there is so much going on, the information that you actually *perceive* (i.e. that actually gets into the first processing 'box' in Fig. 1.2) is only some fraction of it.

What you as an individual do perceive is very much determined by your particular psychological make-up (in our terms, the 'individual constraints' of Fig. 1.2). For example, the speaker's argument may be beyond you (intelligence) or you may be too anxious (personality). You may be too hungry to care (needs) or more concerned with impressing than understanding (motives). You may lack the technical skills and knowledge to perceive the crucial points in the argument. You may have a negative attitude towards the speaker, or believe that the whole project being discussed is unethical. Then again, you may be exhausted from your journey and your attention flags, or be suffering from a toothache that swamps everything else. In other words, every individual constraint listed in the general decision model can play its part, first in causing you to perceive some things yet miss others and, second, in determining which aspects of the information that gets accepted are emphasised or dropped.

As we shall see throughout the present book, biases and distortions of various kinds are the hallmarks of human decision making, and it is important to recognise this first, perceiving, stage as carrying perhaps the major part of the blame. If the information accepted in the first place is faulty, then whatever happens later in the processing sequence is using faulty information. How then can we expect to achieve a correct analysis of the problem, still less a correct decision about what to do?

Because everyone is unique in terms of his own particular mix of individual constraints we have to write in slightly (or grossly) different values for the person sitting next to you, and indeed for every other person in the room. The same objective information from the speaker is therefore being perceived at least slightly differently by everyone in the room – including himself. Examples abound of how different kinds of individual constraints make for different perceptions: think of the way management and unions perceive the same pay demand as justified or extortionate, or how parents and teenagers differ in their perception of the same social issues.

b. Analysing Stage
If we now assume the voice gets through your perceiving stage you then find yourself thinking about the content of the question. You wonder what exactly

is the speaker's view; is there an ulterior issue lurking somewhere? Do I have enough information for me to speak? How much attention should I pay to the frown of my colleague across the table? Am I sure about my facts? All this analysing may take place in ten, five or even fewer seconds as you establish the status of your position.

It is important to appreciate again at this analysis stage that the uniqueness of the individual constraints package means that a different *kind* of analysing is going on in one person's head compared with the head of the person next to him. Without spelling out details here, you can probably see how different kinds of sophistication in problem analysis would be seen in people of different skills, knowledge and abilities, different personalities (e.g. impulsive or cautious) and so on through the list of individual constraints in Fig. 1.2.

c. Deciding Stage

Your analysis of the situation may have suggested you should say nothing, or simply nod and smile at the speaker, or stare at your papers in non-commitment, or develop an alternative point of view. How do you *decide*? Some criterion or rule is brought into play which has guided you reasonably successfully before, e.g. 'Never support a member's point unless it has the obvious goodwill of the Chairman'. And yet again, because of differences in individual constraints, no two people will necessarily adopt the same decision criteria. The person who has the intelligence and experience to spot likely repercussions from any wrong decision will adopt more demanding criteria than the person who does not understand the issue, or who is bored, or who tends to snatch at any solution that presents itself.

d. Test Loop

Although you have 'decided' that you are going to put forward (let us say) a different point of view, so much hangs on this decision that you do not want to rush into it. Before committing yourself publicly you need to test the temperature of the water (see Test arrows in Fig. 1.2). You test out possible courses of action by studying the faces of others around you. If they smile back this suggests that support would be forthcoming, or you try out a non-committal line, simply running the idea up the flagpole. If the atmosphere feels cool or you sense you have taken on too much you withdraw and revise your decision.

e. Action

Let us assume you have firmly decided to speak up and press your own viewpoint; this then becomes your committed course of action — you have nailed your colours to the mast and the public commitment means that reversal will be painful to some extent. In general, implementation of action consequent on a decision is partly a matter of social skills in being able to relate to people and persuade them face to face and partly communication skills in making sure that all people concerned are efficiently informed to an appropriate depth of detail. And of course the implementation involves *acceptance* of change by people affected – changes in attitude and indeed changes in behaviour. We have much more to say about this in Chapter 15.

f. Feedback

This last component in the general decision model concerns the effects both on you and on your environment of the action you have just implemented. In other words, if you decide to try something out, then the fact that it works or does not work causes some *change* in the individual constraints that acted to shape that decision in the first place. For example, if your solution works, your knowledge and skill will increase slightly, it acts as a personality booster, changes you from a tired to a revitalised person, and even alters your whole attitude to your work. But there is a feedback effect on the decision environment as well. Success means task difficulty will be less for similar problems in the future. And whether you were successful or unsuccessful will affect whether your colleagues trust you again. Organisational policy may change to reflect the advantages of your new solution. If you are a senior decision maker this feedback on external constraints may extend as far as changes in the law or government policy. Thus the *dual* nature of feedback from our actions on both ourselves and on our environment is important to bear in mind.

● A question that may have occurred to you when we were describing the 'external constraints' in our general model was whether these constraints are fixed for every decision maker or whether in some way they can be said to vary rather like individual constraints. This at first strange idea makes some sense if you think about it. For example, being married is a significant inter-personal constraint on what one can decide to do in certain areas: but it may operate differently for different marriages and for different partners within a marriage. Again, there is only one legal system, but it may be applied differently depending on how well spoken you are (when apprehended) or on whether you have a good or bad record (when being sentenced). Economic constraints will affect you differently depending on whether you are rich or poor. Because you read a different newspaper from your neighbour you may come to view 'the causes of industrial upheaval' differently from the way he views them.

Try to keep in mind the basic framework of this general decision model since it will greatly facilitate your grasp of the chapters that follow.

1.3 Decision as Change

There are three ways in which a decision situation may be said to be undergoing continuous change:

a. in the sense that a decision does not just happen, it evolves from an early stage of recognising a problem right through to the stage of monitoring the consequences of whatever action is implemented;

b. in the sense that the constraints operating on the decision-making processes themselves fluctuate through the stages referred to above;
c. in the sense that the very importance of the decision – whether it really matters what you decide – will also vary with time.

We now examine these in turn.

1.3.1 Decisions Evolve

The whole sequence depicted in Fig. 1.2 may take only seconds, as in our running example of being asked a question at a meeting, or it may take years, as when a car manufacturer is introducing a new model or a government committee is deliberating on some topic of national importance. Accordingly we must release 'frame hold' and let the cine projector keep running so as not to become too hypnotised by this single-frame picture of the decision situation. Even the initial stage of perceiving that a problem exists may take a long time. Symptoms of industrial unrest or machine breakdown or the need for a new approach may exist for ages before someone spots something odd on a particular occasion but shrugs it off, only to pick it up as a problem requiring solution several weeks later. Problems that walk up and hit you in the face are one thing, but arguably the most important problems never do this – you have to winkle them out. Problem finding is an art in itself and it typically marks 'creative' people from the rest. We need more people to ask, 'What would happen if we tried it this way? Couldn't we save costs by making chairs with three legs instead of four?', and so on.

Even more obviously, the analysing stage which follows can take a very long time. Prototypes may need test-bed or wind-tunnel work lasting many months; hearing evidence from all parties who wish to be represented in a government enquiry can similarly run into months or years. During this time tentative solutions may emerge, die away or persist through to the deciding stage, whereupon a lengthy period of acceptability or feasibility testing may ensue before a concrete decision is actually implemented.

1.3.2 Changing Constraints

The second kind of change occurring during a decision process arises because the very constraints on our decision making are themselves not fixed: they also change in time. Background constraints, such as government economic policy may alter rather slowly, although a bad annual report from a major manufacturer or an indiscreet ministerial statement can have abrupt effects. More usually it is task-related constraints which are constantly changing. In particular, information is *not* available when needed; it arrives in dribs and drabs, depending on human links that often break down, and then two pieces of conflicting information can arrive together. .... Again, the shape and size of the task changes in appearance as decisions are taken by other people in contingent problem areas. Pressure and stress increase as time passes. Individual constraints also change relative to the task. As the problem develops in complexity or magnitude our natural abilities, the amount of our experience, and the level of our skills may start to fall short. We grow tired or stale or short-tempered from worry and from living with the problem too long. We start to have conflicts about being allowed to be drawn into the problem in the first place. As we saw earlier, constraints also change because related decisions taken by you or others are all the time *acting back* on the decision environment and altering it. For example, decisions about pay agreement levels act back on economic constraints such as the levels of inflation/unemployment that triggered the need for the decision in the first place.

1.3.3 Changing Importance

The importance or significance of a decision can increase or decrease between the stage of perceiving the problem and final action. Some decisions hardly figure in our thinking at the present time (e.g. how we will divide next year's budget) yet as the time grows nearer they will occupy more and more of our planning time until they may wholly consume our thoughts on the day prior to the decision deadline. This is because the diversity of information that could be taken into account as well as the number of consequences that might follow from any particular course of action only become fully arrayed before the decision maker when the decision is imminent.

The reverse process also happens, as when we dread some confrontation on the horizon so that it consumes our energies much earlier than it ought to. This feeling of enormous importance may then dissipate over time as new factors enter the picture and anxiety decreases. Indeed, many of our decisions-to-be which lie in the blurred future may never come about at all as they become superseded by other people's decisions or by natural events.

1.3.4 Linkage Among Decisions

Any individual can be regarded as being bound into his own 'decision space' not only by the constraints that operate on him, which we have already recognised, but also through limitations imposed by decisions made in the past and by decisions that have to be made for the future. This idea may need expanding:

a. *Decisions made in the past.* What was decided in the past, either by us or for us (e.g. by parents), affects the kinds of solutions we can even think about now. The fact that a child is sent to one school rather than another, or that a young person decides to join a private company rather than the civil service, may well mean that he cannot bring into operation what is now his preferred career decision since he has the wrong background or experience for it. Or on a shorter time scale, you may be a senior manager with a staff crisis on your hands and you decide the best thing to do is to have your personnel officer take over. The trouble is, you sent him yesterday on a similar mission to the north of Scotland. Thus, past decisions constrain present ones.

b. *Decisions about the future.* If I know that next year I will be faced with the choice between a state or a fee-paying school for my children, this places a major constraint on how much money I can commit this year to furnishing the house. Since I am not ready yet to take that 'future' decision I must keep funds to reserve my options. Companies and governments too realise that large investment decisions on the horizon prevent them from taking what would really be the best decision for the present circumstances. Thus, both for the individual and for the organisation, past, present and future decisions are cross-linked.

c. *Decisions made by others.* The wife may wish to go to the theatre but the husband may wish to go no further than the television set – a situation which may be compounded by the fact that a visiting sister-in-law had plans to go to the cinema, and so on. In this kind of situation 'collective bargaining' must take place. Let us note, however, that this kind of linkage among decisions can also be helpful and constructive as when the government shares the cost of oil exploration with private companies.

This concludes our general survey of the decision-making environment. We are now ready to begin examining in more detail many of the arguments and issues raised but briefly in the present chapter.

Work Section

A. Revision Questions

A1 What are the essential differences between simple or low-order decisions and complex, higher-order decisions?

A2 Why can something which appears to be a simple decision in fact turn out to be complex?

A3 What is meant by an 'implicit rather than explicit' decision?

A4 In what ways can an apparently irrational decision come to be seen as rational?

A5 What is meant by the term 'human information processor'?

A6 Briefly characterise the three stages which information from the outside world passes through in the human brain before it is transformed into some piece of responsive action.

A7 Provide different examples from those in the chapter for: (a) individual; (b) external constraints on the decision maker.

A8 Why is the test stage so important in the general decision model?

A9 Explain how the consequences of our actions feed back and modify the constraints that shaped the decision in the first place.

A10 Give examples to show how *differences* in people's individual constraints affect the perceiving, analysing and deciding stages in human decision making.

A11 What are the consequences of the fact that decision processes stretch over some period of time?

A12 In what way are our possible decisions limited by choices we have made in the past, or will have to make in the future?

A13 Show how constraints both act on and are acted on by the decision process.

A14 Make out a list of ten decisions you carried out today, ranked in order of the most trivial to the most important.

A15 Develop a different example to make the point being made in 1.1.1.

A16 Think of some examples of decision makers who do fit the heroic mould denied in 1.1.3.

A17 Think of two examples of decisions that do appear to have provided absolute solutions to problems (1.1.5).

B. Exercises/Case Studies

B1   Feed a problem of your choice (preferably known by others in the group) through the complete general decision model and detail its progress as it is exposed to influences from the various constraints that are in operation.

C. Essay Questions

C1   Take a function within a firm (e.g. accounting or marketing) and discuss whether the constraints on efficient decision making are more individual or external.

C2   Basing your argument on the decision-making model, suggest how a person's decision making efficiency might be improved.

C3   Why might 'technical experts' often make poor decision makers?

C4   Argue against 1.1.4 that decisions always exist if we only have the time and patience to track them down.

Chapter 2

Needs and Motives

Synopsis: *When we ask the question, 'Why did the company go broke?' or, 'Why did such a promising young man leave the company?', a full answer will always be in the terms of the whole range of constraints that we described in the general model of Chapter 1. But if there is a single 'best' key to understanding why people make the decisions they do, it lies in an understanding of their motives. What exactly was he trying to achieve by deciding to act as he did—was it career advancement, some need for power display or revenge, a wish to impress his subordinates—or what? Senior politicians and businessmen who live their working lives in the decision-making arena can often be found musing as to exactly why some adversary or competitor is taking a particular line. They know that when their opposite number across the negotiating table offers easy concessions it can only be a manœuvre, or that when a colleague argues for delaying decisions 'until we have more reliable information', this is because he personally needs to work in a secure situation rather than because there is any genuine need for delay. Listen to the man himself, not what he says, is a useful precept.*
We begin this chapter by taking a broad look at the nature of 'needs'. We go on to see how Taylor's early ideas of why people work had to make way for the human relations approach of the 1930s and 1940s, and eventually how these ideas too had to blend with the so-called 'human resources' approach of the 1950s and 1960s.

Plan of the chapter: *This is illustrated in Fig. 2.1.*

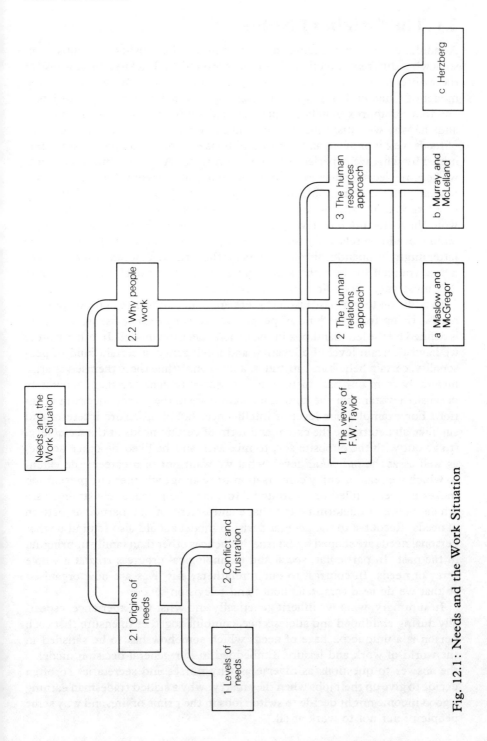

Fig. 12.1: Needs and the Work Situation

2.1 The Origin of Needs

As adults we have a particular pattern of needs that pushes and pulls us in somewhat different directions from those around us. Luckily, the reasons for these differences can be understood by recourse again to the general decision model of Chapter 1. Early in our lives the external constraints loom large; children do approximately as they are told by parents and older children, and the way we satisfy physiological needs for food and shelter, the kinds of foods we eat or avoid and the kind of house we prefer to live in, are determined by what we experience in our upbringing. As we become adolescents we become decision makers in the fuller sense of the word, but we also have to deal with the constraints imposed by our past family history. If we lived in a large family and were used to having people around all the time this would have engendered a level of social needs different from the case of a single child reared in a relatively isolated setting. What is peace and quiet for the latter might be unendurable loneliness for the former. You can probably make a case yourself for how the kinds and extents of Personal Needs (see Fig. 2.2) must vary depending on past influences.

In addition to our past history, there are major influences on our present needs arising from the kind of people we are *now*. And 'what we are now' is defined by the left-hand box in the general decision model! In other words, we have a certain level of education and intelligence, a certain kind of personality, certain beliefs and attitudes, and so on. While these themselves arise inevitably from our past history, it is essential to consider them separately because they stand for the kind of person we are in the present decision situation. For example, our level of intelligence, hobbies, leisure interests and suchlike all determine the extent and form of certain needs at the *social* level (to go out with the opposite sex, to mix with and be liked by other people) as well as at the *individual* level (what we want out of a career; the extent to which we read or enjoy conversation or reading; whether our present job makes us feel fulfilled or frustrated). In short the personal constraints as a whole *interact* to determine the shape and extent of our particular pattern of needs. Recourse to the general decision model should also remind us that personal needs are shaped by external influences other than family upbringing in the past. In particular, social and technological progress *creates* a whole array of needs. In contrast to our forefathers, our lives are now organised so that we do *need* cars, telephones and television sets.

In summary, what we inherit genetically and what we experience, especially during childhood and adolescence, combine together to ensure that each person is a unique package of needs which somehow has to be satisfied in the world of work and leisure. Embedded in our general decision model is the answer to questions as diverse as why nurses and secretaries so often decide to give up their jobs when they marry; why a skilled tradesman earning a good income might decide to switch jobs in the prime of life, and why some people prefer not to work at all.

2.1.1 **Levels of Needs**

The idea of different 'levels' of needs as shown in Fig. 2.2 – some physiological, some social and some personal – is a simplified version of a scheme put forward by Abraham Maslow and provides our discussion with a useful framework. Figure 2.2 in effect plugs into the box marked 'Individual Constraints' in Fig. 1.2. A need at any 'level' can influence the decision output in the general decision model. To take the simplest example of hunger, a whole cluster of hunger-related decisions is triggered when this need is dominant – to go to a shop or restaurant, to reach for a sandwich, to stop taking sugar, to eat less expensively, and so on; you could write a list of a hundred or more potential decisions that are linked with the relatively uncomplicated need for food. 'Implementing the decision' satisfies the hunger, and causes

Fig. 2.2: The Levels of Human Needs (after Abraham Maslow)

it to slip into the background for a few hours. In other words, as you may remember from our general decision model, there is a kind of *feedback loop* in operation: a need builds up, modifying perception, analysis and decisions, and giving rise eventually to actions which satisfy the needs and restore equilibrium. If the hunger need remains unsatisfied this leads to increasing tension and widespread disruption of other 'unrelated' decision-making activities. Hunger (or other physiological needs in Fig. 2.2) can cause committee chairmen to hurry through agendas, and even generals to commit troops to battle, without full and proper consideration of the information available to them.

This is all very well, but does the same kind of argument also apply to the next 'level' in Fig. 2.2, social needs? According to Fig. 2.2, these cover such things as the need to belong to a family or other group and to have self-respect as well as the respect of others. We could imagine deficits here giving rise, as before, to a particular kind of information processing and, hence, decision making. Examples might be to get out of one's present job rut, to mix more with one's seniors, to obtain some professional qualification. Implementation of one or more decisions such as these could satisfy the need, at least to some extent, and cause it to fall into the background. Therefore the feedback cycle implied in the general decision model would seem to operate *reasonably* well for social needs. But bear in mind one important qualifying point which may be particularly relevant to the personal needs of Fig. 2.2. Attempting to satisfy a need *can* make it yet more insatiable. The taste of power is an example of where the appetite can often be increased by feedback. And going back to needs at the physiological level, alcohol and drug addiction are examples of where 'satisfying' the need only results in a new and higher demand level. Even overeating can be looked at in this way. Thus the equilibrium model should only be taken as a rough and ready guide to how needs operate.

2.1.2 Conflict and Frustration

It is a common experience to find that two needs *conflict* – for example, a company may be losing money by employing an inefficient man, but dismissing him would disturb good staff relations. Often the decision is a compromise; perhaps the member of staff is given an inflated title with reduced responsibilities, or he might be bypassed completely. People generally try to resolve the conflict by making compromise decisions which satisfy most of their needs for most of the time. For example, we need to work for money and companionship, and we also need to have leisure to recharge our batteries. Therefore we make decisions leading to actions that satisfy both needs. If we can do without too much leisure, we put in a lot of overtime and earn more money; if we need a lot of time to relax we avoid overtime and perhaps take a job which gives us daytime freedom. As another example, we need to marry in order to have children and enjoy love and security into old age; yet we need *not* to marry in order to keep our personal freedom for as long as possible and to avoid financial obligations such as mortgages. Therefore we may well compromise by marrying late rather than early.

When people have some need or personal target which they cannot reach either because of personal limitations or situational difficulties (constraints) then they experience frustration. If frustration persists it *can* be stressful, all depending on how the frustration is handled. In the face of frustration the usual response is to try harder – and often to try more aggressively by starting to blame others.

2.2 Why People Work

2.2.1 The Views of F. W. Taylor

Going to work obviously satisfies important economic needs, since without money a whole range of dependent needs such as to eat and to have a place to live become difficult or impossible to satisfy. However, while the ultimate purpose of work is economic, in the process of earning one's income other needs such as the needs for achievement, self-fulfilment and for the fellowship of others are also satisfied. The view of the worker current in the nineteenth century and fostered by F. W. Taylor at the turn of the century was that he works simply for money, and Taylor, who started work as a labourer and ended as a chief engineer, set out principles which showed managers how to use this 'fact' for the benefit of *both* the firm and the worker himself. After observing each task and selecting the best method of doing it, the manager's responsibility was: (a) to select and train suitable personnel; and (b) to establish a monetary incentive scheme so that work, as laid down by management, would be done as quickly as possible, thereby increasing the workers' pay and the firm's profit. This is fine as far as it goes, but unfortunately Taylor followed the views of many of his contemporaries in seeing the worker as generally stupid, lazy by nature and without a mind of his own, but eager nevertheless to make money. Not surprisingly, therefore, all his advice was aimed at managers, who were supposed to attract labour to the factories by offering over the agricultural rates, then set up simple tasks with clear quotas and incentives, and finally make sure the work was closely supervised.

Workers hated Taylor's ideas, set tasks, quotas and supervision and were worried about job security since this new and impressive efficiency meant fewer workers were needed. Accordingly, they retaliated by introducing some 'management' of their own: they worked out ways of controlling the rate of work so as to maintain their income levels but not threaten their actual jobs, and on a nationwide front they began to band together into 'unions' to give themselves broad-based strength and protection (see also Ch. 9, p. 125). Yet in spite of these difficulties, it would be a mistake to push Taylor's approach aside as a mere historical curiosity. His message was 'Make a big cake and we'll share it,' but this was misinterpreted as 'All the cake for the owners.' It is true that his view of the work situation was too narrow and quite mistaken in operating *only* through the management side, but there is no doubt that, while not the whole story, people (managers as well as workers) do regard monetary reward as a major incentive to work and the ideas of objectives, quotas and incentives have all stayed around, although they do not always work as planned. People seem to set their own work tempos, which are only loosely related to the incentive scheme operating – indeed some employees may be frightened to show they can work at high rates since this could lead to higher expectancy from management without suitable reward. Moreover, for the worker to regulate his own work rate is itself rewarding since, as you can see, it allows him a sense of independence and control over his 'managers'.

2.2.2 The Human Relations Approach
The now famous studies carried out in the 1920s and 1930s at the Hawthorne (Chicago) Works of the General Electric Company began innocently enough

as research into how lighting levels affected the assembly rate and quality of electrical goods. The whole project was cast in the work study tradition of Taylor, and in fact the research director, *Elton Mayo*, was an ex-assistant and disciple of Taylor's.

However, these innocent beginnings led to a set of ideas which demonstrated the limitations of the Taylor approach. As predicted, improved lighting levels did indeed give improved work levels, but the investigators also encountered their first head-scratcher in that a comparison group (treated in the same way except that the lighting was not modified) also showed the same improvement. Indeed follow-up work showed that any change up or down seemed to bring improvement – even moonlight levels of illumination were sufficient to maintain production levels. Something else must have also been happening. It is instructive to pause and appreciate this compelling demonstration of the value of having some comparison or control group in any research: without such a group which had the same supervisory arrangements and was shown the same degree of concern and interest by the researchers, Mayo would have been led into an appalling error of interpretation – that improved lighting in itself led to improved output! What was the 'something else' that must have been common to both experimental and control group which was responsible for the improvement?

The answer, which was canonised as 'the **Hawthorne effect**', was in a way pathetic. The Hawthorne plant was a rather anonymous place of work without any evident personal interest being shown by supervisors and managers towards their employees, so those workers taking part in the research, including the control group, at last felt useful and important. Accordingly, every time some change was introduced they responded by giving what they thought the investigators wanted – more improvement. It is not difficult to see why Elton Mayo, the early leader of the human relations movement, came to argue that the meaning of work, and therefore the springs of motivation, lie in people's attitudes and social relationships – in interest, respect, fellowship and personal freedom in the job situation.

Nowadays, all this may not seem very striking, but such 'human relations' views would have been scoffed at before the 1920s. Not that Mayo's philosophy suddenly provides all the answers: it is a fuller account of what motivates people at work, but it still takes for granted that workers should work and managers should manage, and the element of worker exploitation as a means of reaching greater productivity still persists even if in a 'nicer' form. This is because most of Mayo's recommendations are, like Taylor's, aimed at implementation by management – increase your information flow; make the workers feel they are doing a significant job; consider group and not just individual incentive schemes. Mayo's formulation goes a considerable way to showing us what was missing from Taylor's approach since his claims must be true, to some extent, for every worker; but, on the other hand, it does not seem to provide a *complete* explanation of why people work – why, for example, do some prefer working with things rather than with people and some even avoid work involving active social relationships? We need to pursue the question a little further.

2.2.3 **The Human Resources Approach**
a. Maslow and McGregor

An emphasis on something called 'human resources' gained momentum during the 1950s and 1960s. Now both workers and managers were recognised as complex bundles of all kinds of motives and the basic philosophy had a feeling of striking out in a new direction. One of the main ideas was that workers are quite capable of making decisions and should be encouraged to take an active part in decision making, particularly within their own work situation where their decisions could well be better than those taken by line management. Similarly it was argued that workers should not only produce goods but also be responsible for their quality, as well as for maintaining their own machines. Most fundamentally, the human resources approach questioned the assumption that work is unpleasant – it should be seen instead as a 'therapeutic' opportunity to enjoy relations with others, to exercise one's skills and to receive monetary rewards and praise. We have an interesting twist here: Mayo's human relations model seemed to assume that job satisfaction makes for quality of worker output, while now it is the quality of the work output that makes for job satisfaction.

We have already encountered *Abraham Maslow's* 'hierarchy' of needs (Fig. 2.2). Maslow thought that needs can be ordered in importance in the sense that if, and only if, certain ones (hunger, thirst, shelter, sleep) are first satisfied can people have the time or indeed the inclination to entertain other 'higher-level' needs. In other words, *if* our stomachs are regularly filled hunger becomes a trivial need in that it takes very little of our time during the day worrying and planning. Affluence allows other needs to come to the fore – needs not just to survive, but to improve and to feel a sense of progress and direction.

Note that Maslow's scheme is concerned with reasonable spans of time. While a person may be driven predominantly by, say, individual needs during a certain period, there will be occasions within the period when probably social and inevitably physiological needs will temporarily take over. There is some evidence for a hierarchical arrangement of needs at the lower levels. For example, it has been shown that when people are hungry or thirsty their social relationships deteriorate noticeably, and in prison-camp conditions sexual needs are depressed to negligible levels. There is also implied the idea that a need can always be satisfied. However, as we remarked earlier in the chapter, feeding some needs only leads to greater appetite.

Other people have nevertheless adopted the basic idea of 'levels' of needs. In particular, Douglas McGregor has developed Maslow's approach into implications for management with his celebrated comparison of **Theory X and Theory Y**.

Theory X. This traditional approach paints the 'old-fashioned' view of a worker as accepted by Taylor. In other words, he is lazy and dislikes work; he is selfish and unconcerned about organisational needs; he avoids responsibility and has no ambition. Accordingly he has to be controlled and directed by management. Although overstated, it does contain some elements of truth, as we suggested before. One major defect, of course, is that it heaps blame on the worker but lets management off scot-free. McGregor picked many holes in Theory X (which he really sets up as a straw man) in order to come up with his own solution – in the form of Theory Y.

Theory Y. This says that people only *become* the way they appear in Theory X because of the way they are treated. The average worker *can* enjoy work and learn to seek out and enjoy responsibility. He does possess imagination, creativity and specialised job knowledge. Suitably motivated (particularly by being able to satisfy the higher Maslow needs), he willingly commits himself to organisational objectives and can be used in labour–management participation. Management are to blame for not allowing all this to happen, for not replacing control and direction by co-operation and participation, for employing only a part of the man.

b. *Murray and McLelland*

An alternative approach to Maslow's is actually to classify people *in terms of* their dominant needs. Henry Murray, working during the 1930s and 1940s, accepted the overriding importance of physiological needs but in his account of human motivation focussed on the needs for power and autonomy, the need to be fed and cared for (nurturance), to be with others (**affiliation**) and the need to achieve in life. This last, the need for achievement, has been the one most extensively explored, although the needs for power and for affiliation have attracted a good share of attention. The way the strength of these needs is measured in each individual (a technique introduced by Murray and still in use) is simple enough. The person is shown a series of pictures, mostly of people in various life situations, ambiguous enough to be capable of various interpretations.

Examples could be:

● A person apparently overhearing a conversation between two colleagues.
● What is apparently a shopfloor complaint being presented to a manager.
● A person apparently slumped at his desk and surrounded by work.

Each of these is only 'apparent' since, as we said, various other interpretations could be made of the deliberately ambiguous situation portrayed in the picture. He is asked to build a story out of his imagination around the scene portrayed, and he quite naturally invests the story with his *own* values, feelings, aspirations and fears. We say the person telling the story 'projects' these elements into the story he is making up, and hence this technique is one example of a **projective test**.

The leading figure in getting Murray's approach applied to work situations has been David McLelland. He has particularly emphasised the need for achievement ('nAch' for short), which he strongly associates with success as a manager. It may be obvious why: wanting to get ahead, wanting to work more effectively, wanting to come up with new findings and ideas of great value – these are all achievement-type qualities we value in our ideal manager. According to McLelland, a high-achieving person:

a. Likes situations where he can take responsibility for solving problems – finding a solution by chance is not nearly so satisfying as managing it through his own efforts, and he tends not to pass the buck.

b. Takes on *moderately* difficult tasks and accepts only reasonable risks. You might expect a 'high achiever' to take on anything – but think for a moment. If he takes on very easy tasks he will easily carry them out but there will be little sense of achievement. At the other extreme, very difficult tasks also offer a very real possibility of failure – something terrible for the high-achiever to experience. Thus a somewhat more difficult than average task offers him the satisfaction of success providing he is prepared to work at it – which he is, of course! He may complain about overwork, but he really welcomes it as an opportunity to feed his need for achievement.

c. Seeks information about how well he is doing. He likes to see his sales figures move up as a result of his efforts: he likes feedback which tells him he is winning – and the more personalised this feedback the better. McLelland believes that 'nAch' is trainable in managers and has put on appropriate courses in various countries.

c. Herzberg

The human resources approach to work motivation proposed by *Frederick Herzberg* in the 1950s and 1960s is perhaps better regarded among managers than among industrial psychologists. There is an immediate appeal since while the Maslow approach and Murray–McLelland approaches are very much clinical or laboratory-based, Herzberg talks directly and immediately in his theory about motives in organisations. In common with these researchers he recognises a set of *motivators* (needs for achievement, recognition, responsibility, advancement and growth) which are intrinsic to the job itself and which lead to satisfaction. The new twist is that he recognises a further set of considerations, rather like the ones we have termed background and situational factors in earlier chapters. He calls these **maintenance factors** – things such as proper heating and clean, well-lit conditions. They are not themselves motivators, but they allow motivators such as incentive and promotion schemes to work: only when a maintenance factor is withdrawn does it become motivating (in a negative sense) for example, when people go on strike to obtain better working conditions. Spend a few moments looking at Fig. 2.3 to get a better understanding of the contrast between maintaining and motivating factors. Herzberg carried out a considerable amount of research on some 2,000 employees of all grades and job types and in various countries, reaching the conclusion that *motivation* factors were the main cause

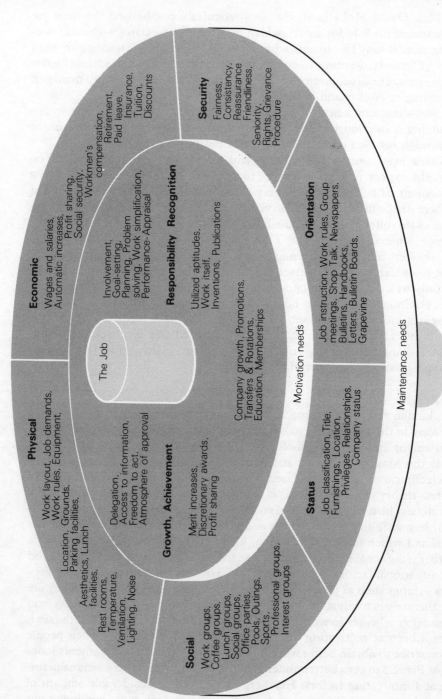

Fig. 2.3: Maintenance and Motivational Factors
(Harvard Business Review, Jan/Feb. 1964)

of job satisfaction while *maintenance* factors were the main cause of job *dis*satisfaction.

Arising directly from Herzberg's notion of 'motivation needs' is the concept of **job enrichment** as a key motivational principle (see **8.3.3** for details). He is at pains to make clear that job enrichment does not mean adding more tasks or increasing production goals or in rotating jobs, or even in decreasing difficulty. It arises from reshaping the job so as to *maximise responsibility, achievement and recognition*. When we get down to it, therefore, Herzberg is taking a position not so terribly different from that of the other human resources theorists we have encountered: Maslow, McGregor and McLelland. We perhaps are not surprised to learn that Herzberg's formula for maximising satisfaction of these three work needs includes allowing workers to become specialists or experts in two ways: (a) by increasing accountability for their own work instead of holding supervisors responsible – in fact minimising or indeed removing supervisory controls; (b) by providing a complete 'natural' unit of work gradually extending the novelty and complexity of tasks, and providing workers with direct information (feedback) on their results.

Work Section

A. Revision Questions

A1 What are the origins of our needs?
A2 Explain Maslow's views on the existence of a hierarchy of needs.
A3 Name and briefly explain the main methods of wages payment.
A4 What was the method that F. W. Taylor used to increase efficiency?
A5 Why did unions begin?
A6 State the chief findings of Elton Mayo.
A7 Why didn't Mayo's ideas provide the whole answer to motivation?
A8 What does McGregor's Theory Y say?
A9 What did Henry Murray feel were the main motivational needs?
A10 What was David McLelland's contribution?
A11 What is the difference between a maintenance and a motivational need?

B. Exercises/Case Studies

B1 Take a piece of paper and write in the middle 'decision to take a business studies/management course'. Now draw out from it a series of spokes, each spoke representing a major motive behind your taking the course (you must have several). Then draw branches off each spoke showing the subsidiary motives behind the major one, and finally twigs off these branches to show how motives can be further broken down. The more dense the resulting tangle the better: the 'motive map' that results may help you discover something about yourself, if you are willing to dig down a little....

B2 Think of two quite contrasting people you know reasonably well. Write down:
a. What you imagine to be their principal motives in life.
b. How their other 'individual constraints' might feed into each of these main motives.

B3 The student, in developing his own picture of how motivation operates, has to look for patterns of similarity among the various theorists discussed in this chapter and decide which elements of which approaches make the most sense to him. It would of course be foolish to think that because the old Taylor and Mayo approaches have now been 'superseded' by a human resources emphasis, that we simply forget all about them. Nor should we make the mistake of thinking that the human resources approach at last gives a complete account of motivation at work. It does not: theories are evolving all the time and our views of ourselves and our fellows are constantly changing.

Bearing the above points in mind, write an account in which you try to recognise the pros and cons of different approaches to motivation.

C. Essay Questions

C1 Think of a businessman or politician about whom you have a reasonable amount of biographical information; then construct a 'motive map' as far as you can, based on this information. Finally select some of his recent decisions and try to relate the person's motivational structure to the kinds of decision he took.

C2 Imagine you are a reincarnation of F. W. Taylor. Write a hostile critique of the new-fangled 'human' approaches and support your attack with hard facts.

C3 Do you agree with the view that money is an important motivator, or do you go along with those who regard wage demands as only symptomatic of more fundamental ailments within the organisation, or even in society at large?

C4 What do you feel motivates teachers in school or college?

Chapter 3

Intelligence and Personality

Synopsis: *In this chapter we continue our concern with reasons why some people are good decision makers and others are not. As you can see from Fig. 3.1, we shall be dealing with two 'dimensions' on which people can be differentiated – intelligence and personality. The first half of the chapter will stress mainly theoretical background, while the second half, together with the Work Section, mainly addresses practical matters. We begin with intelligence, identifying one component as what we inherit and a second component as deriving from what we experience during upbringing. We then examine two contrasting ways of getting at the question of what intelligence is and how we ought to measure it – the 'intelligence test' approach, and a different method based on how people actually solve problems. The next topic, personality, is dealt with in a similar way. We again begin by recognising the contribution of both genetics and experience in determining personality, then go on to look at the traditional test score approach as contrasted with the observational approach which looks at personality as expressed through people's behaviour. The third topic area in the chapter links intelligence and personality, in talking about how they determine our interests in life, as well as the way they combine in the matter of creativity and 'decision style'. To end, we look at problems of staff selection and point up the relevance of what we have been saying earlier in the chapter.*

Plan of the chapter: *This is illustrated in Fig. 3.1.*

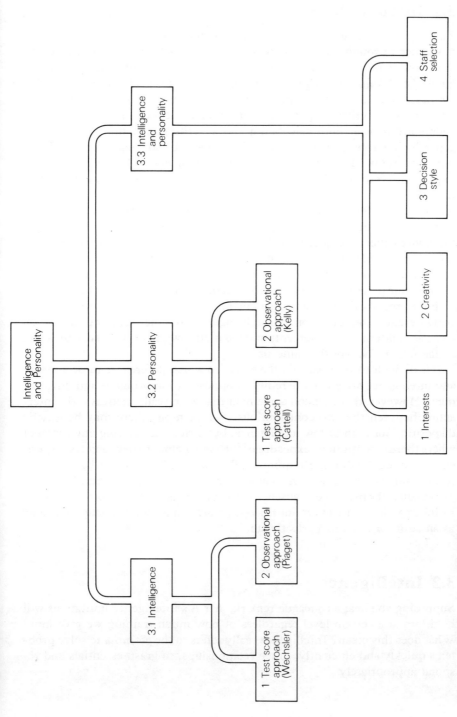

Fig. 3.1: Differences Among People in Intelligence and Personality

3.1 Introduction

The similarities among people are very obvious. We all walk, talk, eat and reproduce in roughly the same way; we all get excited, or afraid, or angry in roughly similar situations. But what makes people interesting is not so much their similarities, which we all tend to take for granted, but their differences. Why are some people naturally 'good at figures' while others can put a verbal or written report together with effortless ease? Of course, other people are poor at both calculating and at writing, and may, indeed have generally low intelligence. Personalities can also be strikingly different. One person might need people around to bring out the best in him, while another might work most efficiently alone at his desk; one might be dominant and the other patient and sympathetic, one imaginative and the other practical and so on. It would not be difficult to draw up an enormously long list of ways in which people are different in their daily behaviour. Certainly those differences affect the quality of people's decisions and other activities. Differences in people's intelligence and in their personality can arise in two ways:

a. We can be born with them; the different genetic packages we each inherit from our parents wholly or partly determine such things as our sex, body build, metabolic level and also our intelligence and personality.

b. Differences can arise from our upbringing; from the way our parents treat us as children and adolescents and from our own pattern of successes and failures in the world around us.

It is difficult to know exactly the extent to which differences in personality and intelligence arise from heredity as opposed to upbringing and environment. However, there is good agreement that what really matters is the interaction between the two contributions. For example, there may be genetic disposition for high or low intelligence, but a rich, stimulating environment where there is continuous exposure of the young child to new objects, experiences and ideas will achieve quite a different final level of intelligence from if the child had been raised in a flat and uninteresting setting. Similarly with personality, the presence or absence of a nervous disposition at birth is shaped by life experiences to determine *whether in fact* that person becomes 'neurotic' as an adult or remains perfectly stable.

3.2 Intelligence

Supposing you hear a colleague remark, 'Mr A's intelligence limitations will hold him at a certain level regardless of how much training we give him.' What does this mean? Intelligence really refers to the *potential* to solve problems quickly and efficiently, to see relationships, to grasp essentials and respond appropriately.

3.2.1 **Standardised Test Approach to Intelligence**

The traditional approach to developing a test of intelligence has been to start with a large set of possible intelligence questions – we will see examples in a moment – which are then given to a large number of people. For some questions it turns out that most people score about the same, and since these items do not discriminate one person from another, they are discarded. For other

Verbal sub-test	*Nature of the tasks*	*Ability(ies) measured (approximately)*
Information	Questions that call for general information, e.g. 'How many wings does a bird have?'	General knowledge
Comprehension	Questions that call for knowledge of practical matters, e.g. 'What should you do if you see someone forget his book when he leaves his seat in a restaurant?'	Practical information and social judgements
Arithmetic	Questions that require the manipulation of numbers: addition, subtraction and simple algebra.	Concentration and arithmetic reasoning
Similarities	Questions that require that two items be compared for their essential similarity, e.g. 'In what way are the lion and a tiger alike?'	Logical and/or abstract ability
Digit Span	Questions that ask the testee to repeat from memory two to nine digits–forwards and backwards.	Attention and rote memory
Vocabulary	Questions that ask the testee to define words such as 'umbrella' and 'conscience'.	Verbal information and general range of ideas

Fig. 3.2: The Sub-tests of the WAIS

Performance sub-test	*Nature of the tasks*	*Ability(ies) measured (approximately)*
Digit Symbol	The testee learns the symbol for each of nine digits, and then is presented with a series of digits and asked to write the corresponding symbol beneath each.	Speed of learning and writing symbols
Picture Completion	Incomplete pictures are presented. The testee must specify the essential part that is missing.	Visual alertness and visual memory
Block Design	Designs are presented. The testee must use small wooden blocks to duplicate them.	Ability to use component parts to form an abstract design
Picture Arrangement	Three to six small pictures are presented in a random order. The testee must rearrange them to make a sensible story.	Ability to comprehend and size up a social situation
Object Assembly	Puzzle-like parts of an object are presented. The testee must put them together quickly to make a whole object.	Ability to put together concrete forms

Fig. 3.2: The Sub-tests of the WAIS (*cont.*)

questions there is a good spread of scores and these items are kept because the scores do distinguish one person from another.

One of the best regarded intelligence tests in both Britain and America is David **Wechsler's Adult Intelligence Scale** – usually shortened to WAIS. This test measures eleven different abilities which David Wechsler considers make up the total concept of intelligence. As you can see in Fig. 3.2, the range of potential being tapped is quite broad, covering among other things information levels, reasoning ability, memory, and ability to copy and put together designs. How well you do on these tests is a good indicator of how well you will perform in real-life situations calling on these abilities, i.e. how intelligently you will carry out a particular task.

3.2.2 Observational Approach to Intelligence

Other approaches to measuring intelligence are possible. Jean Piaget has interpreted intelligence as meaning the way in which we solve problems and think about the world; in particular he has looked at the way intelligence develops as the child grows older. Not until roughly between seven and ten is the child able to juggle ideas simultaneously and show signs of being able to solve things in his head instead of having to resort to fingers or modelling clay. Around puberty, sophisticated adult thinking begins to appear. The child can now look at a problem from several angles, he can hypothesise about the way things could be; he can reflect on the past and project forward into the future. In other words he is now in a position to make reasonable decisions in which the possible and the probable can both play a part.

3.3 Personality

The second major factor affecting differences in the levels of performance between two people is their different personalities. Adventurous, assertive, sociable, trustful, worrying, clumsy; about 18,000 words exist in the English language to describe people's behaviour. In the same way that people's outward behaviour reflects their intelligence, so it also reflects their personalities. Given the large number of words that exist to describe how people feel, think and behave, you may well wonder how we could ever start measuring differences in any comprehensive way.

3.3.1 The Personality Test Score Approach

One way, similar to the one we have already encountered for measuring intelligence, is to take all the words that describe people, sift through them to take out virtual synonyms, and then get a large number of people to assess themselves on the remaining words. As you might expect, people who rate themselves as cheerful also usually rate themselves as happy, and perhaps as talkative and energetic. In other words, certain groups of words cluster together in the sense that if a person ticks one characteristic as applying to him, the chances are he will also tick the others in that group. Different characteristics which cluster together in this way give rise to what we might call a specific **personality factor**, something we can look for in the population at large.

In Fig. 3.3 you can see a widely used personality test which assesses people on sixteen different aspects (or factors) of personality. The author of the test, Cattell, ended up with these sixteen after sifting through the 18,000 or so words referred to above and dropping obscure words and synonyms (e.g. merry, jolly, cheery, cheerful). People can be differentiated by asking them to rate themselves from 1 to 10 on the scales you see in Fig. 3.3. As we have shown, the points are linked up to give a 'personality profile', and one person's profile can then be compared with another's. (You may note that Cattell uses

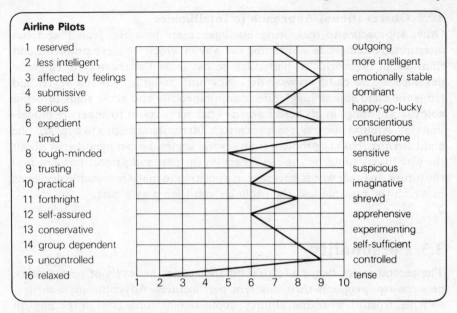

Fig. 3.3: Personality profile of airline pilots, based on Cattell's source traits
(Reproduced by permission of the Institute for Personality and Ability Testing, Champaign, Illinois.)

'intelligence' as one of his personality scales, but our purposes are best served by maintaining a distinction.)

3.3.2 The Observational Approach to Personality

A second general approach to personality adopts a viewpoint rather like the one Piaget adopted in his approach to intelligence. Scores on personality tests are one thing, but may it not be more interesting to discover how it is the person gets those scores? In other words, can we observe the way the person construes life around him and use this as an index of his personality? This is essentially the approach to personality taken by *George Kelly*, who used a rather simple procedure, as follows. Supposing I gave you a set of cards and asked you to write on each card the name of some significant person in your life, until we had, say, twenty cards with names on. I then select three of these cards, say the ones for your boss, for your father and for your best friends and then I ask you to think of some ways in which any two of them are *alike* and at the same time are different from the third. Supposing you start by saying that your father and your boss are both 'distant' in their relationship towards you, relative to the friendly intimacy you enjoy with your best friend. You can probably extend this contrast to other names on the cards, and as you are doing this you are not only characterising those people, you are showing *the way in which you look at people*, i.e. something about yourself. The list of descriptive words which *you* generate as you go through the cards looking for ways of grouping and separating people, as well as objects and events, will be different from the list generated by other people – not only in the actual words used but in the special meaning these words have for you. The personality measure, then, is simply the list of descriptive words you produce, and this can be compared with lists produced by other people.

The kinds of scores people get on any personality measure vary with age: younger people tend to be more energetic, outgoing and risk-taking, whereas older people move more towards moderation and conservatism. It is also quite possible for people to 'switch types', temporarily at least. Bankruptcy, the death of a close relative or failing health can cause personality change.

3.4 Intelligence and Personality

To end this chapter we look briefly at some topics which draw equally on ideas about intelligence and personality. These are interests, creativity, decision style and staff selection.

3.4.1 Interests
One of the ways in which our own particular abilities combine with our own particular personality characteristics is shown in our patterns of interests. To put it the other way round, you could say that knowing a person's interests tells you a good deal about the psychological make-up of that person. Not for nothing do job application forms usually ask you to write down your main hobbies and interests. For example, supposing someone you were proposing to interview for a job gave his main interest as 'early church music' you might infer that personality-wise he was the quiet book-reading type rather than the flamboyant party-goer. You might also infer that this interest goes with a high level of education which also assumes a fairly high general intelligence. Interests tend to cluster together; for example if you looked further at the interests of our above job applicant you would not be surprised to read, 'history', 'bird-watching', 'choir'. Other interests such as 'tennis' or 'swimming' would be moderately compatible, but you would be very surprised if he also listed 'sewing' or 'ice skating' or 'local politics' since, for different reasons, none of these really fits his main interest.

3.4.2 Creativity
The usual tests of intelligence (or 'abilities') have been criticised for permitting only one correct answer, thus scoring 'creative' and original types of answer as wrong. You may have encountered the kinds of items used in tests of **creativity**. A common one is the *Uses of Objects* test where you have to write down all possible uses for a given everyday object such as a brick or a toothbrush. Other tests place you in hypothetical circumstances and ask

you to describe your experiences (e.g. if you had an eye on the end of your finger). While this open-ended kind of test situation is all very well, it has to be remembered that true creativity needs to be harnessed. Real life creativity has a direction and a final product of some kind such as a new design, a cost-saving idea, or a new article which fills a need.

Effective decision making would seem to make heavy demands on creative thinking, in so far as it involves an ability to step outside the problem situation and not assume anything, as well as an ability to attack a problem from all sides and draw on novel methods and resources to do so. You might expect 'ideas' people to be very intelligent, and up to a point you would be right. If we take the top people in a profession (i.e. best known, having the highest outputs, highest salaries, most responsibility, and so forth) you find that this élite are very intelligent, but not always exceptionally so. Indeed, there is some indication that provided a person has a level of intelligence roughly corresponding to that of a good college student, simply making him more intelligent is not going to make him any more creative. In fact it is much more useful to distinguish creative people from others on the basis of personality and pattern of motives rather than intelligence. Careful studies find that top creative people have a high need for achievement; they are determined, persistent, and in outlook they are unconventional and not afraid of being individualistic. They have a good sense of humour, and enjoy problems as opportunities for trying out adventurous, even risky ideas. It seems that their home life as children encouraged independence as well as a respect for learning and making good in life. (If this sounds like you, congratulations!)

This discussion of the way personality, intelligence and problem solving are linked now leads us into more specific consideration of the styles people display in various decision-making situations.

3.4.3 Decision Styles

Concern with the *style* in which people solve problems and indeed deal with the world at large has considerable bearing on the way people behave in decision-making situations. For example, some people like to deal with a problem configuration *as a whole*: a single decision to stop overtime work completely is one way of dealing with alleged lack of parity among overtime rates in different parts of an organisation; another global approach would be to bring in representatives from the disputing sections for a joint meeting. However, a different, piecemeal **decision style** would involve seeking a solution for each section in the organisation independently and perhaps playing one section off against another by meeting representatives separately and individually. As with measuring intelligence, whether the managers get the solution right or wrong is one thing, but the *way* they go about it possibly tells us more about the person if we want to assess his suitability for similar assignments in the future.

There are quite a few ways we could analyse style of decision making. One way, as we have just seen, is to discover whether the person prefers to tackle the *problem* itself piece by piece or in one fell swoop. Another way is to discover how much *information* he seeks, at what stages and how efficiently he uses it – something we pay attention to in Chapter 11. A third possible way is to look at how he uses *people* around him in approaching his decision. We could point to five styles here:

a. Own decision without detailed explanation.
b. Own decision with detailed explanation.
c. Prior consultation with subordinate.
d. Joint decision making with subordinate.
e. Delegation of decision to subordinate.

There are of course other relatively minor methods (e.g. chairman's action where a group vest authority in its leader to act on their behalf) but the principal methods appear to be those listed above.

Virtually all managers use three, four or all five styles according to circumstances. Moreover it seems to be the kind of task that determines which decision method is used.

3.4.4 Staff Selection

The most common way of getting at assessment is by interview with or without supplementary paper and pencil tests such as the Wechsler Intelligence Scale and the Cattell Personality Test described earlier. In theory at least, the interview is the most flexible way of dealing with an individual as a person. Well before the interview, the present and indeed the future specifications of the job as well as the technical and social skills needed to meet those specifications need to be agreed (see Fig. 3.4). Of course, there are good interviewers and bad. Being a good interviewer most obviously means making accurate assessments of candidates, and not being swayed by considerations such as physical attractiveness unless these are relevant and weighted accordingly. It also means being consistent and not shifting criteria to suit the day of the week.

The other half of being a good interviewer is an ability to receive the candidate properly and continually put him or her at ease while allowing the information to flow no matter how tricky and personal the area being explored: from this stems the flexibility of approach which a questionnaire assessment cannot have.

Figure 3.4 provides a check list of the sorts of things relevant to most job interviewing.

Paper and pencil tests of intelligence or personality such as those described earlier in the chapter have no off days; reliability from day to day and across all candidates is high, and they measure what they are supposed to measure without being distracted by such things as how candidates cross their legs. On the other hand the paper and pencil test has not got the flexibility to allow for the fact that the candidate may be tired or ill.

So called 'projective' tests are also used (see page 26). The candidate is shown a picture of some non-specific social situation and then asked to invent

1 Consider the job specification. Does it take account of future developments?
2 Consider the intelligence (abilities), experience and formal qualifications required.
3 Consider the personal qualities and the social skills required.
4 Reduce the basic qualifications to the minimum possible.
5 Discuss the structure of the interview with fellow selectors.
6 Consider the application in the light of the *formal qualifications* required (e.g. age 30–40; good first degree in engineering).
7 Consider the application in the light of the *personal qualities* required.
8 Examine the application (and referees' testimonials)—ensure there are no unexplained gaps in dates.
9 Arrange to reduce or eliminate telephone or other interruptions.
10 Arrange the seating to allow good communication in a relaxed atmosphere.
11 Be aware of your own prejudices about the candidates and about the job.
12 Make the 'small things' immediately clear to the candidate: where to sit, where to put his coat, and so on.
13 Decide upon your opening gambit—for instance whether to adopt a common link or a tell-me-about-yourself approach.
14 Do the minimum talking yourself. You and the other selectors should occupy only 5–10 per cent of the available speaking time.
15 Observe—don't switch off—when your fellow selectors are asking questions.
16 Lead into groups of subjects you want to discuss, with a sentence or two of preamble which prepares the candidate.
17 Avoid asking any questions which invite a simple 'Yes' or 'No'. If he insists on being laconic you can follow up with a further question— 'Why?'
18 Consider evidence from the past only as pointers towards possession or lack of the key qualities you are seeking.
19 Question with a purpose. Don't back down when crucial information is needed.
20 Get at the truth of the matter by indirect questioning if necessary.
21 Don't be aggressive. It will make the candidate hostile or nervous, neither of which helps you or him (unless you want to set up a 'stress interview').
22 Avoid any tendency to trick the candidate.
23 Tell the candidate about the job, terms and conditions.
24 Tell the candidate when he may expect an answer to his application.
25 Discuss facts and impressions with your fellow selectors and make up your minds.

(Adapted from John S. Gough, *Interviewing in Twenty-six Steps*.)

Fig. 3.4

a story around that picture: the idea is that by analysing his account one can get at unconscious sources of motivation and personality, for example, such things as the person's need to be with others, his need for achievement and his need for power. Personal difficulties can also be tapped using this technique.

Organisations such as the civil service and the forces as well as some business organisations often resort to some form of observational procedure as part of their selection process for top people. Candidates are placed in simulated problem situations, e.g. how to scale a wall or cross a river with minimum equipment. The way in which individual members offer advice, direct others, and themselves respond to instructions from others is a living demonstration of their intelligence and personality make-up, and unlike the relatively short interview situation, performance is pretty hard to fake over a period of hours or even days.

All in all, considerations about people's abilities and personalities turn out to be very important when we are trying to fit people to jobs in organisations or predict the kinds of decisions they will make. Job fitting itself is a serious business since mistakes in selecting key decision makers can be expensive. Nevertheless the present state of the art is less than perfect even when paper and pencil tests, and interviews and observation methods are *all* used.

Work Section

A. Revision Questions

A1 Why are differences among people of interest in a decision-making context?

A2 State how differences in intelligence come about.

A3 State how differences in personality come about.

A4 Compare the effectiveness of the paper and pencil test approach with observational assessment for both intelligence and personality.

A5 What is the distinction between 'verbal abilities' and 'performance abilities' in Wechsler's intelligence test (Fig. 3.2)?

A6 How is it that the decision making of a young child cannot be very sophisticated?

A7 What do you think would be the main similarities and differences between typical managers and airline pilots according to Cattell's scheme in Fig. 3.3?

A8 What is the relationship between intelligence and creativity?

A9 What are some of the ways of looking at people's styles of making decisions?

A10 Why are interviews often a key element of selection procedures?

A11 What qualities do you feel are needed by a good interviewer?

A12 How might (a) an interviewer, (b) an interviewee, prepare for an interview?

B. Exercises/Case Studies

B1 Bearing the considerations of section 3.4.4 in mind, let us assume that you work for a firm of selection consultants who have asked you to short-list people for the following job:

Industrial Relations Manager
Scotland, £12,000

The effective use of human resources is a prime objective of this appointment in a mass production environment. Covering every aspect of industrial relations from major negotiations to all legislative matters affecting employment, the successful candidate must have the stature and experience to gain the confidence and respect of both management and trade unions. Aged at least 30, candidates must have a proven career to date in a demanding multi-union situation in the engineering industry. Presence and personality are essential to meet the challenge of this role, coupled ideally with degree-level education. A first-class benefit package includes generous assistance with relocation, and further personal advancement is possible.

    a. State, with justification, the selection method(s) you would use.

    b. What might you be looking for from the applicants? (Check with Fig. 3.4.)

B2 a. Write as a list down the left-hand side of a sheet of paper the different components of intelligence shown in Fig. 3.3. Then along the top write the occupations: Accountant, Personnel Officer, Production Manager, Typist. Now for each occupational type run down the components of intelligence marking whether the person would have to be high (H), medium (M) or low (L) on each particular aspect to do the job with average competence.

    b. Compare your ratings with those of others in your group.

B3 **Selection Interview Exercise**

There is a job vacancy at Black and Grim Ltd. Elect four or five members of the group to choose the job, agree on its specification and generally follow points 1 to 5 in Fig. 3.4. Two or three others in the group should then write letters of application for the job in question and then be interviewed by the panel who try to bear in mind the remaining pointers in Fig. 3.4. Those people not directly involved in the exercise should observe and offer comments during each post-interview evaluation. Not least, some attention should be given to the written applications from the candidates: would they give a good impression in real life; did they appear to be pulling the wool; did they overplay or underplay their qualifications and experience?

B4 Think of some job in industry (or course at college) for which you are approximately qualified and draft a letter of application, as follows. Divide a sheet of lined A4 paper down the middle. On the left compose your letter of application (200 words maximum). On the right annotate what you have written in some detail so as to show: (a) the purpose behind *what* you have written; (b) the purpose behind *how* you have expressed it. Exchange your sheet with a partner and make comments on each other's applications.

C. Essay Questions

C1 'A thorough, methodical, and highly rational approach to problem analysis, while it has its advantages, tends to be stultifying to the creative mind. So, where creativity is vital, avoid overly analytical approaches.' Do you agree?

C2 'Creativity, like good looks, is an attribute that some people are born with. The only way to increase creativity in a firm is to find and use people who have it.' Comment on this statement.

C3 Write an essay on 'decision styles' in a wide variety of contexts ranging from family, through the army, politics and business. How applicable are the approaches in section **3.4.3** to each of these contexts?

C4 What other ways of looking at decision styles could have been introduced in section **3.4.3**? One example is how 'risky' the person is prepared to be. Try to develop some other examples.

C5 What are the pitfalls in trying to select the best man for the job?

C6 Re-read section **3.4.2** then develop some ideas of your own for: (a) tests of creativity; (b) ways of picking out people with progressive and imaginative ideas in the work situation.

C7 When selecting candidates for a job, do you believe it is more important to check their intelligence or their personality?

Chapter 4

Knowledge and Skills

Synopsis: *We can now build on the basic ideas about intelligence and personality which we picked up in the previous chapter. Knowing something about abilities allows us to talk about the kind of task-related knowledge and skills the decision maker obviously needs. The first type of knowledge and skill we encounter is* technical, *the kind that comes from one's technical training as a chemist or accountant, say, and which enables one to analyse the task structure efficiently. The second kind of knowledge and skill we call* social. *This includes the kind of people-handling skill unfortunately rarely taught, but essential to execute any decision efficiently. The second part of the chapter builds on what we have learnt about personality, and we examine one major way in which it enters the decision-making situation, through a person's response to stress. We show how stress must reduce the efficiency of the decision maker, and consider the consequences of experiencing too much stress for too long.*

Plan of the chapter: *This is illustrated in Fig. 4.1.*

4.1 Technical and Social Expertise

In the following sections we shall be looking at the importance of both job knowledge and job skills for the decision maker. We consider the stages that have to be gone through before a skill can be said to be thoroughly learned. We also examine some of the ways in which learning of both information and skills takes place.

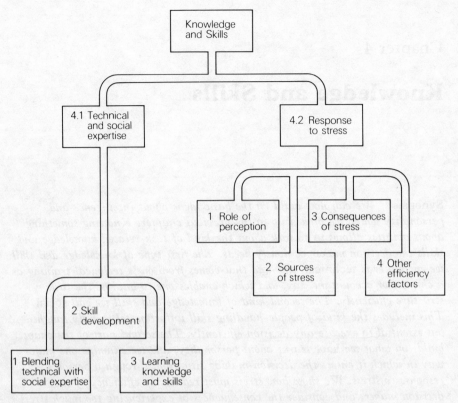

Fig. 4.1: Knowledge and skills

4.1.1 Blending Technical with Social Expertise

Probably all occupations depend on some 'mix' of technical and social knowledge and skills. Even someone whose job seems to be entirely concerned with materials, tools or instruments, such as a forensic analyst or panel beater, needs some social skill; the person has to know, for example, how to accept or decline work if he is overloaded and how to deal with objections and complaints from customers either directly or through his supervisor. The job of 'public relations officer' might appear to be wholly concerned with skills in handling people but you can probably think of several technical skills which are also involved. Similarly, family doctors, who are highly trained in the technical knowledge and skills of their profession, actually spend a large part of their time in advising, counselling and giving support even though they are definitely under-trained in these social skills.

One is often surprised by the sheer amount of information or 'know-how' one finds in a person who has been doing his job well for years. You go to him for *technical information* and he either gives you the answer directly or provides valuable short cuts and ways of restructuring the problem which you could not have imagined. He also displays *social information*, for example knowing who will act quickly or who will do you a favour in the different firms you may deal with, and he generally displays 'perspective' knowledge of what can and cannot be expected of different people. As a generalisation, young people at the time they begin a business career will need mainly the technical knowledge and skills appropriate to their profession such as accounting, marketing or product development, and rather little social know-how will be essential. However, as the person moves up the administrative hierarchy the proportions become reversed as more time is spent as a facilitator of the work of others. In fact people right at the top are often out of touch with the sheer technical knowledge and skills with which they began their careers.

4.1.2 Skill Development

Most skills are not acquired overnight but go through a series of learning stages during which performance of the skill improves.

a. Early Stage. The early stage is uncertain, jerky, fragmentary – and exasperating. You have read the instruction booklet, talked things over with your instructor and now you are having your first driving lesson. You sit in the driver's seat, noting the position and feel of the various indicators, switches and pedals.

As you move away jerkily in third gear the simultaneous awareness of foot pedals, speed indicators, rear-view mirrors, not to mention the possibility of killing somebody, causes great difficulty. It is true that you can perform bits of the skill fairly competently, but the bits still feel odd and they don't fit together properly.

Take quite a different example: learning the skill of running a committee. Before the first meeting you check through the members, trying to spot who may give difficulty and framing your approach to prevent such difficulties arising. But, as in learning to drive, what you anticipate will happen at the meeting and how you will handle it is quite different from how real events turn out. You discover that in trying to placate one member who has taken offence you have lost the thread of your own argument and in trying to recover it you make a silly gaffe which offends somebody else. In trying to discourage one member who breaks into irrelevant anecdotes at every opportunity, you frighten off quieter members. Your behaviour is again jerky, uncertain and ineffectual; as in the case of the first driving lesson, there is an exaggerated awareness of massive information inflow, with everything seeming to matter.

b. Intermediate Stage. You continue to practise and at last the bits of the skill begin to knit together. A crude sort of fluency begins to emerge. You now depress the clutch before attempting to change gear, and the car does not wobble so much when you remove one hand from the steering wheel. Moreover, you start to modify how hard you press the clutch or accelerator depending on the response of the car, i.e. feedback controls your efforts. In committee, you are able to listen and follow one speaker while 'stacking' others who want to contribute by means of eye contact and hand gesture. An acid comment does not throw you to such an extent that you reject out of hand everything else the person contributes. There is still some 'wobble' in your running of things, but you are more relaxed, your timing is getting better and there is structure, direction and sense of integration in your efforts.

c. Final Stage. It eventually happens that we climb into the car preoccupied with other matters and drive home from work without any consciousness of executing a skill as such. We can execute thousands of skills literally without thinking about them, as though we just actuate an automatic programme. The 'programme' responds automatically to the traffic and pedestrian situation, and all we have is peripheral awareness. In fact the extent to which a skill has moved from conscious to automatic control is an index of how competent we have become. The smooth control exercised by an experienced committee chairman is of this same kind: he no longer thinks what to do – he just responds spontaneously to the shifting demands of the meeting by drawing automatically on one or more of his arsenal of people-handling skills, such as the well-timed quick smile or frown. His brain is not choked with the here and now, and he can reflect on the course of the discussion, plan his summary and scan forward over agenda items yet to come.

4.1.3 Learning Knowledge and Skills

a. Learning by Associating New with Previous Experiences. One of the oldest views of learning is that it is a process of associating new experiences with our existing knowledge. If you have the misfortune to be caught in a lift, you will in future be apprehensive about lifts until, in the absence of further misadventure, the apprehension eventually subsides. A really bad experience, like being humiliated at work, may cause you to avoid the person responsible for months afterwards since, like the lift, that person becomes *associated* with the bad experience. Association also works positively, of course. You associate a new problem situation with a similar situation you experienced last year and this helps you tackle it.

We also meet learning by association in the world of advertising. By associating things which we admire, or cause us pleasure, with the manufacturer's product, the product itself comes to arouse in us some aspects of that pleasant experience and shapes our 'decisions' about that product. This is why cigarettes are typically advertised in country or sporting settings, and why some of the disarming innocence and purity of children eating a particular food is supposed to rub off on the product itself.

b. Learning through Instruction and Copying. Advertisers also depend on learning by imitation or copying. If you wish to be like this gentleman and exert a strange power over women, then you should smoke our brand of tobacco. We have learned from imitation throughout our lives, modelling our behaviour and opinions on what dad or a favourite uncle says or does, dressing in the way our favourite pop star dresses, so why should a little learning by imitation not take place as we watch television commercials?

Learning by copying is of course quite essential in *skill training* where the copying is normally preceded by instruction and followed by feedback on your degree of success. If you fail to observe the techniques used by your supervisor to control and win the support of subordinates you will progress less quickly; if you do not copy the instructor's grip and movements correctly in learning to use a rifle or operate a bench saw, you may not have a career at all.

One commonly followed technique for learning social skills is role-playing, where the trainee acts out different situations and thereby learns how it feels to be on both the giving and the receiving end. For example, a management trainee might try out three roles of 'complaining customer', 'innocent victim' and 'senior manager brought in to referee the action'. Before the role-playing is actually undertaken a good deal of groundwork is done through instruction and 'critical incident' analysis using video playback. Critical evaluation of good and bad points provides the feedback which completes the training loop.

c. Learning through Familiarisation. By simply encountering new ideas, new objects, new people, new experiences in everyday life we inevitably learn something, often a good deal, about them without any *deliberate* effort to learn. The way we learn a language is probably mainly through increasing familiarisation: for children language flows around them and understanding gradually occurs through immersion in it. Of course, sheer imitation of adults and also memorising play a part, but language learning in the child seems mainly a matter of understanding by 'getting used to it'. (Incidentally, the fact that school learning of a foreign language leans so heavily on memorisation helps to explain why the process is so difficult: learning by memorisation is quite unlike natural language learning primarily because it fails to integrate language with experience – a criticism that can also be aimed at language laboratories which mainly provide 'learning by imitation'.) The way we learn to perceive seems to depend upon simple familiarisation: the more we travel a particular route the more we are able to trace landmarks in our mind's eye even though there has been no conscious effort at memorising them. Most of the things we learn incidentally at work can be put down to sheer familiarisation. Learning to skim faster and more efficiently through documents is one example: one does it so many times that one becomes familiar with the probable structure, what to look for, what to ignore and what to query. Again without conscious learning effort, decisions start to become easier as we become familiar with different decision environments, e.g. what sorts of decisions are acceptable in what sorts of committees. Learning by familiarisation generally enables us to sort out things better, to pace our working week more efficiently, and to obtain a better understanding of our role in any organisation.

d. Learning by Memorising. There is a whole range of situations in which it is very important to be able to commit material to memory. We may be preparing for professional examinations or we may have to brief ourselves hurriedly to represent the firm when a senior is indisposed. We can, of course, learn things 'parrot fashion', in the same way that children learn tables or hymns, without understanding. It works, but unless we are reading to understand, what we do remember has very limited usefulness outside its specific purpose (e.g. examination learning is poorly integrated into our overall knowledge and is quickly forgotten). There are certain ways in which we can improve the speed of memorising as well as reduce the rate at which it is forgotten and this is taken up as a special exercise in the Work Section.

4.2 Response to Stress

The range of possible **stressors** is large and varied, as we shall see in 4.2.2. Whether or not a given person actually feels **stress** is very much related to his psychological make-up ('individual constraints' in our general decision model). In particular, it will become clear that *personality* is a major factor in determining whether a given situation is perceived as 'stressful'. For example, a 'tense' or 'reserved' person is going to feel more stress in the presence of other people than an 'outgoing' or 'relaxed' person (see Fig. 3.3).

4.2.1 The Role of Perception

The perceptual involvement in stress is quite striking. In trench warfare the perceived threat used to vary enormously among different men – as it now does in office warfare – even though the absolute danger is about the same for everyone. Mr Green may find working with Mr Baron stressful because he feels he is not appreciated and he has to work all the time to impress Mr Baron. But because Mr Baron's perception of the relationship is quite different he himself feels no stress. Or take the reverse case of a bright trainee who makes his supervisor feel old-fashioned, old and incompetent: the supervisor will therefore experience stress. Discrepancy between perceived *actual* performance and perceived *acceptable* performance must be a source of stress. The discrepancy can be reduced by 'working harder' but, as we know from the previous chapter, intelligence and personality factors must set upper limits on what can be achieved. Downward adjustment of what constitutes 'acceptable' performance would be a healthier solution, particularly since, as we saw in Chapter 2, managers who have a high need for achievement never allow themselves to reduce the discrepancy; they keep on adjusting their target upwards all the time.

4.2.2 Sources of Stress

As we said, the range of possible stressors is quite varied, but perhaps we can distinguish two broad types.

★ See Question B4

a. Mental Stressors. These include making unreasonable demands on ourselves in terms of personal objectives, or *feeling* that other people are making such unreasonable demands. You can feel overworked even though your workload may be less than that of colleagues: stress does not in fact derive from hard work, only from a succession of seemingly insoluble problems, especially when compounded with other problems in one's personal relationships.

We must recognise *frustration*, the failure to satisfy one's needs, as a major source of stress. Two common sources of frustration are:

i. Personal Inadequacy. To get to the top – however you may define 'top' yourself – you need certain qualities of intelligence and personality to allow you to develop the knowledge and skills we have been speaking of earlier. If you do not have these yet your ambitions persist, then you will experience frustration due to personal inadequacy.

ii. Conflict of Needs or Objectives. If you cannot make up your mind which of two careers to follow, or whether to go for long- or short-term benefits, you obviously have a conflict of some kind. Such examples of dithering between two or more apparently equally attractive alternatives give rise to frustration, even if of a rather self-indulgent kind. More compelling is the case of two or more courses of action all equally unpleasant for oneself or others, one of which must still be chosen. Perhaps most disruptive is the case where a person is both attracted and repelled by a course of action at one and the same time. In business one can imagine conflict arising in a situation where the envisaged action being contemplated is cruel to the individual who may be a friend (e.g. sacking or transferring him) but kind to the organisation (e.g. by relieving a bottleneck in administration). The person who has the power to make the decision must, in such a situation, feel some sense of what is called 'approach-avoidance' conflict. Similar conflict might arise in permitting barely legal dealings which could be vastly profitable to the firm. Any doubt between possible courses of action and the resultant inability to come to a decision – is a source of conflict and hence of stress.

b. Physical Stressors. Prolonged heat or cold are obvious examples of physical stressors. Noise *can* be disruptive, though it is least disruptive for low-level, routine tasks and most disruptive for any skill which is incompletely learned or involves making complex decisions. One can get used to continuous noise at reasonable levels, but a given noise level is more disruptive in on–off sequences, especially when the onset of the noise is unpredictable. What constitutes 'noise' is to some extent personal and depends on what you are doing; a raucous pop station which is just the thing while you work under your car at the weekend would become an impossible distractor if placed on your desk on Monday morning.

4.2.3 Consequences of Stress
It is not only normal but highly necessary that people should be able to draw

on appropriate bodily reserves in times of emergency, e.g. in personal danger, or when there is some need to work all night on a problem. But some people spend the larger part of their working, and even their domestic, lives in this 'emergency zone'. In consequence their physiological systems, whose role it is to respond in emergency conditions, work too long and too hard. Blood pressure, heart rate and adrenalin levels are unnecessarily high, blood is shunted from the viscera to the brain, head and limbs, the mouth is dry; skeletal muscles are tense, and so on. Physiologically as well as psychologically the person is in a near-permanent state of anxiety. Not surprisingly, various psychosomatic ('mind-on-body') illnesses are the result. Continuous high arousal causes high acid levels in the stomach which eventually cause a lesion in the membrane lining, an ulcer, which rather like the old soldier's war wound has become a badge of office in the business world. Of course, while some people are busy developing ulcers, others are working towards heart attacks or asthma, since different kinds of stress seem to lead to different psychosomatic symptoms.

The decision maker's *outward* behaviour is also affected by stress. He loses sensitivity, imagination and flexibility and instead goes about each new problem in the same old, rigid way. He is also nervous and jumpy at work; he snaps at people without reason or warning and picks on silly things to complain about. In short he is anxious, inefficient, and probably depressed: it is not difficult to see how alcohol becomes a too quick and ready friend in such circumstances.

4.2.4 Other Efficiency Factors
There are also other factors which affect efficiency. Each of us has what might be called a 'personal efficiency curve' which describes how the quality of our work changes in step with changing activity levels in our brain and nervous system. Just before going to sleep, during sleep itself and just after waking up, the activity level in the brain and nervous system is very low (i.e. we feel 'sluggish'). This physiological activity also drops after a heavy meal, in the middle of a boring task, and in fact at any time when we are feeling drowsy. Our activity level increases as we move around and perform different tasks: our heart rate steps up, our muscular co-ordination improves, our brain feels alert. We are now in the optimal range of the efficiency. Given that there exists an optimal operating zone for individuals in each task, it is also true that this optimal zone is reached, by different individuals, at different times in their day. For example, it is quite common for some people to make their best decisions early in the day while others may be at their optimum as late as 9 p.m. – well outside the normal working day.

There is good evidence that people changing shifts show quite good adaptation but it is seldom complete. The reason for this could be the conflicting daily cycles of activity of the people they live with and of fixed events such as television programmes, as well as evidence of their senses concerning when it is night or day. It is noticeable in organisations operating a shift system that 'days off' involving a return to the normal day–night cycle are particularly disruptive in preventing proper adaptation to the artificial shift cycle. Airline pilots, who are continuously involved in making important decisions about the state of the aircraft, show marked depression of performance during the first day after they fly into a time zone eight hours behind the one they left, but recovery is good by day three and apparently complete by day eight.

Hard evidence suggests that there is surprisingly little fall in efficiency with age in a wide range of occupations. The fall occurs mainly in occupations where there is time stress of some kind, e.g. piece-rate working in heavy engineering plants, or generally where slight impairment of vision or hearing, together with slower thinking, starts to affect the work rate. Age reduces both the information capacity and the processing speed of the executive decision maker, although as we said above this will be compensated in many cases by sheer skill fluency derived from experience. According to available evidence older employees are *not* more prone to accidents or absenteeism – if anything they have a better record in these respects than younger workers and they are much more likely to stay on in their jobs. Thus a fair amount of mythology exists about the 'problems' of employing older staff.

Work Section

A. Revision Questions

A1 Explain, with examples, what is meant by technical as compared with social skills.

A2 What kinds of technical skills are required by a public relations officer?

A3 Outline the stages involved in acquiring a skill, giving illustrations different from those in the chapter.

A4 Identify four ways we learn new information and/or skills and give brief examples different from those in the chapter.

A5 Why is perception crucial in deciding whether or not stress will be experienced?

A6 What kinds of person are most vulnerable to (a) mental stressors, (b) physical stressors?

A7 Describe the effects of prolonged stress and explain how these effects can come about.

A8 In what ways can increasing age *both* improve and reduce efficiency at work?

A9 State six ways in which task efficiency may be affected.

B. Exercises/Case Studies

B1 Four ways in which we learn new things were discussed in section 4.1.3. These were: by association of old with new experience; by instruction and copying; by familiarisation; by memorising. Discuss the extent to which each of these might be involved in (a) learning formal and informal organisational structures, and (b) learning 'public speaking'.

B2 Make up a list of things or situations in everyday life which you find stressful. Compare your list with that of others in your group.

B3 A health insurance firm has suggested in its advertising that ulcers, appendixes, gallstones and the like are 'some of Britain's key decision makers'. They claim that 'all too often important decisions are made by staff while working below par due to debilitating illnesses. And the effect on a company's performance can be serious.'

Questions
a. Do you believe this is true?
b. What could an individual do about it?
c. What could the organisation do about it?

B4 How to Memorise Material

This is a 'case study' focussing on and elaborating a point in the main text.

As we saw in section 4.1.3, one of the most heavily used ways of learning new things – and one of the most arduous – is learning by memorising. The following suggestions can make the process less painful and provide useful hints for your own approach to studying. Read them through, then answer the questions at the end – each question refers back to the suggestion of the same number.

a. Space Your Learning Effort

If you had only an hour to memorise background materials for a meeting tomorrow morning it is unlikely that you would get best results by attacking the material for a solid hour and then moving on to another task. Depending on the length of the material, you would recall more from two half-hour sessions, and perhaps more still by arranging four sessions of fifteen minutes each during the evening.

b. Learn Material Well Past the Point at Which You 'Just' Know It

If you want to remember something really thoroughly, so-called 'over-learning' has enormous benefits. Everyday examples of this over-learning are our own name, address and telephone number; we know them instantly without any effort at recall.

c. Look for Similarities and Contrasts Between the Present and Previously Learned Material

Nothing is ever entirely new. Memorising briefing documents becomes easier the more times you do it, in the same way that learning parts for an actor gets easier the more parts he tackles. Psychologists talk about this as 'learning to learn' – having successfully completed similar tasks previously facilitates access to the new task as well as improving one's confidence about completing it successfully.

d. Motivate Yourself by Working Out the Consequences of Success and Failure

Unless you are *interested* in what you are remembering you are going to be reduced to rote or 'parrot' learning no matter how much time you spend on it: your attention will drift and you will find yourself taking frequent coffee trips.

e. Recognise That a Small Amount of Anxiety Is A Good Thing

At sluggish levels more nervous arousal will improve your performance (see 4.2.4), but if you have left yourself only five minutes for an important briefing your brain is bound to feel paralysed and the only result may be confusion. While the anxiety increases the strength of your *desire* to learn the material, it also increases the strength of all other responses including sweating, tension, palpitations and the imagined consequences of failure: all of these crowd into your awareness and compete for your attention.

f. Organise the Material Into Meaningful 'Chunks'
Read the whole block of material through two or three times for an outline of meaning and to obtain an ordered framework. Then memorise each 'natural' section as it occurs on the basis of meaning not format: learning line by line or page by page is not a good idea since artificial boundaries are involved having no relationship to the meaning sequence.

g. Rehearse the Material You Are Memorising During As Well As After Reading It
The surest way of finding out whether you really are remembering material is to test yourself after each section or page or even after each paragraph. *Knowing* that you will have to answer questions at the end of the page or section (like our 'A' questions) means that you start to 'read for recall', the attention is more sharply focussed and you become more consciously aware of committing material to memory. Further, by continuously going over material *during* the process of memorising you receive early warning of where the holes in the learning fabric exist; thus, special attention can be given to more difficult sections. Not least, this approach gives the learner continuous *practice* in active remembering: it is really unwise to spend all of your available time in 'storing' the information and expecting it all to be available in *one* 'retrieval' – at the meeting or examination.

Questions
a. Why do you think several 'spaced' attempts at learning are better than spending all your allocated time in one big effort?
b. What are other examples of 'overlearning' in everyday life?
c. Does 'learning to learn' apply to learning languages – would you expect each new language learned to get easier or for it to be confused with the one previously learned?
d. If you do find material to be learned very boring, what can you do about it?
e. Assume you have one hour available every evening for a week to prepare for your end of term business studies examination. Now consider the following two strategies, and indicate how well you would expect to fare from following each of them: (a) each evening 40 min. spent in learning and 20 min. in recalling; or (b) 20 min. spent in learning and 40 min. in recalling. Relate your answers to the complementary question of spacing work effort – Question (a) above.

C. Essay Questions

C1 Make a list of (a) technical skills (b) social skills required by an efficient decision maker in your own profession (actual or intended).

C2 Why do you think some people are quicker than others at getting through the stages of learning a skill? (Answer in terms of differences in personality and abilities.)

C3 We claim in this chapter that making good decisions requires the right kind of intelligence linked to the right technical skills, while good implementation of those decisions requires the right personality allied to the right social skills. In what ways is this an oversimplification? (You will find tackling this question a helpful warm-up for later chapters on the decision-making process.)

C4 Argue the case for and against greater flexibility in the timing of a day's work for different types of worker.

Chapter 5

Leadership

Synopsis: *We have now given enough attention to the psychological make-up of the decision maker to take an extended look at the topic of leadership which brings many of these ideas together. The first main section concentrates on the generally agreed* functions *of a leader, which traditionally break down into fulfilment of task needs, of group needs and of individual needs. We then turn to* models *of leadership. Most of the early research in this area seemed to be seeking a pattern of personal characteristics that would somehow define the 'ideal leader'. Findings were inconsistent, so that emphasis then shifted to a consideration of* style *in leading others, or the way in which different proven leaders operate. Some good progress was made but eventually this approach in turn gave way to a focus on* group and situational *factors which, it was argued, must be the ultimate determinants in deciding which people emerge as leaders and how effective they are. Finally we present a more recent account of leadership which attempts to synthesise these three rather different approaches.*

Plan of the chapter: *This is illustrated in Fig. 5.1.*

5.1 What does a Leader Do?

It has been proposed by Michael Argyle that the leader has functions in three somewhat overlapping areas: task needs, group needs and individual needs. If a leader neglects any of these areas there will be harmful consequences, for they are all interrelated. For example, if the *task* is not being achieved the morale of the group will tend to fall and lower *individual* satisfaction – possibly resulting in internal conflict that may disrupt the *group*. In different

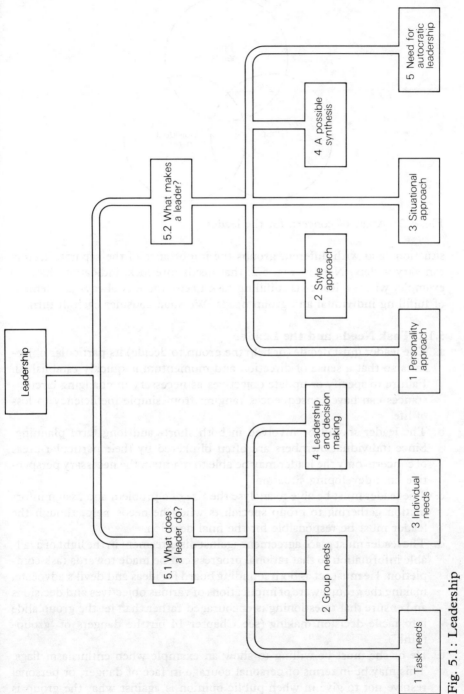

Fig. 5.1: Leadership

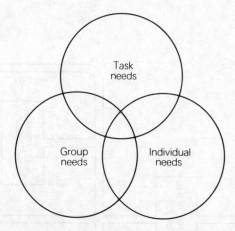

Fig. 5.2: Areas of concern for the leader

situations and with different groups the importance of the separate factors can vary widely. Note in Fig. 5.2. that needs interlock, indicating that, for example, where a leader is fulfilling task needs there is always an element of fulfilling individual and group needs. We shall consider each in turn.

5.1.1 Task Needs and the Leader

a. The leader must decide (or help the group to decide) its particular objectives so that a sense of direction and momentum is quickly established. Failure to specify or update objectives as necessary in changing circumstances can have consequences ranging from simple inefficiency to loss of life.

b. The leader should be involved in both short- and long-term planning. Since individual members are often blinkered by their particular areas of concern, only the leader may be able to maintain the necessary perspective on a developing situation.

c. The leader must be able to analyse the size of a problem and assign information gathering to group specialists when he needs help, though the leader must be responsible for the final decision.

d. The leader must place agreement against disagreement in the light of available information so that rational progress can be made towards task completion. He must act as both sounding board for ideas and devil's advocate, making the group aware of implications of various objectives and decisions and ensure that questioning is encouraged rather than let the group slide into facile decision making (see Chapter 14 on the dangers of 'groupthink').

e. He or she must be willing to show an example when enthusiasm flags. This may be in terms of personal courage in face of danger, or personal resolve not to give in when public opinion is against what the group is doing.

f. The leader must see that the tasks facing a group are carried out. The leader will normally delegate most of these – particularly within a complex formal group. In order to see that execution has been satisfactory, standards and controls must be set up, and each action must be reviewed in the light of the objectives.

g. Particularly within informal groups and in emergency situations, the leader must often provide relevant expertise. In complex situations he will also draw upon skills and information present within the group, although it will still be the leader's responsibility to formulate and co-ordinate these contributions so that action can be taken.

h. If tasks are to be successfully fufilled there is normally a need for the leader to open up external contacts. Such outside resources provide information and ideas as well as making clear to others the specialist skills or activities of the group.

5.1.2 Group Needs and the Leader

a. The leader will, directly or indirectly, decide the organisational structure – the hierarchy and lines of authority – and the methods by which the group will function, through individual or group assignments. Hence he will substantially control the internal relationships of individual members of the group. This function is obviously particularly important within formal groups where certain kinds of contact may be debarred.

b. It is normally left to the leader to allocate rewards and punishment. This needs to be done on both a short- and long-term basis, using both financial and non-financial methods. Examples are the way in which the Prime Minister uses the Honours List, the managing director uses promotion and the supervisor uses allocation of overtime and types of work. The leader/manager must also warn, reprimand and even be prepared to dismiss staff when the normal practice of reward and support is not effective in bringing about the desired effort.

c. It is the leader who acts as arbitrator or conciliator when there are internal group problems. He must always have in mind the need for group cohesion and stability.

d. Initially, the leader normally accepts the major norms of the group and assists in disseminating these both among the group and to people outside. As time progresses, he has to see that norms evolve in line with the objectives and attitudes of the group. A glance at the political scene shows that the leader cannot move too far in advance of group norms if he or she is to retain acceptance by members.

5.1.3 Individual Needs and the Leader

While many needs of the individual may be satisfied by interaction with others in the group, there are others which could well be handled more specifically by the leader.

a. The leader can stand in and protect members from individual responsibility. There are many who will give group allegiance in exchange for being relieved of certain responsibilities in decision making, and most members need to consult and receive guidance from time to time.

b. Some members need to use their leader as a 'father figure'. If a leader can honestly fulfil this need it indirectly gives him great power over such members.

c. The leader provides goals for personal achievement and for recognition of performance, and has to be prepared to become the scapegoat when things go wrong. In disastrous circumstances, a group may preserve some self-respect by deposing the leader.

The more a leader enables individual members to find fulfilment of their individual needs the more power he will exercise and the more cohesive and single-minded the group will be. As examples, authority needs can be recognised by giving out impressive job titles, self-actualisation needs by pacing the assignments given to members so that they can become progressively more competent without experiencing hard falls.

5.1.4 Leadership and Decision Making

Leadership really implies something over and above being a good decision maker. Some of these 'extras' are as follows:

● A brilliant decision maker may be a failure as a leader because he lacks the *personal qualities* necessary for leadership, as discussed in 5.2.1.

● A leader must be able to represent the group to his superiors and to outside bodies.

● A leader has to set *examples* as well as make decisions.

● A leader has to exercise considerable *social skills* in such activities as delegation, execution and implementation, and particularly in keeping his team together and motivated and helping them to satisfy their own individual needs.

5.2 What Makes A Leader?

Having given an overview of the functions and responsibilities of a leader, we can now look at different theoretical approaches which have tried to define the essence of leadership. These go under the headings of the personality approach, the leadership style approach and the situational approach.

5.2.1 The Personality Approach

The leader has fascinated observers through the ages. In traditional society the leader was often associated with abnormal ability. He was able to read people's minds, to foresee the future and to provide cures for mental and physical ills. In the early part of this century, men still believed that leaders had special powers, though the claims were becoming somewhat milder. There were attempts to collect lists of these claims, by observing or reading about actual leaders or by simply theorising about the ideal leader.

A large number of personality traits of the kind talked about in Chapter 3, for example, having initiative, courage, intelligence, imagination, perseverance, and so on, were thought to be either desirable or necessary in a leader. In fact, lists eventually became so long that only supermen would have been capable of fulfilling the specifications.

More recently, rather more systematic studies of the leader have been carried out and they emerge with the following kind of list of traits and behaviour patterns possessed by leaders:

a. They have proven competence in one or more task-related areas.
b. They tend to be brighter than the norm in the group (but not so bright that they are unaccepted by the group as a normal member).
c. They are alert and energetic.
d. They are better adjusted psychologically and tend to be interpersonally more sensitive.
e. They are self-confident and decisive.
f. They tend to display better judgement.
g. They possess fluency of speech and skill in using speech to persuade.
h. They tend to interact more than non-leaders and both give, and ask for, more information.
i. They display strong group solidarity and belief in the importance of the group.
j. They take the lead in interpreting, or summarising, situations.

It may immediately be seen that most of the above traits are tied to the *tasks* of leadership and are not just personality traits in a vacuum. This changing emphasis foreshadows the appreciation, around 1940, that a personality approach to leadership was by itself insufficient.

5.2.2 The Leadership Style Approach

We had occasion in Chapter 3 to discuss the way in which managers used different 'decision styles' in their jobs – whether they tackled problems as a whole or in bits, whether they consulted, explained, delegated, and so on. This functional approach to defining leadership, by examining how leaders vary in the way they execute tasks (rather than trying to detail the personal qualities they may possess) was given special impetus around 1940 by the now famous experiments of Lewin, Lippitt and White. Their early work involved observing adult leaders in a boys' club, and the findings have since been broadly corroborated by other studies. They set out to compare **autocratic** versus **democratic leadership styles,** although they also came up with information on the consequences of leave-'em-to-it or **laissez-faire** leadership style. We can look at each in turn.

a. The Autocratic or Authoritarian Leader
i. He sets his own objectives, makes his own plans, then gives orders that he insists be obeyed.
ii. He usually only unfolds his plan piece by piece, so that followers have

difficulty in knowing why they are doing things or how their work fits
in with that of others.

iii. He lays down exactly how work should be done.

iv. He organises the work teams within the group and often arranges a formal
communication structure of the type shown in Fig. 5.3, (a) and (b) (the
second diagram shows the leader working through a lieutenant).

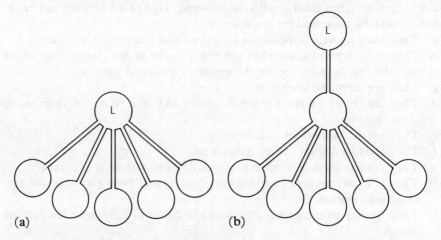

Fig. 5.3: Autocratic Communication Patterns
(L = Leader; circles represent other members)

v. He tends to keep himself apart from the group and requires from group
members single-minded commitment without interpersonal ties.

vi. He tends to act without personal feelings for the members of the group
and their differing needs. He is inclined to arbitrary praise or punishment,
unrelated to task achievement.

Consequences of Authoritarian Leadership

i. The group becomes very dependent on the leader.

ii. The group gains little cohesion.

iii. There are very few suggestions from the group, which really adopts a
very passive role.

iv. There is a tendency towards high output (when supervised) but this is
often of a low quality, with a high waste factor.

v. Among themselves, the members are often irritable and aggressive.

vi. The group is often dissatisfied with the leadership and with its own
general situation.

b. The Democratic or Participative Leader

i. Under this kind of leadership as many tasks as possible are shared by
the group. These tasks will include policy making, planning and execution
as well as keeping group members themselves informed on all matters.

ii. The group is allowed to organise its own methods of work and members choose their working companions.
iii. Formal communications are of the type shown in Fig. 5.4. Far greater use would be made of informal networks than would be found in authoritarian structures. Committees would be much in evidence and these would be used for genuine distribution of resources and less for haranguing or horsetrading.

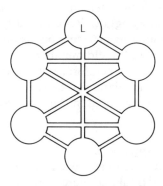

Fig. 5.4: Participative Communication Network

iv. The leader attempts to encourage the full development of each member as a contributor to the group.
v. The leader praises the group for its performance according to its successes at attaining agreed objectives.

Consequences of Democratic Leadership
i. There is a low dependency on the leader, who becomes very integrated into the group.
ii. The group has high cohesion.
iii. There is a high frequency of suggestions from members.
iv. Output is of average quantity, whether supervised or not, but the quality is high.
v. There is great group cohesion and a low incidence of aggressiveness and irritability.
vi. The group tends to be satisfied with its activities.

c. The Laissez-Faire (or let-them-get-on-with-it-themselves) Leader
This 'leadership' style cropped up incidentally in Lewin's early study when one adult leader of the boys' group became carried away with the democratic style and simply left the boys to sort themselves out, contributing little more than his physical presence. The result was mild anarchy.

Consequences of Laissez-Faire Leadership
i.   There is little dependence on the leader.
ii.   There is an extremely high level of suggestion from the group.
iii. Productivity is at an average level.
iv.   There is often great discontent about achievement and general activities.
v.   There is great irritability and aggressiveness amongst members.

It must *not* be assumed that there is one ideal style of leadership. In fact it may be that a good leader is one who is versatile enough to use all three styles as and when the situation demands it. It is not hard to see that the different stages of a meeting might well require just such style variation, and the same might be true for groups starting out as opposed to mature groups, groups with young as opposed to old members, groups enjoying good times or groups in crisis, and so on. Therefore, *style versatility* rather than ability to conform to a style formula might well be the key to successful leadership, and some element of this is captured in the 'situational' approach to leadership, which we now discuss.

5.2.3 The Situational Approach

During the 1950s the personality approach was rejected as being unhelpful. According to a new way of thinking, there were no particular qualities which could be said to characterise all leaders, since a military leader, a business leader, a miners' leader, and a religious leader must surely all be different kinds of animal. What matters, it was proclaimed, is not the person so much as the context or situation in which he operates; this is what determines whether he will emerge as leader. Indeed, it is easy to agree that a person who is very successful as a union leader could well be a disaster as a church leader. Nevertheless, the wish to sweep away personality aspects entirely was a mistake, since there does exist a cluster of personality traits which seems to recur in various studies of leadership personality.

A second implication of this emphasis on situational factors is that, even for the same group, different situations, such as getting the group launched, dealing with slack morale, steering the group through financial crisis, will themselves require different *kinds* of leadership from within the group as these various stages evolve. Indeed it does happen that an elected leader may temporarily hand over part or all of his function to one or more members of the group in situations he is not competent to handle. If he does not, a point may arise at which group members force him to hand over control: mutiny is a graphic example of such a process, or in business the dismissal of an incompetent chairman by angry shareholders.

5.2.4 A Possible Synthesis

A well-regarded group approach that has tried to synthesise the best of the personality style and the situational interpretations of leadership is that of Fiedler. Fiedler worked mainly with natural groups such as production teams, working parties and policy-forming committees, as well as with groups in non-business spheres. He found one type of leader who showed a directive, task-oriented style and a second type which was less directive and more social-emotionally oriented. Fiedler considered more than leadership style, and this is where the strength of his approach lies. He wanted to know: (a) whether interpersonal relationships were good or poor – by seeing how much liking was expressed among members for the leader; (b) whether the leader's power or authority was strong or weak; and (c) whether the tasks performed by each group were well or poorly structured in terms of objectives. The essential findings of Fiedler's research are summarised in Fig. 5.5.

	Interpersonal relations were –	Task was –	Authority was –
Ⓐ An *autocratic* was better than a democratic style when...			
	Good	Structured	Weak or strong
	Good	Unstructured	Strong
	Poor	Unstructured	Weak
Ⓑ A *democratic* was better than an autocratic style when...			
	Not good	Structured	Strong
	Good	Unstructured	Weak

Fig. 5.5: Fiedler's model of how simultaneous consideration of three variables is necessary in order to determine the most efficient leadership style

We take up the possible reasons for such findings in the Work Section, but for the moment you can see that neither of the two leadership styles, autocratic or democratic, can be considered better for all circumstances: it is the interplay among the three components that is the paramount determinant. On the other hand we may reasonably wonder just how exhaustive or representative are the three criteria that Fiedler examines; is there nothing else about groups that might affect leader effectiveness? In fact in his later work Fiedler introduces 'member similarity' and 'amount of stress' as additional factors, and you may be able to think of others that could well be relevant.

5.2.5 Need for Autocratic Leadership
The swing to human relations emphasis in management studies should not lead us into thinking that autocratic (or authoritarian) leadership is an unnecessary evil. We were at pains in Chapter 2 to show that Taylor's essential ideas, although they may not dignify the worker, can be effective in certain circumstances. Fiedler's findings also show that the autocratic control is

suitable in a wide range of situations. Indeed, some earlier research has been accused of starting from a human relations bias which influences the kinds of experiments done and the kinds of interpretations imposed on the findings. For example, it is difficult to establish from available evidence that supervisor behaviour (good or bad) *causes* similarly good or bad productivity in workers – could it not be that when good productivity already exists this permits increased concern about employees by the supervisor since he has less need to worry about production? We can develop this 'devil's advocate' line of argument into something more substantial by recognising indicators of when autocratic leadership is actually desirable.

a. Task-Related Indicators
i.   When the traditions of the organisation are of an autocratic type. Thus consulting with the group might here be seen as a sign of weakness or ignorance.
ii. When there is a type of organisation which does not allow for consultation. This might occur for geographical reasons or when it is necessary to keep a plan confidential, as in new product development.
iii. When the problem may demand specialist skills which only the leader possesses.
iv. When there is great pressure on time. This is particularly evident in an emergency, or with a crash programme. Often the most important requirement here is decisive, co-ordinated effort. The group will normally accept autocratic leadership in such situations, for a short time.
v.   When the leader sees his job as very task-oriented.

b. Group-Related Indicators
i.   If members are young and untrained, in which case direct instruction helps them more than consultation since they have no experience.
ii. If members have a low level of personal independence.
iii. If members have no willingness to assume responsibility.
iv. If members prefer clear-cut orders to living with a high level of ambiguity (such a preference often results from previous autocratic environments).
v.   If the group members are uninterested in the task, or do not feel an identification with the group's goals.
vi. If members like or want autocratic leadership. There is evidence that workers who are themselves authoritarian in disposition also prefer this kind of leadership.

c. Leader-Related Indicators
i.   When the leader is convinced he has been picked and given the pay and responsibility to make decisons for the group.
ii. When, by nature, he has an autocratic personality.
iii. When he has little confidence in the group members or in their skills.
iv. When he feels very insecure or uncertain.

Work Section

A. Revision Questions

A1 Summarise and give examples of the three kinds of needs to which any leader must address himself.

A2 Outline the job of the leader in a decision-making group.

A3 To what extent are particular personality characteristics now thought to be necessary in a leader?

A4 Explain the differences between an autocratic and a democratic style of leadership.

A5 Summarise the effects on the group of the three kinds of leadership style; autocratic, democratic and laissez-faire.

A6 What is meant by the situational approach to understanding leadership?

A7 How does Fiedler's synthesis of the personality, style and situational approaches to leadership claim to offer advantages?

A8 What ingredients do you feel are still being missed out of the available models of leadership?

A9 In what circumstances would you advocate the use of autocratic control?

B. Exercises/Case Studies

B1 **Case Study: the Greenwood Post Office**
The Greenwood Post Office staff consisted of a small, closely-knit group of about 15 employees, many of whom had worked in the office for a number of years. Beginning about 1970, the post office began to experience rapid growth because of the influx of new industry into the town. As a result of this development, it was not long before the post office had grown to the point that Mr Perkins, the postmaster, could no longer supervise the post office staff personally. An additional administrator named Mr Grey was brought in to fill a newly authorised position of assistant postmaster. This move constituted a promotion for Mr Grey, who had just completed 20 years of service at another post office where he had, in the main, been a postman. After being given about a week to become oriented, Grey was placed in charge of the post office personnel. Efficiency began to deteriorate rapidly within the office, and confusion increased as the employees refused to accept his authority. Furthermore, since the physical facilities of the post office were inadequate, both Perkins and his new assistant were forced to maintain their desks in a corner of the work area where they were easily accessible to

the other personnel. The office arrangement made it easy for the office personnel to continue to take problems directly to Perkins and to bypass Grey. Because of this practice Grey became virtually a figurehead. The continued growth of the post office, however, eventually forced Perkins to delegate more decision making to Grey. Since he had previously been ignored and bypassed, Grey was reluctant to use much initiative in making decisions and, whenever possible, relied upon the postal manual for support. Often mail postmen consumed so much time disputing interpretations of the manual with Grey that they were unable to complete their mail routes within the time prescribed. Grey also initiated the practice of holding a 30–45-minute meeting each morning to discuss operating procedures and problems. The postmen soon regarded these meetings as an attempt by Grey to emphasise his authority and as an effort by him to gain prestige and status. Their response was to add the time taken up by Grey to the normal eight hours that they were supposed to have for completing their routes. The extra time that they utilised constituted overtime.

Upon discovering the substantial increases in overtime that were accumulating, Perkins became quite concerned and demanded to know the cause for these increases. Discussions that Perkins had with the postmen disclosed the fact that they resented the morning meetings and considered them to be a waste of time. Acting upon the basis of their complaints, Perkins directed Grey to discontinue holding the daily meetings except when there was some urgent problem to discuss. Grey quite naturally resented this directive; even more, he resented the fact that the postmen had ignored his authority by going directly to the postmaster with their complaint about the meetings. Following this incident, Grey became quite disagreeable in his relations with subordinate personnel and relied entirely upon the use of an autocratic approach in performing his administration responsibilities.

As the post office continued to expand, larger quarters were eventually obtained which permitted a private office for both the postmaster and the assistant postmaster. The position of superintendent was also established and filled by means of an internal promotion. The superintendent located his desk in the operating area of the mailroom where he supervised the work directly. Both morale and efficiency in the post office began to improve substantially, and Grey's job developed largely into one of handling paperwork.

His contacts with the postmen and clerks were kept at a minimum.

Questions
1. Why was Grey not accepted by the staff?
2. Why did he initiate the 45-minute morning meetings?
3. Why did he turn to the official manual?
4. How could Grey have handled the situation better?

5. How could Perkins have helped more?
6. Was the eventual solution a satisfactory one?
7. How would you have handled the introduction of the new assistant chief into the set-up described?

C. Essay Questions

C1 Compare and contrast the kinds of 'leadership behaviour' that probably occur between:
   a. a football team manager and the team captain – a football team manager and members of the team;
   b. a site foreman and student vacation workers on a building site – a site foreman and regular labourers;
   c. a university professor and his academic colleagues – a university professor and undergraduates.

C2 Compare Argyle's representation of needs in Fig. 5.2 with the model adopted by Herzberg in Fig. 2.3. In what ways are they similar yet different?

C3 Would you advocate any particular style of leadership in preference to another?

C4 'A good leader may sometimes give the impression that he is rather a stupid fellow, an arbitrator, a mere channel of communication and a filcher of ideas.' Comment on this.

C5 Alex Bavelas has said that in large modern organisations leadership no longer consists of making personal decisions, but rather maintaining the operational effectiveness of the organisation. He sees the picture of the leader keeping his own counsel and coming to his own decisions as outdated: he also sees brilliant innovation on the part of the manager as rapidly becoming an organisational embarrassment. What do you feel about such suggestions?

Chapter 6

People in Groups

Synopsis: *The first way in which other people influence our decisions is through laying down the 'individual constraints' that determine how we perceive, think and decide. We consider how family, friends and work colleagues exercise a crucial role in shaping the beliefs, attitudes, motives, and indeed the whole personality of the person, from infancy into adulthood. We then try to link particularly attitudes to behaviour, partly through considering evidence from organisational attitude surveys.*

The second way in which people affect our decisions is directly as external *constraints. Lawyers, local government officers, tax officers and many other professionals, spend a large part of their working lives acting as external constraints regulating people's actions. Even stronger and more pervasive constraints on our decision making arise from the 'social groups' to which we belong. Perhaps only relatively occasionally does the ordinary person come up against laws and regulations, but the direct influence of family, friends and colleagues is ever present in the kinds of choices that anyone makes. How hard you work and what jobs you are prepared to take on, for example, will be constrained by the tempo and pattern set by other colleagues in the office. We look at some laboratory examples of these social forces operating on the individual and draw inferences for the decision-making process.*

Plan of the chapter: *This is illustrated in Fig. 6.1.*

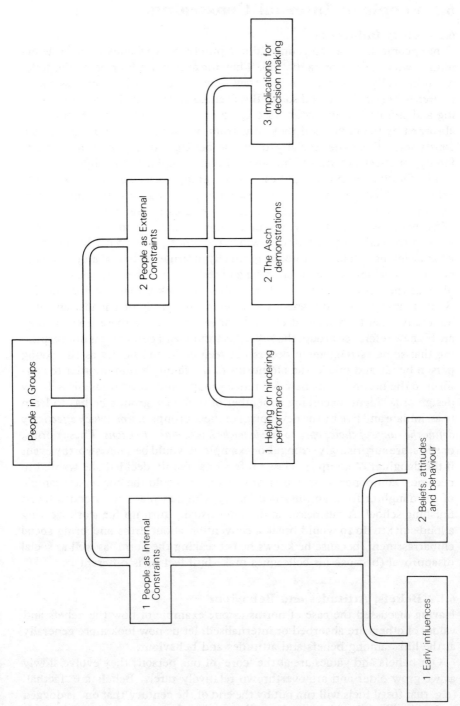

Fig. 6.1: People in Groups

6.1 People as Internal Constraints

6.1.1 Early Influences

Other people are, for the young child, a purely external constraint in determining what he can or cannot do. They make him wash or go to the toilet when he really does not want to; they praise or punish him for reasons he is often not clear about, and so on. But eventually, through instruction, copying and simple familiarisation (see Chapter 4) these rules of behaviour are absorbed by the child, and they shift from being external to being internal constraints. Thus the 'social groups' he belongs to (e.g. culture, society, family) in effect determine the range of choices open to the child.

The family, the most significant social group, places boundaries on the extent to which, for example, aggression or swearing or sexual intimacy is permitted to the growing child: it provides rules or **norms** of behaviour. What happens in his family, no matter how bizarre, seems to him normal, since in the early years he has no wider reference point. What he observes, what he learns, what he is told, he gradually internalises to make up his basic beliefs and values. Some questioning and reshaping of these norms does take place as the young teenager is better able to think things out for himself. By that time he is simultaneously widening his circle of friends, and it is imperative that he behave, dress and, indeed, think like these friends; they are his new reference group, the key to his future, and perhaps it is not surprising that some estrangement occurs between child and family as the young person bends and breaks the old norms of the family group in order to conform to the norms of his new reference group. And as he finds himself, by design or accident, becoming a member of such new groups he has to learn to assimilate and live by the new norms of those groups, *norms which effectively define the range of choice open to him when he has to make decisions*. These norms, or rules, are surprisingly strong. For example, it would be a newsworthy event if the daughter of an upper-class professional family decided she wanted to become a components assembler or packer. So would the converse example of the daughter from an unskilled family who had plans to attend a Swiss finishing school. A businessman does not usually turn up for work wearing a loud suit: to do so would break a convention about dress and bring social embarrassment (because he knows he is breaking the norm) as well as social disapproval (because his colleagues make him feel he is different).

6.1.2 Beliefs, Attitudes and Behaviour

Having discussed the case of norms as one example of how the beliefs and values of others are absorbed or internalised, let us now look more generally at the links among beliefs and attitudes and behaviour.

Our beliefs and values are at the 'core' of our person; they evolve slowly as we grow older and are overthrown relatively rarely. Beliefs are 'factual' (e.g. that fossil fuels will run out by the end of the century/that one is dogged by bad luck) while values are 'moral' (e.g. that democracy is the right form of government/that promotion should be based on merit). Now from each belief (or value) springs an associated cluster of attitudes which link the belief to actual behaviour. For example, valuing democracy means that you have certain attitudes to certain newspapers/people/ways of public decision making, and so on. *An attitude is simply a disposition to behave in a certain way.* And of course this 'disposition to behave' often becomes expressed in actual behaviour, as when the person votes/protests at a meeting, and so on. Such is the link from belief to attitude and to behaviour. But why do we need these so-called attitudes, you may ask; why do we not simply measure people's beliefs or values or, indeed, their behaviour directly? Measuring behaviour directly is very inconvenient since you have to be there with your clip-board at just the right time; measuring beliefs and values on topical issues is also tricky since people show understandable reluctance to provide 'private' information for a survey. Measuring the intermediate attitude is less difficult, though not without problems, as we note later. It is more reasonable to ask people to tell you their attitudes, and their answer enables you to infer backwards, if you wish, to the underlying belief, and infer forwards to what the person's behaviour would probably be in certain circumstances.

Generally it has been assumed that employees with 'favourable' attitudes are better employees than those with 'unfavourable' attitudes. Some of the research evidence is at variance with this widely held view. Certainly as we have already implied there is no consistent pattern linking attitudes and opinions on one hand and actual job performance on the other. Reference to two or three studies will illustrate this point.

a. A Department Store Survey
The sales performance of 94 sales girls in a department store was compared with their scores on a job satisfaction questionnaire. The correlation was 0.03, i.e. approaching zero, indicating the absence of any significant relationship.

b. Life Insurance Company Survey
In this study it was possible to identify 'high-producing' sections and 'low-producing' sections in the company, both doing identical types of office work. Four attitude measures were developed, namely: (a) pride in work; (b) intrinsic job satisfaction; (c) involvement in the company; (d) financial and job status. After deriving attitude scores on these variables a comparison was made with the output of employees in the 'high' and 'low' sections. It was found that pride in work bore a significant relation to the work performance of the various sections, but that the other attitude areas did not.

c. A Heavy Engineering Company Survey
A study was made of the attitudes of both white- and blue-collar employees of an electric power company. A measure of 'overall work satisfaction' was obtained and compared with absentee rates. The results indicated that only

22 per cent of employees in groups with high absence rates were satisfied with their jobs. By comparison, groups with medium or low absence rates could boast around 50–60 per cent of their members satisfied with their jobs.

Thus in certain circumstances favourable attitudes *may* be related to better work and/or to lower absenteeism. This does not mean that good attitudes cause the work output to be better; it could well be the other way round, or they could *both* be caused by some third factor such as high rates of pay.

At a general level there is a reasonably consistent link between an underlying belief, an expressed attitude and a resultant piece of behaviour. However, the link cannot be guaranteed.

There are several reasons why people's attitudes do not tie up with their intended or actual behaviour. First, as we have seen, personal limitations and intervening events may prevent an 'honestly intended' course of action. Secondly, people may deliberately falsify their public attitudes for ulterior purposes: a presidential candidate may promise to cut taxes if it will bring him a few more delegates even though he knows that such cuts may in fact be impossible. Third, people may *unwittingly* falsify their answers to questions about attitudes they hold: they may wish to present themselves in a more favourable or more progressive light and adjust their answers accordingly. If you ask healthy males if they would intercede to help a girl being attacked on the street, nearly all would say yes, but if you rigged an incident where this happened probably few if any of them would in fact do anything. The more delicate the area being explored the more difficult it is to be sure that questionnaire and interview data are dependable. Data from surveys of people's sexual habits are notoriously vulnerable on this point.

The important topic of how we change people's attitudes is left to Chapter 15 where we discuss 'change' in general.

6.2 People as External Constraints

We now move to a more general consideration of the influence of other people on our decision behaviour. In this context, people operate very much as *external* constraints in the terms of our general decision model.

6.2.1 Helping and Hindering Performance

We all know what it is to work with the boss breathing down our necks or to answer a difficult question in front of a selection panel, or to put together a tennis or golf shot in the presence of an attractive member of the opposite sex.

The presence of such people is definitely disruptive; we seem to stiffen up and become all arms and legs. But, on the other hand, is it not also true that even though we may become more self-conscious, our performance can also be *improved* by knowing that the boss or the selection panel or the attractive spectator is capable of being impressed by our performance? The solution to this paradox seems to be that when we are in the *early stages* of acquiring a skill, including manual skills such as typing and social skills such as being able to maintain a conversation, then the presence of another 'evaluating' person is disruptive to our learning and fitting together the component bits of the skill. The weak link which naturally exists between each bit becomes exaggerated by the evaluating presence and one error seems to trigger another and yet another. (See Section 4.1.2.)

Consider the somewhat different case of others working *with* you in the same task, rather than standing outside the task and evaluating you. You know from experience how working on a common problem with similar minds brings out the best in you. If you are a member of a management consultancy team you find the assertive self-confidence of your colleagues investing your own behaviour, and your application of appropriate social skills being much facilitated by their competent presence. None of this works, however, if the skill level of the others is too far superior to your own: a junior who has to stand in at the last minute for a senior management consultant may find himself tongue-tied, generally inhibited, and in fact working *below* his normal competence levels, when discussing matters with people very senior to him in status and technical experience.

Related to this helping or hindering effect of working with others is the more general notion that the presence of others regulates or sets the tempo of what we do. The group acts to pull individual work rates up or down to suit the general tempo. Depending on the work rate of a particular group, an individual's efforts can get him rated as a blackleg, as idle, or as a swot. The individual usually wants to discover the 'normal' rate so that he can conform and be accepted by the work group. Elton Mayo's research findings in the Hawthorne plant of the Western Electric Company (see pp. 23–25) provide examples of how group work rate can be affected through unspoken agreement among workers. We even use other people in a situation to decide what action is appropriate. In one study, for example, when they were sitting alone in the room about three-quarters of subjects rushed to investigate when they heard a (tape-recorded) crash followed by screams and moans of pain in an adjacent room. If, on the other hand, two 'stooges' were in the same room as the subject and these two *ignored* the drama next door then very few (under 10 per cent) of the subjects went to the rescue. The reasons for this contrast in behaviour may be clear enough: if no one is around you use your common sense, but in the presence of others you look to them for confirmation of your own appraisal or suspicions – and if such confirmation is not forthcoming you generally adopt the group view.

Thus, depending on various factors, the presence of other people can help or handicap us in carrying out a task, tell us how fast to work or even tell us how actually to behave.

6.2.2 The Asch Demonstrations

In the **Asch demonstrations,** Solomon Asch carried out a series of experiments based on a mock task in which subjects were misled into thinking they were in a 'visual perception' experiment, and had to match lines according to length. Let us look at a typical set-up. The group is gathered at one end of a table, while at the other end two display cards are being shown by the experimenter. On one card is the standard line of a certain length, say 12 in., while on the other is a choice of three lines (one the same length, one shorter, and one longer). The experimenter goes around the group asking which line, a, b or c, is the same length as the standard: everyone calls the same letter. The experimenter changes the pair of display cards, again goes round the group asking for the correct match and finds everyone agrees yet again. A third new pair of cards is propped up on the table, but this time something curious happens. Everyone seems to be agreeing about which line is the correct match until the experimenter asks one person towards the end who, with some hesitation and looking rather surprised, calls a different letter. He is even more surprised when he finds himself disagreeing yet again the next time around. When it happens a further time, he is showing ill-disguised disbelief, some embarrassment and his answer itself is subdued. He is enormously relieved when on the next round his choice is in line with everyone else's. . . . What our 'deviant' student does not know is that all *other* members of the group have been briefed beforehand to give distorted answers once the opening rounds have been used to establish credibility. And of the 123 guinea-pig students that Asch used, three-quarters of them began to acquiesce in the group opinion at some point in a series of eighteen rounds – some of them going along with the majority opinion nearly immediately. Consider the dilemma of the wretched student. His senses tell him plainly that he is right, his fellows tell him plainly that he is wrong, and he has to come to a decision. Some of the 'victims' quickly accept in the situation that the others are right and they wrong; others *suspect* their classmates are wrong, perhaps because of an illusion of viewing angle, but nevertheless cannot assert their independent judgement when it comes to the point. Some unfortunates saw their disagreement with the others as a result of some kind of personal deficiency which they tried to hide by going along with the rest. Although Asch was criticised for 'showing no more than the fact that students are conformists', the same trends were later demonstrated among engineers, architects and army officers. It could be argued that in these latter groups independent-mindedness is something especially valued, so that if the phenomenon operates there it should indeed be fairly general.

6.2.3 Implications for Decision Making

Committees in which there is a tradition of uniform approach from all members, whatever the issue, are very prone to the Asch effect, because there is an implicit acceptance of the rightness of others. (This can lead to a condition known as 'groupthink', which we discuss in Chapter 14.) When non-routine decisions have to be taken, independent-mindedness guarantees a more adequate airing of all possible considerations. On this particular point, Asch found in his experiments that briefing just one group member to give the correct answer acted as an enormous prop to the victim and caused a dramatic release from group pressure. There may be some benefit, therefore, in setting up groups in which views and approaches are paired, i.e. so that any member expressing an individualistic viewpoint can depend on sympathetic support from his 'partner'. The personality mix of groups that have to work together should also be considered. Compatibility of individual temperaments is crucial in groups whose members depend on each other in dangerous situations – aerospace crews provide good examples here.

People who feel the strongest pressures to fall in with group needs are of a range of personality types: the gregarious, the anxious, the non-intellectuals, those who respond to authority, and those who cannot tolerate indecision easily.

Summary. All in all there are many ways in which other people act upon us. We have seen that they are major influences on individual constraints in the general decision model, in particular affecting personality and attitudes. We have also seen that they operate as major external constraints on our range of choices by facilitating, inhibiting and controlling particular kinds of behaviour. Put in these terms, the influence of other people can be seen to be very pervasive indeed.

Work Section

A. Revision Questions

A1 What are the main influences on attitude development?

A2 What are 'norms'?

A3 How do norms affect the behaviour of the adult?

A4 Summarise the experiments by Asch on conformity.

A5 What does the Asch experiment tell us about group decision making?

A6 Explain the two main sources of people's beliefs.

A7 How is it possible for some people in Britain to believe that capitalism is good and for some to believe it is bad when all these people are inhabitants of the same country?

A8 Why is actual behaviour sometimes not linked to attitudes?

A9 How do our attitudes help or hinder us to perceive the world around us?

A10 Describe how the presence of other people can help or hinder performance on both technical and social skills.

A11 How might group influence improve an individual's output?

A12 How might group influence decrease an individual's output?

A13 Is a worker's output related to his/her satisfaction?

B. Exercises/Case Studies

B1 Identify some rule breakers of your immediate acquaintance. Why do they break the rules? How does the group react? How does the person counter-react?

B2 Can you identify any influences which you experienced *as a child* which you think have been formative on certain views that you now have in regard to: (a) social gatherings; (b) religion; (c) family? If so, do you know why?

B3 Can you identify any areas where advertising has achieved significant penetration in affecting people's attitudes towards (or even beliefs about) ways of doing things or particular products? Comment on the methods used.

B4 Indicate some ways in which your own attitudes affect the way you perceive the behaviour of others around you. Start by listing a few of your basic attitudes (or likes and dislikes) and show how these may be biasing what you pick up from the world around you.

B5 If you were the unsuspecting victim in Solomon Asch's experiment, how would your reaction be affected by the following variations on the basic experiment?

- if you were in a recently formed (as opposed to a well-established) group of friends;
- if you could not see the other people in the group (i.e. everybody was blindfolded);
- if you did not care about the problem of estimating line length.

B6 You are doing a survey of 'attitudes to work' in a medium-sized company manufacturing electrical appliances.
  a. What background information might the company already have?
  b. Write down a check list of the things you might usefully find out.
  c. How would you find out the answers?
  d. Would you want to ask everybody or just a proportion of the staff?

C. Essay Questions

C1 What differences would you expect to find: (a) between social classes; (b) between different nationalities, in conforming behaviour?

C2 In what ways are the implications of the Asch experiments disturbing or encouraging for business?

C3 How do external social constraints become internalised into our psychological make-up from childhood through adulthood?

C4 Do you believe that the British 'middle-class' attitudes to industry have been a blessing or a curse?

C5 What do you understand by the terms 'opinion', 'attitude', 'belief' and 'value'? Describe how in your view they can be considered as related concepts growing out of each other.

C6 How do advertising and the media influence our views of the world at large?

Chapter 7

People in Organisations

Synopsis: *The organisation, be it a commercial firm, a school or college, or a civil-service department, is responsible for providing the major external constraints on the individual decision maker. In the first place it typically provides the very problem which has to be solved. It also provides a background of policy and precedent, and it has its own house rules about how the process of decision making is to be conducted. Finally, it also provides most of the interpersonal constraints, e.g. how well people get on together, which determine whether the decision maker will be able to gather the information he needs effectively, and whether he will be able to implement any course of action with reasonable efficiency.*

Our first approach is to regard organisations as simple aggregates of lesser groups, all co-existent and interdependent to varying degrees. Some of these groups are small and intimate (primary) providing essential job satisfaction, some large and impersonal (secondary). We point to the 'profit centre' as an important example of a group which combines both what we call formal and informal elements.

In the second area of the chapter we draw a distinction between formal and informal organisational structures; we also point to the kinds of job confusion that typically exist in any organisation and the way in which people use their job roles to exert power.

In the third topic area we focus specifically on the topic of decision making in organisations. We note the overriding need to keep most of the people happy for most of the time, the dilemma of exchanging trust for control when responsibility is delegated, and the ideal span of control in the management hierarchy. Finally, we consider some of the advantages and disadvantages of centralised as opposed to decentralised decision making.

Plan of the chapter: *This is illustrated in Fig. 7.1.*

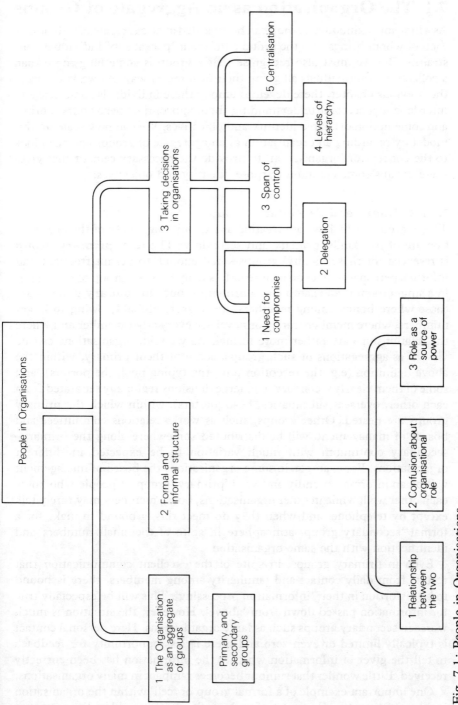

Fig. 7.1: People in Organisations

7.1 The Organisation as an Aggregate of Groups

As a first approximation a group can be regarded as an aggregate of individuals each of whom brings into the group a different 'package' of individual constraints. But we must also recognise that a group is something more than a collection of individuals all going their own merry way. As we know from the previous chapter, there develops among these individuals some sense of interdependence, some understanding about appropriate behaviours (norms) and some notion of shared identity and objectives. We can now scale up this model by regarding an organisation as an aggregate of groups and then look to the concept or 'organisation' to provide the necessary cement that gives these groups some common purpose, identity and objectives.

7.1.1 Primary and Secondary Groups

These 'groups' which we are treating as the building blocks of the organisation are of two kinds, primary and secondary. The term **primary group** is reserved for those 'family' groups small enough to permit frequent and informal personal contact on a more or less daily basis – a group of secretaries in a single room is an example of a primary group. **Secondary groups** are those where bonds among members are weaker, probably owing to larger numbers, where members rarely or never see every other member and where the relationships are rather more formal. As we said, organisations can be viewed as aggregations of such groups, some of them primary, within the above definition (e.g. the reception unit, the typing pool, the porters), and some of them clearly secondary (e.g. large divisions regionally separated from each other, overseas subsidiaries, headquarters), within which the primary groups are nested. Other groups, such as works relations committees and boards of management, will be distributed somewhere along the primary–secondary continuum with much variation to be expected in different organisations. For example, in some organisations the board of management will be an informal, friendly and very 'primary' group of people who know each other well, while in other organisations, board members may rarely talk except by telephone, and when they do meet this is bound to make for a formal 'secondary group' atmosphere in spite of the small numbers and identification with the same organisation.

Even in primary groups, in spite of the excellent communication that results from daily contact and familiarity among members, there is bound to be distortion in their 'information processing'. This will be especially true for information passed down from 'above'. However, the situation is much worse in secondary groups such as large organisations. Here personal contact is typically limited or even zero and there is less opportunity for feedback to tell the giver of information whether the information has been correctly received. Little wonder that rumour becomes rampant in many organisations.

One important example of a formal group or 'cell' within the organisation is the **profit centre**. Examples of such profit centres would be the computer department, the 'South Western Division', even a particular retail or production unit. Such a centre has a life of its own in that it has formal tasks, available resources of personnel, materials, machines, etc., a nervous system or control network and of course a target which it will agree and be judged upon for given periods of time. However we organise the large units, it is the health of profit centres which is vital. If they are not efficient and resourceful then the whole will not flourish. Many of the formal budget systems work into the profit centre from whence the original information stems and the final agreement of goals is made. Equally, personnel tend to develop into *in*formal groups within the profit centre and personal morale and performance are much geared to their health.

7.2 Formal and Informal Structures

7.2.1 The Organisation's Formal Structure

Like each of us, an organisation has chosen objectives which will need to be constantly refined and rethought in the light of internal or external conditions. The establishing and communicating of these objectives then enables plans to be made – without plans little progress is possible – and will also enable the organisation's performance to be measured (see Chapter 8 for a discussion of 'management by objectives'). A group of individuals may now be harnessed towards specific objectives which, hopefully, they will agree with but which would not be identical to their own individual objectives. Again like people, each firm has a different objective and strategy, but by far the most common is a combination of reasonable profitability and survival.

We saw in Chapter 2 that people work to satisfy a range of needs, some of them economic, some of them social and some of them individual. Too often an *organisation* is only able to satisfy needs at the economic level. But the employee has to find other things he needs such as comradeship and respect at the social level, as well as the sense of doing something worthwhile and making progress which he needs at the individual level. To find these things he typically turns inwards to his own immediate and most 'primary' group where the level of intimacy permits people to knock the system without fear of retribution and where he can take pleasure in the level of achievement of his own particular outfit.

7.2.2 The Relationship Between Formal and Informal Structures

The formal reporting structure of Kelly and Sons Ltd is shown in Fig. 7.2. Similar structural diagrams could be drawn for a college or a civil-service department. Technical and clerical workers report to section heads, section heads to departmental heads, departmental heads to division heads, who finally report to the managing director. The managing director is then

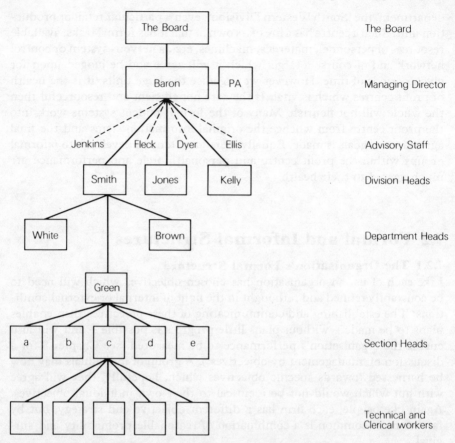

Fig. 7.2: Organisation Chart: Kelly and Sons Ltd

responsible to the Board. These lines of formal authority are also used quite extensively for communication, mainly via information forms, memoranda and telephone calls, and would appear to the outsider to work well. However, the formal structure in Kelly and Sons Ltd, is in fact quite creaky – it would not work except for the 'social lubrication' provided through the *informal structure* superimposed on it. For example, too little information flows between Mr Kelly and Mr Baron at the top of the structure. To be honest, they cannot stand each other, with the result that Mr Kelly channels most of his dealings that matter through Baron's personal assistant, who thus takes on an importance not reflected in the formal hierarchy. Indeed, were it not for the fact that Mr Baron's sister-in-law is assistant to one of Kelly's departmental heads, he would have a pretty scant picture of the true goings-on in that division. There are similar problems further down the chain. Hardly any of the section heads get on with Mr Green of Marketing, and prefer to deal through Mr Brown, even though this means the latter is overworked.

Actually, a couple of the section heads live across the golf course from Smith, the head of division, and often talk about work when they meet out walking or in the pub: Smith places great value on these meetings, and the net result is that Mr Green is pushed further into a vacuum within the organisation. And so on. You can see how easy it is to write a scenario for an informal structure which is completely at odds with the formal organisation structure displayed on the staff notice board, yet which in fact may be much closer to reality.

7.2.3 Confusion About Organisation Roles

Any job, and especially a managerial one, can never be completely specified. One might indeed say that jobs do not exist by themselves, only as the interpretations of the particular persons doing them at the time. You could be sure that each of, say, ten short-listed applicants for a managerial position would carry out the same organisational **role** quite differently.

For the new manager, role confusion is to be expected, and it will be the largest factor in the stress and strain of taking on the new job. But role confusion too often persists. Even well-established managers may not know the precise boundaries of their responsibilities, or who is evaluating their work and on what basis. This is partly due to lack of concern or timidity since it can be argued that boundaries do not really exist and therefore cannot be specified: you discover them by testing the decision environment for yourself. What happens if you say something will be done in such a way: is it done or is there a comeback? What happens if you ignore a potential responsibility: does someone else take it over, and can you therefore draw your responsibility boundary a little bit closer? Nor should we forget that a major constraint on our role or decision boundaries is provided by those whose work interlocks with our own – where are they prepared to draw *their* own role boundaries? One might expect adventurous, helpful managers to have wide decision boundaries, and careful, quiet managers to have narrow ones, and both within the *same* organisationally specified role.

7.2.4 Role as a Source of Power in the Organisation

As can be seen from the formal structure diagram for Kelly and Sons Ltd, each employee occupies an intersection point or 'node' in the organisational structure. The fact that he is at a node must mean he exerts power to some degree since he will control information flow through that node. The extent of this power will depend obviously on *which* node he occupies, but also on whether he uses the position negatively or positively to block or facilitate information flow. This in turn will be determined by whether his personal needs and the needs of the organisation are more or less compatible. Even the postal clerk has power. You would quickly realise this if, after you had been dismissed for inefficiency, you discovered he had been putting half your mail in the dustbin.

Power can come in different varieties:

i.   A senior manager may rarely be seen but his *titular power* means that people jump when they get a memo bearing his signature.

ii.   Some people radiate power without really trying; their voices, gestures, physical presence are such that even in gardening clothes it is obvious what they are made of. We could call this *charisma*.

iii. Other people exercise their power in a very obvious *assertive*, even aggressive way: they like directing and advising and always like to be at the helm.

iv.   Others exert their power *indirectly*, from 'behind the throne': secretaries and personal assistants are known to engage in this kind of power gratification. These are the hidden decision makers.

v.   Still others derive power from supplying emotional needs, e.g. spouses of important people.

vi.   People who monopolise key skills or commodities also exercise power; for example, computer experts, systems analysts, investment managers.

vii. People who feed rumour into the information network or who block or distort information, as we saw in the example of the disenchanted post clerk, have what we would call *destructive power*.

It has to be realised that most kinds of power depend upon the acknowledgement of the recipient in the particular role relationship. To employees the supervisor is a person who holds their careers in his hands, while to the outside client he is a rather anonymous or even annoying person. Medical internees envy the way patients can speak to the consultant; office staff are delighted when an irate client puts down an unpopular manager.

7.3 Taking Decisions in Organisations

7.3.1 The Need for Compromise

Personal needs will always take precedence over group or organisational needs unless the person is a saint. Accordingly, an executive will usually go for lines of action that (a) bring him most personal benefit; (b) involve least personal effort. Very often such a course of action amounts in fact to inaction, since change often has unforeseen repercussions and when risk is significant any new course of action is best left alone.

A decision complex can be regarded figuratively as a bowl of greasy ball bearings where movement of any one (i.e. a decision) causes distinct movement in those close by, and at least some degree of slippage in the whole set. Good administrators therefore have to anticipate this slippage – they have to recognise how far-reaching their decision will be and deal with potential disquiet before it actually arises. They may moreover have to 'de-optimise' their decision strategy in order to placate different sections of the organisation. Another common example, relevant to later discussion of employers and unions in Chapter 9, is how organisational policy makers have to agree to overstaffing in order to get the union concerned to make concessions in other areas.

Typically in an organisation, then, the central decision maker has to be prepared to hand out sweeteners that allow *everybody* to get some benefit – and the more lobbying power a person or division exercises the bigger the sweetener that will be necessary. The inevitable consequence is that in order not to have to get into this kind of difficulty, administrators prefer to stick with existing policies as long as possible – and this means probably too long. When they do have to make a decision for change they try to limit the disturbance effect on the major lobbying powers; a strategy which gives rise to over-careful decisions which are then weakly executed. 'Grand slam' strategists who propose to give all the 'ball bearings' a jolly good shaking up need tough nerve and low family history of cardiac arrest. Indeed it is noteworthy that all such 'big' strategies always seem to originate *outside* the organisation, from people who write to newspapers or from external management consultants – none of whom has to face the staff the next day.

7.3.2 Delegation

Delegation is of course a 'wonder concept' in discussions of decision making in organisations. Managers, when questioned, feel they ought to do more of it and wish they received more of it from their supporters. But there are problems. The fundamental dilemma is that delegation is made up of two parts: trust and control. The trust is the trust that the subordinate feels that the manager has in him. The control is the control that the manager has over the work of the subordinate. The implications are that: (a) any increase in the control exercised by the manager *decreases* the amount of trust perceived by the subordinate; (b) any wish by the manager to increase his trust in his subordinate, i.e. to give him more responsibility, must be accompanied by a release of some control.

Control Costs Money, But Is Safe. To monitor, check or control the work of the subordinate requires the time of the supervisor, along with the time and energy of those who compile figures and records for use in the control procedures. Furthermore, if a control mechanism exists, the tendency is for the subordinate to rely on it and push things to the limit in the expectation that if he pushes them too far there will be a safety net. For example, if there are limits on promotional expenses to be paid to sales agents, a salesman will be tempted to spend up to the limit rather than exercise his judgement, or a secretary will rely on her boss to do the final proof reading of her letters. This tendency to rely on the control mechanism helps to perpetuate it since the superior finds that he has to use it, unaware that a self-fulfilling prophecy has been at work.

Trust Is Cheap, But Is Also Risky. Trust leaves the superior free to do other things; if given and accepted, it breeds responsibility and removes the need for controls. The controls become in a sense self-administered (the secretary refers only the letters she is worried about to her boss, the salesman consults his manager in doubtful cases). But trust is risky because the superior is still held accountable for things that others have done (e.g. the company chairman cannot relinquish responsibility to the shareholders no matter who was or was not given responsibility for any of the company's activities), even if they have done them in ways he would not himself have chosen. Trust can be misplaced, and it can be abused. And since it means the absence of superior-administered controls, trust can leave the superior feeling out of things and ready for the worst, rather like the way an anxious parent may feel when the children are mysteriously quiet.

So we can note several factors in the giving of trust within the delegation process:

i.   To give trust, the superior obviously has to have confidence in the subordinate to do the job. This is easier if he has prior experience of his work and capacity, or if he has selected the subordinate himself. It is difficult with new or unknown subordinates.

ii. Trust must be given if it is to be received: if a superior wishes to reap the benefits he must initiate the process, give trust, release control and then sit back and wait. If proved wrong, he can withdraw the trust and replace the controls. It is hard for the subordinate himself to initiate the process.

iii. Trust is a fragile commodity. Like glass, once shattered, it is never the same again. The subordinate must always live up to the trust invested in him if that trust is to continue. The superior cannot withdraw the trust except by explicit agreement in specific circumstances.

iv. Trust must be reciprocal. It is no good the superior trusting his subordinates if they do not trust him.

The proper amount of delegation, the proper blend of trust and control, will depend on the situation – the degree of risk, the skill and experience of the subordinates, the self-confidence of the superior, and the pressures he feels from above. In particular it is important for the superior to keep those key tasks that are most vital to achieve objectives. These typically include: the setting of objectives; the taking of strategic decisions (but not information gathering); the selection and rewarding of key personnel; the establishing and monitoring of the key controls like large capital expenditure, cash flow.

For the many tasks that are delegated there are some practical rules of thumb that make them easier: delegation will probably work when the following conditions are met:

i.   The superior is allowed to select or at least approve his key subordinates, and moreover *they* have something to say about his appointment.

ii. The territory of trust is clearly defined for each individual, and is not violated. The individual must have full control within those limits. (Unclear territorial boundaries lead to misapprehensions.)

iii. Suitable authority is given to the individual which should balance the responsibility delegated. Equally he must be given all the resources

needed to operate successfully, including personal training in necessary
technical or social skills.

iv. There is control of ends not means. Control of results, i.e. after the event,
is not violation of trust; control of means, i.e. during the event, can be.
This implies that results can be determined and are known to the subordinate as well as to his superior.

Finally we should note that delegation allows *specialisation* and specialisation
is the key to most efficient enterprises. A person becomes an expert in his
or her particular area, no matter how small that area might be. Now this
has three advantages. At the economic level of the needs of the organisation,
having 'experts' means both that decisions are handled with a greater efficiency than the generalist could bring to bear and that each member of staff
can be employed and paid for his most useful or relevant skills. Thirdly, at
the level of personal needs, it is much easier for the expert employee to satisfy
both his social needs for respect and praise, and his individual need for
achievement. The negative side of this is that it can lead to 'too many chiefs
and not enough injuns', a situation characterised by poor co-ordination and
disunity.

In the last analysis, the kind of delegation pattern one finds in a particular
company depends on three factors. The first factor is represented by the company philosophy as transmitted downwards by top management. If they consider delegation 'a good thing' then it can happen: otherwise it will be stifled.
Secondly, there is the matter of company objectives. If there is a wish to
maintain continuity and not rock a boat that is sailing along quite nicely,
then the emphasis will be on control rather than delegation. If on the other
hand profitability is the main objective, this can lead to more 'creative',
riskier, kinds of management involving a high degree of delegation and a low
degree of control. Thirdly, the extent to which the organisation is technology-
based may determine the degree of delegation. In high-technology industries
staff have even less understanding of the **line** man's job, and even within
the **staff** or line domain itself, a senior manager may not himself have competence in crucial skills possessed by his subordinates. In such cases there
is no option but to extend trust and draw the boundaries of control wider.

7.3.3 **Span of Control**

Knowing something about the pros and cons of delegating decisions allows
us to look at the broader topics of '**span of control**' and **levels of hierarchy**
in organisations. The span of control, or span of management, is defined
by the number of 'managers' who are to be directly responsible to, i.e. directly
report to, any one 'executive', be he works manager, headmaster, brigade
commander or bishop.

Although many recent writers have considered this span to be of great significance in the structure of formal organisations, there is considerable conflict as to the most desirable span. In fact we shall not conclude with any
fixed views, but rather with a general impression along with a few guidelines.

Research was carried out in Ohio, USA, within 620 manufacturing companies, each having over 100 employees. The general picture was found to be related to the size of the organisation and was as follows:

● Less than 1,500 employees: most frequent span around 4, 5 or 6.
● 1,500–3,000   employees: most frequent span around 8.
● Over 3,000   employees: most frequent span around 9.

It was noticed also that there were marked differences according to the type of goods manufactured. (Could you say why?)

Such practical observations are of interest and give an indication of the spans commonly employed within management. However, there was no attempt in the Ohio study to relate the size of span with the efficiency of the organisation. So it is with interest that we turn to a study conducted in Sears Roebuck where efficiency was measured. The result is slightly surprising. Within two sectors of the organisation, each part doing exactly the same task, the span of control was fundamentally different. In one area they had removed a whole level of management so that 30 merchandise managers reported to one assistant manager. In the other, the store was organised along more conventional lines with an extra level of departmental management – so giving two spans of respectively 5 and 6 each. Analysis of sales volume, profit, morale and competence of lower managers all indicated that the stores with the larger span of control were superior!

Perhaps we can resolve this paradox by looking at some of the factors involved in determining 'optimum span of control'.

a. The Skill, Experience and Training of the Subordinate. In general the better trained the subordinates should need less general support in planning, action and review.

b. The Degree of Delegation of Authority. The clearer the tasks delegated and the wider the authority given for carrying them out, the less time a subordinate should need from his superior. Thus an efficient organisation, used to careful and precise delegation, may often come to increase the spans of control within itself.

c. The Similarity of Delegated Tasks. If a subordinate is controlling people with broadly similar duties he may clearly look after more than if each is involved in a totally different pursuit. This may be one of the reasons why Sears Roebuck found a large span possible.

d. The Rate of Change. In general it is found that organisations which change slowly and are in relatively stable environments can afford to have wide spans of control. This is particularly so where the training of subordinates has been good.

e. Communication Techniques and Personal Contact. The effectiveness of the communication techniques used will influence the span. If this has reached a high level, so reducing ambiguity, misunderstandings and the time needed to reach important decisions, then the span may be increased.

f. The General Ability of the Superior. If anything is clear from this book so far, it must be that no two people are the same. Some people, by their natural ability and experience within the business and as delegators, may achieve a speed of decision and personal efficiency greater than others.

These are the main variables to be considered, but the variety is further increased by the direct relationship between the particular span of control and the *numbers of levels* within the hierarchy. We shall say more on the matter in a moment. First let us look at some of the symptoms of wrong span size.

If the span is *too small* there will probably be a tendency towards incomplete or inefficient delegation, with superiors continually interfering with the day-to-day work of subordinates and generally over-controlling. Somewhat different symptoms may be seen if the span is *too large*. We may find the subordinate poorly briefed, supported, trained and controlled. We may see the superior overloaded so that he is forced to spend too little time with important decisions. Worse still, he may be unable to deal quickly and effectively with problems passed through him. This results in a bottleneck which severely affects the efficiency of those below. Even after symptoms are recognised, it may be difficult to take action for there will always be two possible diagnoses: (a) that the span of control is really too large or too small; or (b) that the superior has not the skills or ability to hold down the particular job!

7.3.4 Levels of Hierarchy

So we may move on from the span of control to the related matter of **levels of hierarchy** – the number of levels of authority from the bottom to the top of the organisational pyramid. To give an example, if the span of control was 4, an organisation of over 1,000 managers would need five levels of authority. On the other hand, if the span of 10 was used, then it would need only three. (Try this for yourself.)

There are some who still defend the 'tall' hierarchy, but having many levels of authority is becoming unfashionable. There is pressure to close the gap between top and bottom, so that the ideals of the leaders will directly affect a larger number within the organisation. In this way the organisation may be more unified. It should certainly enable those at the bottom of the hierarchy to feel more a part of the whole. Equally, within the process of strategic decision making information must be drawn up from the bottom. If this information is filtered through a large number of individuals it can soon come to bear little relation to reality and rather too much to the politics or the personalities in the organisation. Also information will arrive more slowly thus reducing the speed of decision making. But even this is not the end of the matter, for the decision has to be passed *down* and if the structure is tall, the final message at the coal face may be blurred or even irrelevant. An alternative would be to miss out some of the steps in the hierarchy, but this could leave superiors ill-informed and lacking in ultimate authority over their subordinates. We say more about these communication difficulties in Chapter 13.

7.3.5 Centralised or Decentralised Decision Making?

This topic represents the final and the most broad ranging heading under which we discuss the various aspects of organisational decision making. **Centralisation** refers to the amount of control exercised from the headquarters (or 'centre') relative to the amount delegated to those, as it were, at the periphery. Now any organisation will have elements of both centralisation *and* decentralisation within its structure. There can never be complete decentralisation, or the manager at the centre would no longer have a job, hence with decentralisation we are concerned to keep only those decisions at the centre which are necessary for the planning and control of the organisation. It is conceivable that we could take all the decisions at the centre and hence have absolute centralisation (Henry Ford Snr was known to boast that every major decision in that vast company was made by him), but again there is obviously a limit.

Ever since companies have appreciated the two alternatives, there have been fashionable swings from one emphasis to another. The United States led the fashion in the late 1940s and early 1950s when they began to tear apart many highly centralised structures. They felt organisations had become so large that the central boards were no longer able to obtain and master data quickly enough for efficient management. But in the early 1960s they were recentralising. For the new management information systems, complete with their computers, had given the centre a new tool for decisions and control. We may note in passing that such exercises are highly lucrative to the management consultants, and one was reported to have earned a fortune by taking the Shell system of centralisation into Esso and the Esso system of decentralisation into Shell, the exercise being made possible by the time lag between the acceptance of ideas in the USA and the UK. A more recent example of topsy-turvy philosophy on this issue was the rapid centralisation and then decentralisation of British Leyland.

How do we recognise a 'centralised' as opposed to 'decentralised' organisation? You might think that a glance at the organisation chart would show us the answer. It does not. The way that the organisation is divided cannot show the responsibility and authority given to each area – which is what determines the degree of centralisation. Instead, we must examine the *decisions taken* within the different levels of management. If we find that middle and lower management are taking frequent decisions, important in magnitude and little checked by supervisors, we are clearly in the realms of decentralisation.

General Factors That Can Affect the Degree of Centralisation
No two men will have the same idea about the balance necessary to optimise organisational effectiveness. However, there are a number of criteria which can assist us in deciding.

a. The Cost of Mistakes. The fundamental objective of most organisations is to survive. Hence activities where mistakes may jeopardise this prime goal should be centralised. They will be different within organisations operating in different fields. As an example, a high degree of financial expenditure within any one area of activity, or at any one time, might prejudice the viability of most firms. Within a drug firm safety standards might be critical.

b. The Need for a Uniform Policy. There are areas, such as wage bargaining, where this is desirable. Firms may also see the need to have uniform price structures, a common advertising theme or even public relations posture. If so, these activities will need to be centralised.

c. The Need for Co-ordination. Some large organisations are more concerned with the integration of their parts to produce a whole, than they are with the single success of any separate part. An example of this is when the manufacture and arrival of components from satellite factories have to be synchronised with spare capacity at the assembly plant.

d. History. The historical method of growth will often be 'imprinted' on the structure. Enterprises which have grown from within tend to be centralised; those that have grown through mergers will tend to be more decentralised. They may each change in their structure over time but a successful organisational structure may be maintained, often for far too long, when the implications of change are too disturbing.

e. Philosophy. Individual entrepreneurs and the companies they have developed have usually come to accept certain views about the organisation of people and materials. If the original entrepreneur was a despot, a poor delegator, a lover of power and authority for its own sake, then we will find a heavily centralised company. Other entrepreneurs might recognise in their own organisations that employees wish to have status, to use their initiative and to take some responsibility. They may also see the frustration and narrowmindedness which *can* result from closely controlled centralised activity.

f. Geography. It has been said that the reason why the Roman Empire lasted so long was that the centre was forced to delegate because of the enormous distances between the centre and the periphery. It was certainly true that in any emergency within Britain the Governor just took action: there was little authority withheld by the centre. Distance is nowadays not the vital factor it was but the greater the dispersion of units or operators, the more likely there is to be a local call for decentralised authority.

g. Talents. Centralised organisations can run without capable men at the lower levels. Decentralised structures need good managers at all levels. So it is hard to change from a centralised to a decentralised stance if the staff have not been prepared. This is one reason why fast-growing companies may feel the necessity to remain centralised although other factors would argue otherwise.

h. Control. In the end it may be the minimum means of control which will decide the degree of decentralisation.

Methods of Decentralisation

There are four main ways in which the activities of an organisation might be grouped. Different approaches go by the names of functional, federal, project activity or communications decentralisation. No method is, *a priori*, superior to the others but each has general advantages and disadvantages which are worth noting.

a. Functional Decentralisation. **Functional decentralisation** is the traditional, and at present the most common, form of decentralisation. The organisation is divided into the specialised functions of marketing, production, accounting, research, etc., each branch containing the relevant specialist personnel. Clearly many of the advantages of specialisation can be reaped, including the economies of scale which can result from grouped personnel and equipment. However, there is a constant danger that these individual parts may strive to achieve functional excellence in their own style and for their own purpose, rather than seek to co-ordinate their activities and plans towards the common goals.

b. Federal Decentralisation. **Federal decentralisation** overcomes the major weakness we have met by grouping activities as autonomous businesses, each with its own products, budget, market, productive unit and responsibility for survival and profitability. This has now become the method of most multi-nationals like General Motors, Ford, General Electric, and even British Leyland. The efforts and ideas of all senior managers can easily be directly focussed on performance and results and the effectiveness of each grouping can be easily monitored (and where necessary a unit may need to be shed to save the whole body).

c. Project Management. Increasingly, organisations are adopting more flexible structures which solve their immediate problems. One such method is the grouping of personnel to achieve a particular objective within the overall plan. Thus if a new product is to be launched, a special team will be formed from within the organisation. Experience, compatibility, technical skills or even training needs can all be taken into account. Such groups often knit quickly and develop great momentum. The only serious objection to project management seems to be that the personnel wish to keep their active and successful groups together when their task is complete. Thus, although it needs greater management flexibility and control, this is an exciting method that we can expect to see more of.

d. Decisions and Communications. Lastly, some management experts have come to feel that successful decision making is the key to organisational efficiency and that this is based upon effective information systems. So they have taken as their starting point the decisions which will need to be made to achieve the company objectives and then listed the information each of these decisions will require. Groupings can then be organised in a way which minimises the time and effort to receive information and relay decisions. While this may in itself result in a type of functional or product approach, it is a new way of looking at formal systems.

● This completes our survey of the organisation as the major external constraint on the individual decision maker. Having presented him with the problem, the organisation then sets the rules about how it must be solved, a truly formidable state of affairs which can tax even the most dedicated organisation man. We shall be continuing with the organisation context as we discuss motivation in organisations, collective bargaining and leadership roles.

Work Section

A. Revision Questions

A1 In what different ways do primary and secondary social groups affect the needs of individual workers?

A2 Give two examples of how inter-departmental prejudices might develop.

A3 Define 'delegation'.

A4 Name four tasks that a manager might be reluctant to delegate.

A5 Why do you feel that many managers are reluctant to delegate?

A6 What makes for successful delegation?

A7 Give two reasons why precise job descriptions are desirable and two why they might be undesirable.

A8 Define 'span of control'.

A9 Why is 6 often regarded as the largest span which may be successful in practice?

A10 What factors would you consider when deciding on a suitable span of control?

A11 Why do you believe that flat or low hierarchies may be desirable?

A12 List four types of decentralisation.

A13 What roles do senior management normally keep to themselves?

A14 Why are profit centres important?

A15 Briefly explain the difference in role and outlook which could exist between a line and a staff man.

A16 Why might it be said to be necessary to please most people most of the time in organisational decision making?

A17 Give four examples of staff positions stating the type of firm each was in.

B. Exercises/Case Studies

B1 Associated Brewers Ltd.

The Group

Associated Brewers is a regionally based group, enjoying a considerable local history and good will. It operates six separate breweries, and nearly 1,000 pubs. It sells mainly its own brands, but also some well-known brands of other brewers. It has a higher market share within its own region. Turnover and assets are both approaching £20 million, and there are over 2,000 employees, including part-timers in the pubs. Return on investment is less than 10 per cent.

The present group has resulted from a series of mergers and takeovers between locally based brewing companies. Until recently, each of the units continued to operate autonomously, with their own assets, management teams, boards of directors and policies. There was only loose co-ordination at the centre. The group is family controlled. Each unit tends to be dominated by a family interest and personality, and the management style is autocratic.

The past two to three years have witnessed many changes at the top. Most members of the previous group Board have retired and a new generation has taken over. A strong managing director is at the helm. The balance of power has shifted from the units to the centre, and there is an increased emphasis on management and results.

A major brewery development programme is now in progress at the central location, and the other breweries are being closed. Most of the old labour-intensive plant is being replaced by modern automated plant. As a result of this rationalisation programme, profits are rising significantly, even though the group is losing market share within its region.

Besides brewing, the group is involved in the following activities:

● Hotels and restaurants
● Off-licences and retail shops
● Wine and spirit bottling
● Mineral-water production

The proportion of group profits coming from these activities is still less than 10 per cent of the total, but it is growing.

There are currently only five executive directors. Some of the senior and middle managers are potentially able, and are developing well under the new regime. Others are struggling somewhat. At junior management and foreman level, the group is fairly weak. Some new managers have been brought in from outside to fill newly created staff positions at group headquarters. The rationalisation programme is stretching top management to the limit.

Distribution takes place mainly through the group's tied outlets. Under the 'tied-house' system, the brewery owns and maintains the pubs, and charges relatively low rents to the tenant, provided he buys all his beer, wines and spirits from the brewery. The sale of other products and services in the pub is the tenant's own affair. The vast majority of the group's outlets are *tenanted*. If a pub is *managed* the brewery takes the retail as well as the whole-sale profit but receives no rent and has to pay the overhead costs. The brewery can decide policy and even change each manager as they feel desirable. Only a few outlets are managed by the group. Sales to free-trade outlets are growing and now account for over 10 per cent of beer turnover.

Apart from the rationalisation programme, the group has identified certain priorities for profit improvement. These include raising prices to the public and rents to tenants, increasing sales volume, putting more of the pubs under the group's own management, swinging the product mix to higher-margin products, and setting up tight cost control, particularly on labour and property maintenance. Profits are forecast to rise steeply during the next two to three years, under the impact of these measures, but after that they are expected to level off.

The group is currently developing its plans for the longer term. The main considerations are:

● Prospects to expand brewing operations into other regions are limited, owing to the tied-house system. Selling to the free trade in other regions could be less profitable, owing to the higher distribution costs involved.

● Diversifying into allied leisure activities and expanding the existing non-brewing activities, either within the region or nationally, could offer better prospects for long-term growth and profitability.

A programme has been set up to look into possible mergers and acquisitions.

The Organisation Structure

Figure 7.3 gives an outline of the company organisation chart (complete only for Brewery E). Some selected comments on the various activities are as follows:

a. Breweries A, B, C, D and E are of similar size and are situated close to each other. Brewery F is much smaller, and is geographically remote in a rural area. The organisation chart at each of the breweries is similar.

b. The wine and spirit company bottles and wholesales a range of British and imported brands. It has its own free-trade sales force, and does a significant amount of export business.

c. The mineral-water company operates its own 'pop' factory, and also wholesales a range of well-known brands. It has a free-trade sales force. Both the bottling plant and the 'pop' factory are situated near the main breweries, and most of their sales come from the tied outlets.

d. The hotel and off-licence companies have recently been spun off as separate profit centres to operate suitable outlets previously controlled by the breweries, with the aid of specialist expertise. The hotels cover a wide range, from prestige hotels down to local inns and restaurants, all trading under a separate company symbol.

e. All of the above brewing and non-brewing units are subsidiary companies, with their own boards of directors, consisting of their own senior managers and managers from other parts of the group.

f. The property development function is concerned with buying and selling land, and developing sites where there is potential for using them for other purposes than as pubs.

g. The pubs are maintained by each brewery company. This function includes keeping them in a proper state of repair, and improving the interior décor and fittings to attract customers. There is no internal rent element in the management accounts.

h. Management accounts are produced monthly for each of the main brewing companies. For the non-brewing subsidiaries and the managed houses,

Fig. 7.3: Associated Brewers Present Organisation Chart

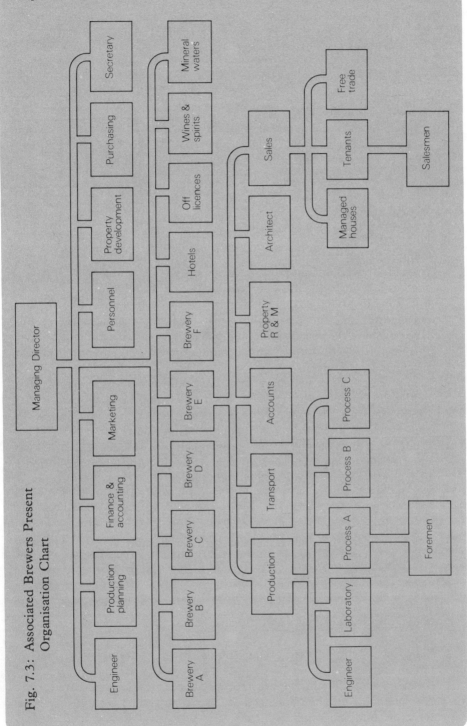

they are produced quarterly by the accounts department at Brewery A. Below general-manager level, some departmental controls are run internally, but there is no group system for this.

The Industry

The brewing industry is at present undergoing fundamental change. The main trends are as follows:

a. A whole series of mergers and takeovers has resulted in a rationalisation of the industry structure. Six major national brewers have emerged, and they are now providing the remaining independent brewers with much fiercer competition than they have faced in the past.

b. The licensing laws are under review, and it is anticipated that it will soon become easier for many types of premises to obtain licenses, and that opening hours will be extended. Within a few years, the beer 'tie' in pubs could be made illegal.

c. Companies are becoming more market-oriented, and interest is swinging from the breweries to the pubs as the main area of potential. New services, such as catering and entertainment, are being introduced.

d. Social habits are changing, particularly in the leisure area. The age and sex mix of pub customers is changing, and it is the younger age groups who now have the spare purchasing power. People are prepared to travel further for a night out and are becoming increasingly interested in new products and services.

e. The product mix is switching from the traditional draught beers to the lighter and more expensive beers, such as keg and lager.

f. Production and distribution of these new products is capital intensive, and the trend is towards automation and larger units.

g. While the industry is still basically controlled by a number of well-known families, day-to-day management is increasingly being left to professional managers, some of them fresh to the industry.

h. Cost inflation has reached unprecedented levels, particularly of labour. The TGWU is becoming the dominant union within the industry and is pursuing militant tactics.

i. Market research has shown that the main factors affecting the customer's buying decision are firstly the pub (atmosphere and location), secondly the landlord and thirdly the beer.

Questions

1. What observations would you make about the present organisation structure?

2. What sort of strains is the organisation structure suffering in the present circumstances?

3. Draw up an outline for a more appropriate organisation structure (probably including an alternative activity grouping system) and give reasons why this could be beneficial.

4. What practical considerations would you have to bear in mind when it comes to implementation?

C. Essay Questions

C1 How could one monitor the effectiveness of delegation? If you were planning the formal organisational structure of a large and complex institution, what factors would you consider and why? What is the key to successful organisation?

C2 'The informal links within an organisation are more important than the formal.' Discuss.

C3 Explain the formal organisation of an educational institution that you know and critically comment on its effectiveness.

C4 Why have formal organisation charts and profit centres?

C5 Is the silicon chip revolution leading to more or less centralisation?

Chapter 8

Motivating the Organisation

Synopsis: *Organisations, like individuals, have 'needs'. We begin by outlining what we mean by such organisational needs, then move on to special topics within the motivation theme. First, we review the philosophy of 'management by objectives' and recognise some of the problems and difficulties in its realisation. Then we turn to 'participative decision making' as a solution to problems of motivation in the organisation. Again points for and against are recognised. We examine the idea of 'job enrichment' as representing the first step in involving the employee in decision making; then, at the other extreme, worker representation on the company board. We end by looking at money as a special motivator with a note on profit sharing and share ownership.*

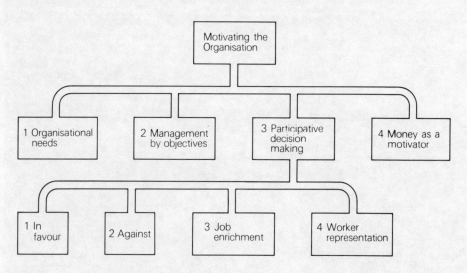

Fig. 8.1 Motivating the Organisation

8.1 Organisational Needs

Not just individual people, but firms large and small, have **needs** of different kinds. It may strike you that what is best for the individual receptionist or office clerk in an organisation may not be best for the organisation as a whole. He or she ideally needs higher pay and longer holidays, whereas the company needs to give its staff limited holidays and limited pay rises. Even what is best for the managing director may not be best for the organisation. He might be motivated by a wish to raise the value of his shareholdings by pursuing short-term policies of dubious value to the organisation, or to ingratiate himself with a government minister by taking on non-profitable work. By no means, then, are the needs of the organisation and the needs of the human units that make up that organisation one and the same thing.

An employee aims at doing his job with enough enthusiasm so as to give him satisfactory job security, satisfactory promotion opportunity as well as allowing satisfactory relaxation and socialising time. *H. A. Simon* has claimed that employees and indeed organisations as a whole are equally motivated by nothing more than this '**satisficing** principle', as he calls it. Organisations do not, he argues, seek to maximise profits, as traditional economics would have us believe; they want a *satisfactory* profit level combined with a *satisfactory* share of the market and a *satisfactory* public image. Simon's view recognises that intolerable stresses and strains would be imposed on the organisation by continually stoking the boilers for 'maximisation' on every front. Of course, for short periods of time, such as when objectives are being set or statements being prepared for shareholders, everyone may believe in the overriding need to maximise profits, but over the whole year a better understanding of what goes on may be obtained through the principle of satisficing.

Having proposed this, it is most important to appreciate that what is 'satisficing' for one firm may appear to be lazy to a second firm or actually rate-busting to a third, since we each have our own ideas on what satisfactory work levels, earnings and incentives really are! We are always being told about the productivity of German or Japanese workers relative to the British worker: it is not unreasonable to see this in terms of different national ideas of what constitutes a satisfactory day's work for the organisation. Organisations whose selection system allows in too many 'low satisficers', however, will find themselves falling behind their competitors.

8.2 Management by Objectives (m.b.o.)

Proponents of the **m.b.o.** philosophy claim that very often an organisation has no clear idea of what its needs and priorities are. There is too often a general lack of direction, or conflicting activity within enterprises. Managements fail to look ahead and fail to co-ordinate for a common purpose. The result can too often be a 'crisis' style of management which heaves the firm from one drive or purge to the next.

Firms need to be clearer where they are going in both the long and short term by setting realistic *objectives* in line with available resources and the environment in which they are operating. These objectives should be clear to all, and activity to gain their achievement should be paramount over any narrow departmental or professional activity. Management should be operating in all ways possible to achieve these objectives (planning, organising, commanding and motivating, co-ordinating and controlling) and success should be judged by the ability of the whole organisation to meet these objectives.

8.2.1 What is m.b.o.?

M.b.o. means putting into practice the following plans of action:

● Reviewing critically and re-stating the company's *strategic plans*, as well as resetting tactical plans and seeing that the organisation is geared towards these.

● Clarifying with each manager his job and the key *results and performance standards* he must achieve, in line with unit and company objectives. The manager's agreement and commitment must be gained.

● Agreeing with each manager a *job improvement plan* which makes a measurable and realistic contribution to his unit and company plans for better performance.

● Providing conditions in which it is possible to achieve the key results and improvement plans, in particular:

   i.   *an organisation structure* which gives a manager maximum freedom and flexibility in operation;

   ii. *management control* information in a form and frequency which makes for more effective self-control and better and quicker decisions;

   iii. *systematic performance reviews* to measure and discuss progress towards results and *potential reviews* to identify men with potential for advancement;

   iv. *management training plans* to help each manager to accept a responsibility for self-development;

   v. *selection, salary and succession plans* to strengthen a manager's motivation.

Arguably, one of the least-developed assets used by firms and organisations is the people who work for them. M.b.o. accepts McGregor's Theory Y with its optimistic view of the creative worker. It also accepts man's work needs as seen through the generalised concepts of Maslow and their extension in the work of Herzberg (see Chapter 2). Accordingly, the company must see that maintenance needs are satisfied and that motivational factors are present. It follows again that consultation and **participation** are the approaches required. Moreover, the needs of the individual (and the informal group in which he operates) should be fulfilled while purposefully moving towards the objectives of the firm. Ideally, the requirements of the shareholders should be unified with those of the employees and employers of the enterprise.

8.2.2 **Advantages of m.b.o.**

a. It is a system which makes management take a continuous look at what it is doing and the way it is doing it, forcing a continuous review of the firm's activities, now and in the future.

b. There is a continuous examination of the formal organisation and an evaluation of each job within it. Reorganisation can take place as needed.

c. Within each unit every man knows what his job is, what standard of achievement is expected from him and how he is getting on. The targets are set by himself. Participation and discussion are the key: autocracy and command are removed. Staff can see their jobs as a movement towards objectives and not a fulfilment of duties.

d. The control and review of activities is overhauled so that each manager may himself receive information that is timely, relevant and comprehensive, so that *he* may strengthen the quality and speed of his decision making.

e. As a result of setting the targets and reviewing subsequent performance, the man's future activities (including training), rewards and promotion may be planned.

8.2.3 **Some Problems and Difficulties**

1. M.b.o. must always be seen as a total and not a partial style of management. Not least, successful m.b.o. must start with top management.

2. There is no one system which is applicable to all companies in all situations. The scheme needs much initial groundwork and considerable effort if all the stages are to be successfully completed.

3. There are a number of problems which need consideration when *setting targets*:

   a. The targets must each be sufficiently narrow so that the managers cannot balance the good with the bad performance.

   b. Targets must be realistic. In the short term it may be necessary to agree unusually low figures as the problems of unproductive areas are slowly overcome, and particular care is needed to set realistic targets in declining businesses (e.g. coal mining). At the other extreme, the individual enthusiasms of managers may greatly exceed their ability or the resources available.

   c. Research work in the General Electric Company of America in the early

1960s showed that the number and complexity of goals affected performance. They found that most individuals worked best when they had one very difficult (but *not* impossible) goal to work on at a time.
d. If managers are going to set the targets themselves and be judged and rewarded as a result of their achievements they will tend to select easy, discrete tasks which they know they can perform. The result may be a lop-sided advance which would tend to lay emphasis on short-term issues. There is also the related problem when working to targets, that undue effort will be put into reaching quantifiable, rather than qualitative (e.g. human needs) targets.

8.2.4 Problems in Reviewing Targets

a. Too often the programme is found to be confused and confusing. Targets have been set based on the use of sophisticated techniques, while insufficient attention has been given to definition, the material for control and the application of the techniques.
b. There must be real advantages in meeting targets (e.g. salary increments; promotion) and real disadvantages in failure. Those who fail may be given more support and training in the short term but must be removed, or the job changed, if performance is still unsatisfactory.
c. It is nevertheless sometimes very hard to isolate an individual's performance (e.g. in the area of industrial relations).
d. Care must be taken not to use the results of m.b.o. as a stick with which to beat managers. The emphasis *must* remain on the individual. If punitive methods are used the managers will adopt the traditional work force methods of restrictive practices to beat the system!

8.3 Participative Decision Making

In the past few years there has been increasing discussion about industrial democracy and the desirability of involving employees in the process of policy planning or even in actual management. Sometimes the concept of participation has political overtones when the speaker has in mind a kind of democratic safeguard for all employees in organisations. On other occasions 'participation' may mean the involvement of all personnel in all organisational decision making. However, there are some points we can make both in favour and against the general idea of participation before we go on to look at some examples in practice.

8.3.1 In Favour

1. To be practical, the consent of the workforce is nowadays needed to get things done: the economic sanctions of the past are no longer effective.
2. With each passing decade, employees are becoming better educated – and this means more sophisticated, more self-confident and more ambitious.

3. Both 'sides' know that continuing conflict and mistrust make for continuing poor performance. Harmonisation of objectives and a caring about the organisation, while desirable in stable times, may be essential to survive periods of rapid change.

4. Employees ought to have some say over their own working lives. People fundamentally are responsible and 'participative' beings. Even people who seem to have a permanent chip on their shoulders in the workplace magically become caring, responsible and conscientious members of a family once they get home. What is wrong with the organisation that it fails to bring out these qualities during work hours?

5. Participation leads to improved decisions. Information which is first-hand and more up-to-date can now be fed into the decision mix. While employees raw in the skills of decision making may make unrealistic suggestions, generally speaking better-quality decisions will emerge. The level-headed, intelligent draughtsman with his HNC in engineering may not even want to be a manager, but he literally holds the company's products in his hands every day and he knows what customers think about them. People such as these, the skilled non-managers of industry, represent a slumbering resource whose potential needs to be brought into the process of decision making.

6. Participation leads to a greater acceptance of decisions by all concerned. This is because: (i) participants are in at an early stage of the problem and can help shape solutions as they evolve; (ii) decisions now appear less as irrational directives from management and more as an attempt to meet prevailing constraints.

7. When employees feel that they can make their views heard, morale improves. Especially acute is the case of junior managers who, because they are actually supposed to be involved in the decision process, can feel even more cut out by lack of a participative lead. In other words, by making or letting everyone feel that his or her contribution counts in policy making we are indeed making positive steps towards motivating the organisation.

8.3.2 Against Participative Decision Making

1. As the 1974–79 Labour government discovered in its dealings with the **TUC,** a participative as opposed to a statutory approach means making concessions to the other's view: these concessions can lead to sub-optimal decision making or even abuse, as in the instance of 'secondary picketing'.

2. **Works council**-type bodies such as the 'joint representation committee' proposed in the Labour government's 1978 White Paper may serve to promote the ideology of the unions more than the needs of employees in that firm.

3. Participation can become time-consuming at the expense of productive work. Moreover, if management leans too far backwards to be consultative on too many things the decision pipeline will become clogged.

4. Many employees are uncomfortable about decision making. They would

much rather be left to work in their own sphere, rather than have 'management' thrust upon them.

5. Participation leads to worse decisions by diluting managerial input through the opinions of people unskilled in decision making and without the necessary perspectives on the problem.

6. Employee participation can have the consequence of bypassing the supervisor and line manager, thus affecting his morale. Alternatively, the participative setting can allow unscrupulous managers to disclaim responsibility when things go wrong.

7. As a final point, it has been noted that although participation may be a beautiful concept it is not a *sine qua non* for industrial harmony. High morale and a sense of common objectives are not unknown in hierarchical organisations (for example army units). Further, a highly democratic organisation is not in itself an inevitable recipe for business success, and one can point to firms which are highly enlightened in this respect but whose business performance is quite modest.

As we hinted at the beginning of this section, participation comes in a range of shapes and sizes. In the following sections we will look at one 'minimal' and one 'maximal' form of participation. The minimal example of participation is so-called **job enrichment**, where the employee is encouraged to take decisions about matters directly related to his own job function (e.g. pacing his work effort, ordering in materials, quality control, liaising with people in complementary jobs, and so on). The maximal form of participation which we shall look at is the notion of worker representation on the policy board.

8.3.3 Job Enrichment

We have already encountered Herzberg and his notion of job enrichment in Chapter 2. Herzberg argues that staff have a basic expectation for their 'maintenance needs' (see Fig. 2.3) to be met. If they are not met symptoms emerge as grumbles of job dissatisfaction. Conversely, 'motivation needs', which relate mainly to individual achievement and career growth, are the ones requiring attention if the employee is to be effectively motivated. Herzberg proposes that job restructuring can be done in such a way as to meet these motivational needs more fully. He says this can be done:

a. By removing some controls while retaining accountability.
b. By increasing the accountability of the person for his own work.
c. By giving a person a complete unit of work instead of a repetitive fragment.
d. By granting additional responsibility to the worker for work planning.
e. By giving feedback direct to the worker rather than to the supervisor.
f. By introducing more varied and more challenging tasks (*not* just giving them more work!).
g. By allowing people to become experts in some area of their work.

Herzberg recognises that not every job can be 'enriched' and that, indeed, every worker does not want to see his job enriched. The worker may feel more secure in conditions of maximum predictability and in any case he may view his job as no more than one way of earning a living. Moreover, certain jobs are so repetitive and routine that introducing job variation, let alone elements of planning, is hard to conceive. Job rotation, where employees move among a set number of tedious jobs, is a compromise solution in such cases.

There can also be organisational resistance to job enrichment. In the first place the unions may object to the blurring of job differentials or to employees taking on certain managerial functions. They may also use the enlarged job specification as a basis for higher wage demands. On the management side, too, supervisors may see their own role being undercut. Obviously, then, a good idea such as job enrichment cannot just be grafted on to any organisational structure: it has to have a hospitable environment in order to flourish, and if the traditions of the organisation are not sympathetic it will wither.

The natural extension of job enrichment is the autonomous or semi-autonomous work groups which organise and manage the task themselves. Experiments by Philips in Holland and by ICI have been successful in delegating this kind of maximum responsibility to the primary work group.

Motivational considerations need to be central in setting up job routines and not some kind of frill to be stuck on later. It is essential to ask which elements of the involvement really attract and which alienate the worker. Remember that some people respond better to human resources management while others are happier with a 'human relations' approach – and many still respond best to a carrot-and-stick, Taylor type approach. Employees may even need different approaches depending on how old or how skilled or intelligent they are. This means that a person's job cannot simply be set up and left but needs constant feedback and adaptation.

Job advancement must be based on publicly demonstrated merit and not just on seniority. A rise in status may be more sustaining than a pay rise, which can be quickly forgotten as it is absorbed into the family income. Perception is crucial here: people generally have certain motivators in common, but the importance of different needs as work motivators will vary from person to person according to the *perceived* attractiveness of factors such as promotion, and the *perceived* likelihood of having the long-term abilities to maintain continuous advancement.

A motivational 'dead spot' can occur in a work cycle in three ways:

i. The outcome may be wrongly perceived ('Why should I work like a dog to increase the profits of the shareholders?').
ii. The person may underestimate his own abilities, or his level of aspiration may be too low.
iii. Even if he *does* correct these estimates of his own abilities he may wonder if, say, passing the examinations really will lead to greater personal satisfaction or to a salary increase: he is under-motivated in this instance because he underestimates the likelihood of his desired outcome being realised and instead concentrates on possible negative outcomes, e.g. 'Once I've shown them I can pass the examination they'll want more out of me.'

8.3.4 **Worker Representation on the Policy Board (Joint Consultation)**

Whereas job enrichment concerns making the operative his own chargehand in the sense that supervisory decisions about his own immediate work milieu are delegated to him alone, joint consultation involves a shift of reference away from the worker's own immediate job situation to short- and even long-term planning about the whole workshop, the whole department or indeed the whole company. Joint consultation implies a joint examination by management and employees on issues of mutual concern so that genuine solutions acceptable to all may arise from a full exchange of views. Some examples of such issues are whether to invest abroad, whether to merge with or take over another company, whether to launch a new product. Note that joint consultation is *not* the same thing as collective bargaining where there is typically a conflict of interest over payments, benefits and hours of work. Collective bargaining is carried out as a distinct and separate exercise (see Chapter 9). The United Kingdom was a pioneer in joint consultation, and some works councils instituted in the last century are still active and many also remain from the First World War. Companies where such shared decision making through worker representation flourishes include the Glacier Metal Company Ltd, Scott Bader Company Limited, and the John Lewis Partnership. After the First and Second World Wars there were bursts of enthusiasm about worker participation but the enthusiasm subsequently subsided. The publication of the Bullock Report, widely criticised for its dogmatic approach to industrial relations, and the subsequent government White Paper on industrial democracy (1978) envisaged that worker directors would be operating by 1984. While it now remains to be seen how the Conservative government chooses to interpret this theme for the 1980s, it is of some interest to list the main points of the Labour government's White Paper. These were:

● To encourage companies to work out a framework for representative decision making for themselves, but to provide 'statutory fall-back rights' for employees and unions.

● A two-tier structure: policy board and management board, with employees having the right to representation on the policy board.

● To introduce legislation requiring employers of more than 500 people to discuss with employees all important proposals concerning them.

● To require trades unions to form 'joint representation committees' (JRCs) which would have the right to require boards to discuss industrial strategy.

● These JRCs would also have the power to require companies to ballot employees on whether they wanted representation on the policy board.

In general, all the problems discussed in 8.3.2 will apply to the operation of consultative committees. In addition there may be additional conflicts from divided loyalties or the by-passing of formal structures. First, the works council representative might not be a shop steward (and not take the union's policy into account) or he might be a shop steward and present the union's view rather than that of the other employees in the particular firm. Secondly, the supervisors and junior managers could easily be by-passed in decision making as the senior management and the workers could easily be seen to be giving the information, making the decisions and communicating these. However, there are many advantages that could come from greater openness and shared viewpoints in an organisation which can only be as strong as its weakest and most dissatisfied members.

8.4 Money as a Special Motivator

The emphasis in Chapter 2 on motivation of the human relations or human resources type should not let us forget that money is an important motivator in its own right. People will go to work in the snows of Alaska or the sweat and dust of Dubai in order to accumulate large amounts of money; the fact that in such places there are few leisure facilities on which to spend the money is almost an attraction. People can be induced to do outrageous things if the money is right, and, as the saying goes, 'Every man has his price'. Money is also tied in with 'higher' needs such as needs for power and self-esteem, since money can effectively buy these things, by allowing us to compare ourselves with the less well-off or by allowing us greater freedom of action. It is true that highly esteemed professions such as medicine and teaching are often lower paid than equivalent levels in business, but the argument here is that other factors such as job satisfaction and personal freedom make up for this. However, if salaries remain significantly and persistently low this must eventually affect the prestige of the occupation: even in special cases such as clergyman or probation officer, where some might argue prestige is built into the job regardless of salary levels, money still operates as a social marker and as a motivator for the typical holder of such a job.

The extent to which money is a motivator for the individual will depend on his present level of wealth, since offering a £1,000 increment to someone earning £5,000 as opposed to someone earning £50,000 will obviously have a quite different effect. It also depends on how much money actually matters to the person, since some people seem to calculate everything in monetary terms whereas others interpret life differently.

Given that money can be the key to satisfying so many of the needs of life, we might briefly look at how the employer uses his money to obtain the 'best value' from the workers he employs. There are two basic methods of determining wages to be paid: (a) according to the *amount of time worked* (usually a fixed amount of money is paid per week or per shift); (b) according to the *amount of work produced* (a certain amount of money is paid, or a certain amount of time 'allowed' per unit produced on either an individual or group-sharing basis). Very often the distinction between the two bases of payment becomes blurred as when workers on time rates are given an additional **productivity bonus**, or when the hourly rate paid is varied according to the previously assessed effectiveness of the individual worker (**measured day**

rate). Payment according to amount of work produced – also termed **piece-work** – offers the worker the opportunity to regulate his work output according to 'strength of need', that is, how badly he needs the money at a particular time. This contrasts with the time-based system, which pays him a straight £100, say, regardless of whether he looks for work or avoids it. It also gives the worker a feeling of being in control of the work situation, at least to some extent, and rewards the more hard-working able and skilled worker against the less effective with, at least theoretically, a nicety of discrimination which is not practicable with time-based systems. However, most workers, through their trade unions, have insisted on safeguards. These safeguards often include a guaranteed basic rate and careful agreements concerning such eventualities as machine breakdowns, material shortages and changes in product design. Workers such as office staff or warehousemen who are not directly involved in production may participate in bonus schemes based on overall productivity calculations. Such schemes arise from a wish to appear fair to all staff: in practice, since the 'incentives' are usually so far removed from their own work situation and in effect unrelated to their own output, the specific incentive value is near zero, although their general liking for the organisation may improve.

One step more ambitious than periodic bonus schemes is profit sharing and even share ownership. How effective is profit sharing as an organisational motivator? It would seem to be a good thing that employees obtain a fair share of the wealth they help to create, and not just through wages but also through a share in the capital value of the company. On the face of it, this should help staff (and this includes managers as well as the workforce) to feel increased commitment to the organisation and its objectives. There are questions about whether share ownership would be fair to existing **shareholders,** or, more insidiously, whether it could eventually lead to worker control. There are also some Inland Revenue difficulties over the problem of 'tax-free wages'. But more important is the question of whether such schemes do in fact operate as effective incentives giving employees a stronger feeling of commitment to the firm. It is doubtful if employee loyalty can be won that easily. A firm that hands out some of its profit to employees directly or via shares yet does not care for their motivation needs while they are engaged in *making* that profit can hardly expect such schemes to be any sort of answer to company motivation. As part of an overall concern for the relationship of the employee to the company, certainly, it must have an important component role to play, but it would be naïve to expect more than this.

The Future
This chapter, and its subsequent work section, gives a few ideas on forms of participation that can, and are, occurring in organisations. There are many other types which are being tried and experiments are continuing in the search to provide some formula which will allow organisational objectives to more nearly coincide with the objectives of those who work. It is clear to the most

casual observer that conflict must be reduced and that greater sharing is necessary: it is also obvious that in 'advanced' societies with relatively educated and well-to-do workers, many will want a say in decisions affecting both their job and the company. Time will show whether the present capitalistic structure of the private sector (with shareholders electing the Board to make decisions primarily to benefit the shareholders) can be adapted to suit these changing facts of life.

Work Section

A. Revision Questions

A1 Explain Simon's 'satisficing' principle of motivation.
A2 What is m.b.o.?
A3 What systems would be needed to carry out m.b.o.?
A4 What are the advantages of m.b.o.?
A5 What are the difficulties commonly encountered when establishing m.b.o.?
A6 List seven points in favour of 'participation'.
A7 List seven points against further 'participation'.
A8 Explain 'job enrichment'.
A9 Name three companies that have adopted a form of participation.
A10 Explain why 'piece-work' can be a good and bad wages system.
A11 Why don't all firms use some form of profit sharing?
A12 Name three schemes or systems by which organisations could be run.

B. Exercises/Case Studies

B1 Case Study: The Assistant Foreman

Pete Cole, the production superintendent for a car manufacturing company, received a visit one morning from David Green, an assistant foreman. Green was disturbed about the way in which the new foreman of his department had been encroaching upon the authority of the assistant foreman. Whereas the new foreman's predecessor had given assistant foremen considerable freedom in scheduling work orders, in assigning specific jobs to their personnel and in training the crew members within their sections, the new foreman assumed many of these duties himself. Specifically, Green complained that the new foreman had taken it upon himself to transfer personnel between sections, claiming that the individuals who were involved needed a greater variety of work experience. In addition to having their crews broken up and their work schedules and job assignments interrupted, the assistant foremen, according to Green, were also being by-passed by the foreman who frequently gave work assignments and instructions to their personnel directly. Green complained also that he and the other assistant foremen had attempted, without success, to advise the foreman of the problems that he was creating for them. Green reinforced his complaint with a request that he be permitted to return to his former job as a production worker.

After listening patiently to Green's story, Cole asked him to defer his demotion request until the difficulty could be investigated. When Cole contacted the department foreman who was the subject of the complaint, he discovered that the foreman's version of the problem was somewhat different than that expressed by Green. The foreman complained that he felt his predecessor had relinquished virtually all of his authority to the assistant foremen, who had become accustomed to operating their departments more or less as they pleased. The foreman went on to describe certain laxities which had developed within the department training scheduling and which he was attempting to correct. He also enumerated instances of resistance that he had encountered from his assistant foremen. He cited Green in particular as being one of the assistant foremen who seemed to be most resentful of receiving any orders or suggestions regarding the operation of his section. Finally, the foreman stated his belief that the real problem stemmed from the fact that the assistant foremen had grown accustomed to exercising the authority of the foreman and that they resented having this authority withdrawn and reassumed by the foreman. Since Cole considered both individuals to be competent in their respective jobs, he surmised that at least a part of the difficulty stemmed from his own failure to give sufficient attention to lower levels of supervision within his department.

Questions

a. What steps do you feel that Cole might take to correct this situation and to prevent the recurrence of similar ones in the future?
b. What possible reasons are there for the differences in the views expressed by the foreman and his assistant, Green?
c. What may be some of the underlying causes for the attitudes of the foreman and the assistant foremen? What may be some of the underlying causes for the difficulties that have arisen between them?

B2 When Clocking-off Time is the Highlight of a Working Day

Sir,

I recently spent several weeks as a labourer in a local frozen food factory.

It was not that the work was particularly hard (although there were some jobs requiring a fair degree of physical exertion); in my experience the worst feature was the sheer, unmitigated boredom. Given that the main object of this factory was to maximise profits, this was, I suppose, inevitable: the jobs were designed for maximum output, although this was certainly not being achieved; job satisfaction was not only not a high priority – it seemed to be a concept completely unheard of.

For someone without any experience of working on a production line, it is difficult to comprehend the level of boredom which comes from doing the same repetitive and utterly mindless tasks day after day. When people are treated like automata, they begin, not surprisingly, to act accordingly. The only way effectively to relieve such perpetual tedium is to switch off mentally.

There is so much noise on the factory floor anyway that it is impossible to think of anything except clocking-off time. Virtually the entire work force functions in a semi-comatose stupor.

Where I was working, the machinery was old-fashioned and in-efficient – breakdowns occurred perhaps thirty to forty times every hour. The mechanics did not want to know; we would have often to wait for them to finish their crossword before they could be persuaded to come and attend to the breakdown. In the meantime, workers would be standing idle and production time would be wasted. Yet the company could apparently not understand why it was losing money hand over fist.

If this is a typical example of British factory life, then the causes of our economic stagnation and deplorable industrial relations seem so obvious, and the remedies so simple that they speak for themselves. – Yours faithfully, etc.
Source: The Guardian, August, 1978.

Question
Draft replies from:
a. F. W. Taylor
b. Elton Mayo
In both cases meet the correspondent's points as directly as possible.

B3 Douglas McGregor tells this story as told to him by a union official: 'A new manager appeared in the textile mill. He came into the weave room the day he arrived. He walked directly over to the shop steward and said, "Are you Belloc?" The shop steward acknowledged that he was. The manager said, "I am the new manager here. When I manage a mill, I run it. Do you understand?" The steward nodded, and then waved his hand. The workers, intently watching this encounter, shut down every loom in the room immediately. The steward turned to the manager and said, "All right, go ahead and run it."'
Comment on the situation.

B4 Since the inception of his company, the chairman has always believed in a fair day's pay for a fair day's work. In carrying out this policy he has concerned himself in industrial relations solely with technical matters, skills and problems. There have been no 'frills' either in his factory or in his personnel activities. And his operations have been financially and personnel-wise relatively successful through the years.

Recently he heard rumours that a strong effort was to be made to unionise his office and shop workers. To counter this, he decided to take some strong and, for him, radical measures. Calling a meeting of his first-line supervisors (50 in number) he ordered each of them to incorporate human relations practices into their daily work, in particular to:

a. Check out job applicants as to attitudes as well as technical competence.

b. Install as soon as possible some recreational and social facilities.

c. Set up a grievance plan under which employees or representatives of employees in each department could submit complaints.

He also announced to all employees by means of a letter that his door was always open to any employee who wanted to see him personally on any matter.

Question

What do you think of the steps taken by this chairman? Where you are critical of them, or in agreement, indicate why or what you would have done instead.

Chapter 9

Collective Bargaining

Synopsis: *We now focus on the most persistently problematic area of organisational decision making—that of collective bargaining between management and unions. We begin by contrasting a micro and macro view of the relationship between employer and employee. The micro view considers how the contribution each makes to the relationship can give rise to feelings of unfairness and inequity. The macro view treats the same question at the level of trade union and employers' associations. At both the micro and macro level what seems to matter is not the objective monetary value of pay demands, productivity awards and the like, so much as their* perceived *value in the eyes of all parties concerned. We give some background on the formation and operation of both trade unions and employers' associations. The dilemma of individual versus organisational needs was raised in previous chapters, but here the discussion is taken further and extended to include the needs of a third party, the state. We then get down to identifying the formal components in the collective-bargaining procedures: the possible causes of dispute in the first place; the kinds of negotiating machinery available; and the sorts of agreement that are possible at both national and local levels. The psychological processes to be found in the bargaining situation start with the early stages of unrealistic extremism, giving way to a tough but hopefully productive stage of trading off concessions, and the final stage of resolution and euphoria. While the advantages of collective bargaining, particularly that of negotiation without state intervention, are recognised, we also notice certain disadvantages. The chapter ends in a thoughtful mood as we wonder whether it is better to work towards improving the present system, or start to build again.*

Plan of the chapter: *This is illustrated in Fig. 9.1.*

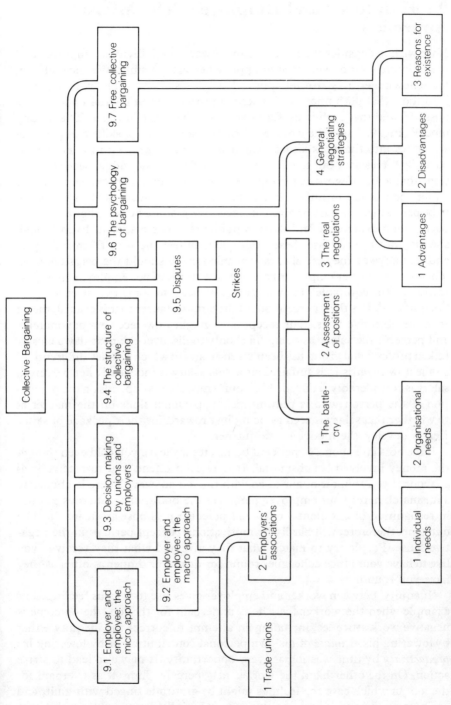

Fig. 9.1: Collective Bargaining

9.1 Employer and Employee: The Micro Approach

If we wish to consider the relationship between the individual employee and the individual employer, several approaches are possible. We have chosen the following **equity model** approach as representative. The main purpose is to show that both micro and macro approaches to industrial relations are possible, and that each is useful in showing the other in relief. The 'equity model' (Fig. 9.2) sees the worker as bringing a package of skills and personal attributes into the work situation which he 'exchanges' with the employer, basically for a salary but also for the other social and individual need satisfactions that a job of work can bring. Now this exchange may be perceived by either party as fair or unfair. For example, a receptionist may feel she ought to be paid a higher salary or given an executive grading because her additional background experience and skills in public relations justify it. Even though she may not directly use these skills she may feel she uses them indirectly and that anyway they are always available for use should the occasion arise. Therefore while her employer perceives the terms of her employment as perfectly fair (or equitable) she will perceive them, to some extent at least, as 'inequitable'. It is their perceptions of the circumstances that is crucial, rather than the objective facts. Our receptionist might now receive a pay increase and perceive the salary as being 'fair' only to discover the next day a closely linked professional group has been given an award which 'erodes differentials' so she now regards it as unfair. Her actual salary is increased; her perceived salary is considerably reduced. The equity model thus depends on the perception of the person who is putting his/her personal skills on the market as to whether that salary is seen as being just reward for their package of skills. Let us develop the model a little further.

If the boss gives you a 10 per cent bonus, it may leave you cold even though the money involved is substantial. It may even offend you to receive it as a favour if you think it ought to go with the job anyway. There is obviously a mismatch here: your employer perceives the bonus as a generous gesture in recognition of excellent work – you perceive it almost as an insult. The outcome, therefore, will hardly be motivational, except perhaps in the negative sense. People try to match what they give and what they receive – you like to have your office colleagues round for drinks or dinner as often as they have you round.

'Inequity' between worker and employer gives rise to various feelings. For example when the worker feels he is underpaid for the job, the outcome is negative work attitudes, including an attempt to correct the inequity either by lowering his *estimate* of his own personal contribution or by lowering his *productivity* by time wasting at every opportunity. It may also lead to strike action. On the other hand the worker may perceive himself as overpaid for the job, in which case the feelings might be gratitude tinged with guilt, and again an attempt to 'restore equity', either by inflating estimates of his own

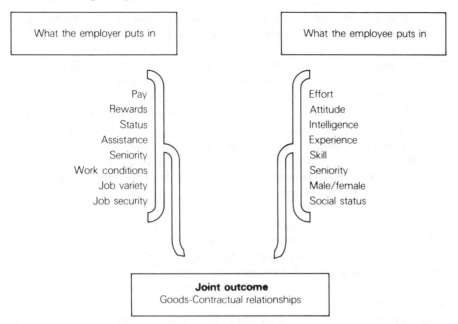

Fig. 9.2: Equity Model of the Work Situation

value to the company or, conversely, by working harder, doing extra work without claiming for it, speaking well of the company to outsiders, and so on. Some people seem to be in a more or less permanent 'state of inequity' with the world at large – they either overvalue themselves or work unnecessarily hard to redress an imbalance which does not exist in the minds of other people.

9.2 Employer and Employee: The Macro Approach

It is possible to consider the employer–employee relationship at the much broader level of an employee's trade union and the equivalent employers' association. We still have contractual relationships and disputes between the parties arising from feelings of inequity; only the level of reference is different.

9.2.1 The Trade Unions
In general terms, trade unions exist to protect the personal interests of their members and they have grown because of working people's problems and defend traditional viewpoints. This generalisation can be broken down into more direct objectives:

a. To have influence over the 'marketing of labour services' by acting as a watchdog (with teeth) over their members' terms of employment (rates of pay, hours of work, manning levels, etc.) and conditions of work (health, safety, etc.).

b. To consider the longer-term effects of employers' actions affecting the *security of members' jobs* (even though in the short term, some jobs may have to be lost – for example in the coal and steel industries).

c. To have some control over the *standards of entry to trades*, so as to prevent a dilution of those standards (e.g. the content of apprenticeships).

d. To protect members' interests against *encroachment by other unions* or employees, by applying the concept of job demarcation.

e. To provide strength through numbers which can apply effective sanctions *against an employer* when normal means of negotiation fail to achieve results.

In any one situation it will almost certainly be impossible for a union to achieve all objectives: therefore it has to compromise. Further restrictions on the free operation of all the objectives may well follow from external constraints within our general decision model such as the level of employment, state of world trade, and the status of the union in question versus that of other unions.

Unions have developed in an unsystematic way to meet different needs in the past. In size they vary from a membership of over $2\frac{1}{4}$ million (Transport and General Workers Union) down to under 50 (Independent Society of Cricket Ball Makers) and fall into roughly four categories:

a. *The craft unions*, which sprang out of the industrial trades, are organised *across* industrial boundaries, e.g. the Electrical, Electronic, Telecommunication, and Plumbing Union (EETPU).

b. *The industrial unions*, which are organised *within* industries. In practice, such unions do not in fact represent all workers in a given industry, but certainly a significant proportion, e.g. the Union of Post Office Workers or the National Union of Mineworkers.

c. *The 'white-collar' unions*, which are representative of the managerial and other staff organisations. This is one of the growth areas of trade unionism, e.g. the Association of Scientific, Technical and Managerial Staffs (ASTMS).

d. *The general unions*, which represent those workers, often amongst the least skilled, not directly represented in the other groups, e.g. the Transport and General Workers Union (TGWU).

Within almost all unions, there is a paid body of full-time officials. These act as the administrators of the policy decided by the union's national executive committee, and members. The ratio of full-time officers to members varies widely between unions: figures ranging from 2,000 to 8,000 members per officer are found. Appointment of the senior permanent posts is by election in most cases, but direct appointment by the executive committee is possible. One hundred and fifteen unions are affiliated to the **Trades Union Congress** (TUC) out of a total of about 485. The TUC is thus the central organisation to which the majority of trade unions are linked. Founded just over a hundred years ago, it is not an executive body but a pressure group with wide advisory powers. The TUC's executives are drawn from the top of individual unions.

9.2.2 The Employers' Associations

The employers' associations, such as the Engineering Employers Federation, find it easy to set clear objectives but difficult to agree and adhere to policy. There are several reasons why:

a. They do not cover the whole range of employment, as some employers do not wish to become 'federated'.
b. They are not single buyers of labour (this is the individual member firm's responsibility).
c. Employers' associations have no control over the demand for new labour (this is again in the company's hands).
d. They only have limited internal power, the ultimate sanction on a member being expulsion, which is probably no real worry.
e. Their role has tended to be passive, leaving much the largest share of initiative to the unions.

So, rather as in the case of the unions, the objectives of the employers' associations can be seen in 'protective' terms, in the protection of members' interests, safeguarding the return on assets in business and in attempting to establish common rules and conditions of employment. As in the case of the unions there are external constraints, like the economy, which affect selling prices, profits, wage settlements or the quality and quantity of labour. Employers' associations cover both private and public industry. Compared with trade unions, employers' associations are a less potent force in the structure of bargaining (the individual firms more normally agreeing their own specific terms). However, the employers' associations do agree many general problems with their union counterparts and these come to form a structure of minimal concerns. They also advise many large and small companies through their advisory and research departments and can co-ordinate company strategies if required. The associations have a counterpart to the TUC in the **Confederation of British Industry** (CBI). The CBI is both a pressure group for private and public sector needs and an advisory body to the government and, of course, its members.

9.3 Decision Making by Unions and Employers

Too often the relationship is one of power conflict. By exercising power and influence in the five areas listed in 9.2.1 unions hope to influence the bargaining process and achieve a settlement nearest to their members' interests; equally, the employers wish to safeguard profitability, survival and control. Thus the different objectives of employers and unions, far from being

128 *Collective Bargaining*

harmonised, can become a conflict of interest, with each side trying to win the bigger slice of the 'wealth cake' for itself, regardless of the loss to the other side. These disputes over which side shall contribute how much of which ingredients too often means a smaller cake for sharing, and in some cases no cake at all.

The fact that the main decisions in each case are made at different levels (employers largely nationally, unions largely locally) leads to misunderstanding. This concept of the level at which bargaining takes place is important (see **9.4**) because at the **national advisory level** the bargain struck is one set in general terms only and is usually in the form of a 'gentlemen's agreement'. The **national participative level** results in agreements which are general in nature, 'skeleton' versions of agreements which may then be filled out in the detailed discussions at the **local participative levels**. Although the Donovan Commission in 1967 recommended plant level as opposed to national bargaining, because of the special conditions special attitudes and special achievements that doubtless do obtain in different firms, the fact remains that where these local agreements differ greatly jealous comparisons are bound to persist.

A healthy, go-ahead company is obviously in the interests of unions as well as of management, yet in Britain the union disposition is protective, traditional, even defensive, rather than participative and creative. This defensiveness can grow into self-defeating stubbornness when unions refuse to accept new technology or when inter-union arguments about differentials or demarcations can cause total shutdown and everybody suffers (including workers completely outside the dispute). From their inward-looking positions unions may well be in the right, but as far as the outsider – which increasingly includes the TUC itself – is concerned, the actions look suicidal. In particular, within our present context, it indicates that collective bargaining as the cornerstone of industrial relations needs radical revision. The employers' associations are guilty of at least as many sins as the trade unions and many of the sins are indeed very similar. As we have noted, the role of the employers' associations is protective: they spend a good deal of energy worrying about levels of corporation tax and guarding the *status quo* – particularly in the areas of control, methods of organising men and making decisions. The stance towards the unions often anticipates confrontation rather than participation, and there is insufficient reaching out in a genuine wish to accept that the other side may have a valid point.

9.3.1 The Individual Employee – His Needs and Objectives
a. Although collective bargaining as a form of decision making is essentially a dialogue between parties meeting on a representative basis, it is worthwhile for us to return to the micro perspective and reconsider the needs of the individual worker, as seen through the eyes of the main management theorists. We insisted in Chapter 8 that in spite of the shift to a focus on psychological needs financial factors are still of great importance when

considering the objectives of the individual. During times of significant inflation and very low productivity growth, such as the 1970–80 period, one of the main objectives of the individual was to *maintain* his financial status (at least) with respect to other individuals or groups of individuals, and human factors took a back seat at the negotiating table.

b. The issue of pay differentials itself is a difficult one. One always has to remember that giving to any one group of workers is effectively taking away from another group, in relative terms. In view of the fact that everyone always thinks his job is more important than others think it is (our old friend perceptual distortion again), the difficulties in assigning monetary values to different jobs may well be insuperable. One solution is the 'tribunal' approach, where supposedly disinterested outsiders study the available evidence and develop criteria or **decision rules** of the kind we shall encounter in Chapter 12 for determining an order of importance for jobs (job comparability) and then, more difficult, the degree of differential in monetary terms. A major advantage of tribunal-type agreements is that the outcome does not depend on the strengths and weaknesses of local protagonists.

9.3.2 The Needs of the Organisation as an Employer

a. The organisation has responsibilities to its shareholders, its employees and its customers. It is the job of management to satisfy these different interests while ensuring that the corporate entity can survive, in good health, into the future. Since the organisation operates in a constantly changing environment the need for adaptation to meet new threats to its survival is vital. For example, through market research, changes in customer requirements can be noted and acted upon; through financial planning, the money market's possible effects must be seen. Similarly, the informal aspects of the operation must be assessed, the employees' requirements being only one of many competing demands.

To ensure survival, then, the organisation must follow a process of continuing evolution. This may take the form of relatively small changes in policy, of no real consequence to the workforce. On the other hand, major changes of direction may be necessary, which have a very great effect (e.g. the decision to resite a plant near to its customers). Such changes must be accomplished if the company is to remain viable in the long term. As this process of adaptation to external and internal influences takes place, the objectives of the employer may change several times before an agreement is reached.

b. We noted earlier the employee could be considered as having two simultaneous aims with respect to the 'wealth cake': that its *overall* size should increase, and that his own share should be maximised.

The first of these objectives is also shared by the organisation; what differs is the interpretation, by either party, of how growth is to be achieved. The employee is concerned that wages should increase, sometimes at the expense of the shareholders' profits, or through price increases, sometimes through 'productivity' deals so long as they don't carry a threat to job security. Management must always balance the demands being made. Unfortunately the notion of balance, particularly where trust between the two parties has broken down, too readily depends on which side of the scales you stand on. The union may see the employers as being selfishly concerned with placing the shareholders' and their own interests first: and the employers may see union demands as being unreasonable or impossible. Thus we have conflict instead of co-operation.

The state is involved in a double role in the collective-bargaining situation. On the one hand, the state is a major employer of labour through its control of the civil service, gas, electricity, steel, coal and railway industries, etc. On the other hand, the state is also trying to shape the decision-making 'climate' through advice, codes of conduct and a very substantial amount of legislation that affects all organisations, employers and workers in the public and private sector.

9.4 The Structure of Collective Bargaining

Workers and management have long bargained over conditions of work. Nowadays this is almost entirely done collectively between the union, representing different groups of workers (including junior management) and the employer or employers. Bargaining in four major areas is common:

a. Union recognition, where a group of workers try to become recognised as the union.
b. Pay bargaining: the usual annual bargaining rounds on pay, related benefits and hours of work.
c. General conditions of work, job security and even participation of the unions within the organisation.
d. Procedural rule bargaining for dealing with any disagreements which may occur between the men and the management over the collective bargain itself or a subsequent dispute.

These negotiations may be restricted by either legal requirements (as for example the Prices and Incomes Act of 1973) or by some government norm where the government could impose sanctions on the employer (or less commonly on the employees). However, in general we have 'free' collective bargaining where the union and the employer come to the final agreement free from government constraint (see 9.7).

Collective bargaining between the parties is conducted at three broad levels, each level having different objectives. These levels are:

a. National Advisory Level
Meetings at this level take place with the aim of discussing broad issues of policy and the respective roles to be played. There is an increasing tendency

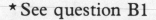

★ See question B1

for such discussions to be looking at macro-economic factors (e.g. the 'national interest' in counter-inflation policy) and to mediate in major disputes where any one of the three participants may take the role of mediator. The participants at this level are:

- The TUC – representing the point of view of the whole body of trade unions and their workers.
- The CBI – representing the collective views of the employers and employers' associations.
- The state – representing the national interest (as seen by the political party in power).

b. National Participative Level

Negotiation at this level is more functional than the general discussion at advisory levels. Rather than discussing broad policies, the parties here are those involved in negotiations. They are trying to conclude agreements on a national basis (e.g. engineering and shipbuilding), or on an industry-wide basis (e.g. coal or railways). Negotiations are normally carried on by the representatives of each side – union officers from the (full-time) national executive committee and nominated representatives of the employers. The participants are:

- Individual trade unions.
- Employers' associations – where the employers are nationally-federated.
- Individual employers – where there is no federation.

c. Local Participative Level

This is again functional but operates on a localised (or even factory) basis. The parties are trying to formulate agreements tailored to the particular needs of a locality or factory and hence there is a great deal of flexibility. This is the area of the 'productivity bargain'. The participants are:

- Trade union representatives – full-time local officials or part-time shop stewards.
- Management representatives – line managers and/or industrial relations specialists.

9.5 Disputes

Common examples of union–management dispute include:

a. When normal negotiations over pay and conditions between management and unions are progressing too slowly or when apparently unreasonable demands come from either side. Disputes can focus on 'the organisation's ability to pay', 'job comparability' or 'government pay policy'.

b. When it is considered by one group or another that the previous agreement has been broken (perhaps by 'unfair dismissal' or failure to 'honour pay differential pledges' or 'accepting black-leg labour').

c. When workers are going to lose their jobs (through factory closure, or a cash-flow crisis perhaps resulting from low market demand).

d. When there are disputes over union recognition, inter-union rivalry or even political strikes (as against the 1971 Industrial Relations Act or the government pay norms of the 1970s).

Any of the above may become full-blown disputes where the parties move from talking to action. This action may be an official or unofficial strike by union members, or a 'lock-out' by management. However, full strikes are relatively rare: go-slows, work-to-rules, banning of overtime, non-co-operation or even sit-ins are more common. Many observers of the industrial scene believe that conflict of interest will always be present because of people's innate greed and their inability to look objectively at situations.

9.5.1 **Strikes**

First, as noted above, strikes are often considered as the last weapon which the workforce will use in cases of pay negotiations or in a grievance dispute. Other devices in the repertoire of industrial action such as go-slows, work-to-rule, blacking, refusal to accept new technology or working methods or simply unco-operative behaviour are more commonly employed.

Secondly, the majority of strikes are unofficial rather than official. This means that they are called, often at short notice, by shop stewards and that there has been an incomplete attempt to use the dispute procedures normally established. Further, the 'unofficial' dispute will not have even been accepted as worthy of a strike by the men's union. This naturally reduces management's trust in unions, but it also gives no warning of close-downs. Linked production units typically cannot build up stocks to carry on so other men in the same plant or in different factories must be laid off; deadlines must be missed and perhaps heavy penalty clauses immediately operate or goodwill and future orders (whether from the home market or the export field) will be lost. Thus the unofficial strike produces the maximum inconvenience to the consumer and the maximum financial loss to the employer. These unofficial strikes compare with the more formal conflicts in Germany and the USA, where agreements are negotiated perhaps once in two years and a large battle may ensue resulting in a substantial number of days lost. Yet in such cases everybody has been forewarned, stocks have been built up and the firm has made arrangements to minimise its financial losses.

9.6 **The Psychology of Collective Bargaining**

Collective bargaining is an especially interesting and relevant topic for this book since it underlines the need for complementarity and compromise in real-life decision-making processes. You may recall the different phases that occur during a meeting as identified by Bales (Chapter 8). We find similar phases around the collective-bargaining table.

9.6.1 **The Battle-cry**

First there is the ritual attack on the employer, mainly to strengthen resolve since it is not taken seriously by either side. The union says do this or we strike, which will be more costly than settlement: the company claims that accepting union demands will cause ruination, leading to national economic disruption and ultimate unemployment. These early stages are often characterised by horsetrading in which both parties ask for the impossible in the expectation of a settlement somewhere in between. Even agreement of an agenda is not straightforward since the form of the agenda can itself be part of the negotiating tactics, e.g. a mixture of strong and weak items, the latter being included purely for trading so that both sides may appear to be winning an equal number of points.

9.6.2 **An Assessment of Positions**

The second phase sees reduced belligerence and more collaboration, with both sides emphasising the low costs of the other side's moving to the position it prescribes, e.g. higher wages will not mean higher costs since productivity will be bound to rise, or lower wages will mean higher sales and therefore more jobs and overtime. The second phase can be protracted and bitter, but deadlines are rarely real (even though the press may treat them as such). However, if strike deadlines are withdrawn too often a union may approach the point when it needs actually to strike in order to maintain the value of the deadline tactic. Decisions taken by negotiators about when to offer, when to concede and when to stand firm and for how long depend on subtle skills. Another tactic is exaggerated impatience so as to force an early showdown on the other's working limits. Another is to arrange or encourage the 'spontaneous' occurrence of demonstrations of sympathy as evidence that trouble is 'already happening'. Personal abuse, irrelevant argument and excessive geniality are all devices that can encourage an unwary opposition to make an error. Of course, a hand can be overplayed, since tactics produce counter-tactics leading to a tension spiral and eventual breakdown in negotiations unless there is some significant restructuring by one of the parties.

9.6.3 **The Real Negotiation**

There is an obvious danger that extremist negotiators on either side will not enter into the spirit of this third problem-solving stage but will insist on repeated harangues at every opportunity, or expressions of hostility which can only undermine the serious-mindedness of real negotiation. The opposite kind of danger is that as more and more common ground is discovered or the wish to co-operate grows, one side may be lured into moving to a position too far removed from its starting point. In protracted political negotiations it is not uncommon for negotiators to be accused of 'going soft' by the people they represent: certainly the moderation of their statements may make it difficult to know, without checking, who actually made a given speech! This third stage is obviously vital because it is *only* then that the opposite sides start

‚to discover that there is some common ground or room for bargaining and that their opposite numbers are not unreasonable idiots that progress can happen.

This third phase, which may be long delayed, ends in agreement in some shape or form. The earliest signs of dawning agreement may be more implicit than explicit, depending perhaps on some 'hypothetical' case being discussed without prejudice to the current situation and perhaps not being minuted. At about this time negotiators may wish to have informal, off-the-record negotiations in which a lot more can be said, always with the understanding that it will not be used within the formal negotiating arena. Neither side obtains what it wanted completely but relationships between the negotiators now warm markedly up to the time that agreement terms are signed.

9.6.4 General Negotiating Strategies

It has been said that constant successes in a negotiation are worrying because it is in one's long-term interest to lose some cases; good judgement comes in choosing the cases to be lost. Negotiators, particularly professional ones, seem to settle into a mutual acceptance of each others' standards and expectations. There are certain things that are not asked for and certain things that are not said; if they are said it is as a deliberate tactical irritant rather than as a serious negotiating objective. This is because negotiators must co-exist, and one sometimes suspects that the bonds between negotiators are stronger than the bonds connecting them to their own organisations. There is certainly on the part of both chief negotiators an unwillingness to embarrass and a wish to keep tension down to manageable levels.

Successful negotiation seems to depend on what sort of 'personal constraint' package each negotiator represents, and on how effectively lines of communication can be established between negotiators. For example, negotiators, like members of parliament and barristers, must not mistake abuse aimed at their position for personal hostility. It takes maturity, confidence and the layers of thick skin provided by years of experience to receive apparent abuse without the flicker of a facial muscle. Truly personal hostility is very damaging to the progress of negotiations especially when it occurs in the early stages since it prevents the formation of a personal relationship between negotiators, which, as we have seen, is crucial.

9.7 Advantages and Disadvantages of Free Collective Bargaining

So far we have considered a bargaining system which is primarily 'free': (a) in the sense that the state does not set either legal limits to the outcome of the negotiations (e.g. a pay norm) or even guidelines by which it may penalise firms if they break; (b) in the sense that the agreement is not backed by law and hence neither party need keep to it if conditions/expectations are considered to have changed. This is the system commonly favoured in the UK by both employers and employees, but there are both advantages and disadvantages.

9.7.1 **Advantages**

i. Both sides feel greater freedom in being able to operate without government intervention, but the procedure can include recourse to the state as a 'neutral' third party to bring to an end a threatened deadlock. This may be by conciliation, arbitration or – *in the last resort* – by legislation.

ii. Contracts can be arranged or changed by mutual consent with the minimum of fuss and bother, and without recourse to legislation.

iii. The system places responsibility on a relatively small number of people. It is then an easy matter to identify these people and encourage them to act in the interests of the community.

9.7.2 **Disadvantages**

i. The relative bargaining strengths of the union (or TUC) and the employer (or CBI) can affect the outcome, perhaps in a very inequitable way.

ii. Negotiators may be more concerned with their own political postures than with the real grievances of shop-floor workers or individual firms, and unions may be out of line with national TUC or CBI objectives.

iii. The government has become increasingly involved in national economic policy-making, and so feels that it should have a greater degree of control over collective bargaining. Once the state has enjoyed a period of control through legal means or tacit understanding it may be loath to see any return to unfettered free collective bargaining.

iv. The ritual clashes that typically occur, and which are in addition exaggerated by the press, only serve to increase the sense of alienation between the two sides. It is a well-known phenomenon of social psychology that threat from one group leads to increased solidarity and cohesion in the other. This in itself is not a bad thing, but a consequence is further deterioration in the 'understanding gap' as the members of one group take on increasingly peculiar ideas about members of the other. And when the leaders (negotiators) do battle they are expected to return victorious: if they do not they lose face and possibly their jobs as negotiators. Thus both sides are sometimes forced to indulge in antics that neither wants.

9.7.3 **Reasons For its Existence**

Such highly ritualised bargaining procedures may not be the best model for forward-looking industrial relations. It has to be appreciated that the now traditional conflict between unions and management has two sources, one economic and one psychological.

a. Economic Conflict

First, within the British industrial system there is undoubtedly bitter competition between the two sides both for power *per se* and for the bigger share of the wealth cake. This is the economic source of conflict. However, there have been two trends this decade which may eventually reduce the 'them' and 'us' feelings in industry: profit sharing and worker participation.

i. Profit Sharing. For many years some companies have experimented with profit sharing, not just at the senior manager level but right through the organisation. These schemes relate any sharing to the size of the annual profit for a company (or part of a company) and to each employee's salary or wage, and have worked well in small companies where profitability is largely determined by the inventiveness, productivity and the quality control of the workers. However, in large companies like ICI, where nobody sees the profit as being related to their individual effort *and* where profits rise and fall because of world demand, they have been discarded. However, more and more companies are trying to reward the workers as well as the shareholders.

ii. Worker Participation. This can be in either control or ownership, or both. Ever since the Second World War many large companies have developed **works councils**, made up of managers, shop stewards and workers, which discuss problems and possibilities in their respective departments. This element of control has lately both been extended at their level (particularly at Glacier Metal, where they can actually block higher management decisions) and by worker participation at Board level. It is well known that the Steel Corporation and the Post Office have a few union representatives on their Boards, as do some public companies. There are also moves to make these representatives of the workforce equal in number on the Board to those elected by the shareholders – but both unions and management are largely resisting this.

b. Psychological Conflict

The second source of union–management conflict is not economic at all, but common-or-garden psychological, stemming from the stereotypes (or fixed views) that each side has of the other. Fixed ideas give rise to prejudices which are fed by colourful imaginations. This leads to distorted generalisations about what the other side 'must be like'. Then these distorted generalisations act back on, and cause further exaggeration of, the genuine economic differences that existed in the first place. And so it continues. Consider the following evidence from a researcher who wanted to know how being on the union or management side of the fence affected perception of the other side. He arranged for negotiators from both sides (184 altogether) to be presented with a photograph and description of a deliberately average-looking, middle-aged man. Half the *management* negotiators were given the additional information that the photograph was of a fellow manager, while the other half were told he was a union official. When they were then asked to rate this person on a range of personality characteristics, those who were told he was a manager saw him as dependable and conscientious, sincere and industrious, but those who were told he was a union man saw him as aggressive, argumentative and opinionated. Interestingly, when the same trick was played on the *union* negotiators, the contrast between the two portraits was less severe, though still evident.

c. *Reducing Conflict*

We will probably never remove the sense of difference between the two sides completely, but we ought to be able to reduce the arguments over power and wealth-sharing to non-injurious levels.

Work Section

A. Revision Questions

A1 Draw a diagram to explain the 'equity model of the work situation'.

A2 Explain why the individual's perception of himself is a necessary part of how this model works.

A3 List five general objectives of most trade unions.

A4 Name four types of unions.

A5 Why do employers' associations find it hard to adhere to any policy?

A6 What do the following stand for: CBI; TUC; ACAS; TGWU?

A7 How might unions help to increase the 'wealth cake' available to all?

A8 Explain how 'job comparability' might reduce industrial disputes.

A9 Why do unions tend to be more traditional than employers?

A10 In what general way is the state involved in collective bargaining?

A11 What four major areas are usually bargained over?

A12 Explain the three levels of collective bargaining.

A13 What 'weapons' might a union use in a dispute?

A14 What 'weapons' might management use in a dispute?

A15 Explain the three phases commonly gone through by negotiators in bargaining.

A16 What are the advantages of free collective bargaining?

A17 What are the disadvantages of free collective bargaining?

A18 When might profit sharing be used successfully?

A19 What is the purpose of 'works councils'?

A20 How do you feel nationalisation has altered attitudes in collective bargaining?

A21 Is the view that conflict of interest will always be present in the work situation pessimistic or realistic?

B. Exercises/Case Studies

B1 Using your college library for background information, write brief notes on each of the following Acts of Parliament and estimate how they influenced bargaining procedure between unions and employers at the time:

a. 1833 Factory Act

b. 1971 Industrial Relations Act

c. 1970 Equal Pay Act

d. 1975 Employment Protection Act

B2 Take *any two* of the following passages and write in some detail about their relevance to industrial relations. Try to understand purpose as well as content and the extent to which the comments may be justified.

   a. The stewards considered that all the good things offered to workers at the Ford Motor Company had had to be fought for. They were seen as the fruits of trade union organization and struggle rather than grace and favour of an ideal employer. Many of the stewards made some reference to the early days of the plant and made it clear that certain lessons had to be learned from this experience. Eric put it like this:

'What we've got we've fought for, and fought hard at that. When I came here first we were worked really hard and if you had a complaint you couldn't get a steward. Now a man can get a steward pretty quickly. It took a lot of hard work. The rate was bad and the job was bad. . . . People have got short memories though, and new ones come. They see the job now and they think "This isn't so bad." They forget that it wasn't always like this. We *earned* it like it is and if we don't watch out with this Company we'll be back where we started.'

   b. 'Industry is organised to make profit. Most people accept this as a fact, and recognise that the more profit their company makes the better chance it has of providing a good standard of living and security for its employees and their families. This is not only because everybody's future earnings depend on the Company continuing to make a profit, but because a good profit encourages more investment – a good safeguard for the future.

'A look at profits in our own business shows that they are closely linked to how much use we make of plant and equipment. This is because it takes a lot of expensive space and plant to make our products and the more we make with the same resources the more profit we get. In fact, unless we are building at a good rate we are not even paying our way – on a two-shift system without overtime our plants are standing idle for a third of the day.'

   c. 'As a shop steward I see the main problem to be the centralization of power on both the management and trade union side. This is bad for the operator as well because both the steward and the operator get frustrated when things get taken above their heads. You need to have much more autonomy for shop-floor unionism.

'The supervisors here are just not trained in the right attitudes. That's why we're young. We've got to be to take it. We're young and we're militant. Not militant in that we take the blokes outside the gate – but in sticking up for them against the foreman. Standing up for their rights.

'I've found that with management it's always a case of passing the buck. They're all *afraid* to make a decision in case they drop a goolie. If anything goes wrong they just don't want to know. They don't want

to find out what or why they just want a scapegoat. Always find someone to blame.'
[*Source:* Huw Beynon, *Working for Ford*, E.P. Publishing, 1973.]

B3 Case Study: 'The Times'
(article from The Guardian, February 4, 1979)

The Times are out of joint   by Patrick Brogan

*On November 30, The Times of London and the Sunday Times suspended
publication. This article on what led to the newspapers' action was written
for The Washington Post by the Washington correspondent of The Times.*

The managements of Fleet Street newspapers enjoy a well-earned reputation for pusillanimity and incompetence. Faced with strong and militant
print unions, they have consistently practised a policy of voluble protest
and craven capitulation.

It was always cheaper to give in than to lose the night's paper, because
a missed edition was an absolute loss. You can never catch up the way
car manufacturers can – by increasing production when the strike is over.
So Fleet Street followed the example of the Saxons, who used to pay
the Vikings to go away. As Kipling put it:

That is called paying the Dane-geld;
But we've proved it again and again,
That if once you have paide him the Dane-geld
You never get rid of the Dane.

So management progressively lost control of production. Manning
levels were set by the union and even hiring was lost to them: On The
Times, even senior editors have to take the secretaries the union sends
them. Wage rates were pushed skyward and profits vanished.

Since management always gave in, the unions progressively increased
their demands. Small claims were enforced by threats to stop production
in the evening, and large claims were enforced by sabotaging the print
run every evening.

Like other Fleet Street newspapers, The Times and The Sunday
Times have had their own traditions; they remain separate papers
although one member of management on the Sunday Times was known
as Father Christmas because he always gave the unions whatever goodies
they wanted.

Father Christmas was sent on his way, and a new management team,
headed by Marmaduke Hussey, chief executive of Times Newspapers
Ltd., was brought in to clear up the mess. Unfortunately, they inherited
their predecessors' reputations as well as their problems.

The unions continued to exact the Dane-geld in ever-larger sums. Mr.
Hussey and his colleagues began to contemplate using the conflict that

would inevitably follow the attempt to introduce computer technology into their facilities as a battlefield on which to try to win back control of the company's printing operations. They have been talking for a couple of years now about the possibility of suspending publication as the final sanction against the unions, and they finally did so November 30.

The Observer, a Sunday paper then printed by The Times, once decided to present a detailed report of the labor practices of Fleet Street. Describing its own operations, it mentioned the case of an elderly printer who was so decrepit that he had to be helped to the door of the composing room every Saturday evening.

The night manager, a union official, would note his presence and put him down for a night's pay, while his brothers helped him totter off to the bar and, later, sent him home by taxi.

When the article was sent down to be set, the printers took great exception, particularly to the bit about their ancient brother. The editor, who was also the proprietor, was told that unless it was removed the paper would not appear the next morning. He capitulated.

When the IRA was setting off bombs around London a few years ago, The Times used to be called, with suspicious frequency, in the later afternoon and informed that there was a bomb in the building. It would be cleared and searched and by the time the day staff had returned, the magic hour of 4 had passed and they were all entitled to overtime.

Usually the dispute concerns money, manning or working conditions, and either management surrenders or the whole edition or part of its run are lost. Management then complains bitterly but invokes no sanctions against the strikers, who have shown once again who controls the presses.

The Times published two profitable educational supplements. A few weeks ago, one of the unions decided to hold a chapel meeting (the office branch is called a chapel in all Fleet Street unions) at 4 p.m. That was legitimate, because the press run should have been over by then. But the chapel stopped work at 3:15 – to wash their hands – and half the paper's run, including the supplement, was lost. There was nothing management could do.

The Times missed eight days' publication last March. A total of 7.7 million copies of the two papers and their three supplements were lost in the first quarter of the year through a series of unofficial strikes and other industrial disputes.

The Sunday Times has the machinery to print an 80-page paper (large by British standards), but the unions insist on a substantial pay raise to work it, so the paper stays at 72 pages. Its colour magazine, which is not even printed in London, was recently increased in size. The London unions demanded a 50 percent pay rise for Saturday nights in compensation; management's refusal to comply led to the loss of hundreds of thousands of copies of the paper practically every week (430,000 Oct. 8 and

290,000 Oct. 15, for instance). The paper's circulation is about 1.5 million.

There has always been overmanning in Fleet Street, and not only there. Low productivity is a national failure and, whatever its causes, is the main reason for Britain's dismal economic performance.

What is not clear is why labour relations have got so much worse in the past decade. Perhaps people are disgruntled because Britain stagnated in the '60s while other countries boomed, and suffered more than most during the recession of the early '70s. The political failures of Labour and Tory governments undoubtedly contributed.

At all events, things have deteriorated steadily on The Times, and with each passing year it has become more difficult for management to turn the paper's labor problems around.

When Roy Thomson, founder of the family that now owns The Times, bought his first British paper, The Scotsman, he was appalled to discover how labor relations and production were conducted there. He made the mistake of listening to his British directors, who told him that there was nothing he could do about it: Canadian methods would not work in Edinburgh, still less in London when he bought the Sunday Times some years later. He may have regretted listening to voices of caution, though it is hard to see how he could have rationalized production with the managers he inherited.

The mistake was repeated when he bought The Times in 1966. He was prepared to put millions into modernizing the paper, and indeed spent horrendous sums over the next decade to keep it afloat. It would have been far, far cheaper to have confronted the unions immediately, even at the cost of a prolonged closure, and then to have introduced sensible manning.

When the Scottish Daily Express closed a few years ago, its workers put out a successor using the same machinery. When the Express had required more than 100 man-hours to put the paper on the presses, the same workers found that they could do the same job with three man-hours. This kind of labor-saving would have made The Times a profitable paper in practically every year since 1966 – instead of the loss-leader of the Thomson empire.

The paper's losses early last year coincided with the arrival of the first oil from the North Sea. Roy Thomson died two years ago, but the manifestation of his genius for making money was also the most spectacular.

Together with two other elderly capitalists, Armand Hammer and Paul Getty, he had a little flutter on oil under the North Sea. Their wells started production before those of the big oil companies. The Thomsons' share of the profits is around $200 million a year.

The family owns about 80 percent of the company, which has now moved its headquarters to Toronto. The whole organization was booming, except the Times, and that paper could be closed permanently, if necessary, without any significant effect on the group's profitability. The various Thomson organization directors, presumably including Kenneth Thomson, Roy Thomson's son, let it be known that enough was enough, and that The Times had better solve its labour problems.

This suited The Times management, because the computers and terminals for using the new technology had been installed, and months of negotiations had failed to get the unions to agree to use it.

In particular, the printers refused to allow anyone else to touch the computer terminals. Management wanted the girls who take down telephoned classified advertisements to type them straight into the computer. The printers, who were losing their linotype machines, wanted the jobs – at three times the wages.

The ultimatum was issued, therefore, in a sudden gesture of vexation last April. Ironically, it came during The Times' first period of profitability in many years (The Sunday Times almost always showed a profit). But for the strikes and stoppages, the company would have made a large profit last year.

The turnaround was partly due to improved management and partly to Britain's economic recovery. The new profits incited the unions to make ever-greater claims and helped management resist. It demanded that all the unions sign new contracts by Nov. 30 or the papers, including the two educational supplements and The Times Literary Supplement, would close until they did sign.

The new contracts would provide for new manning levels, though there would be no compulsory redundancies; there would be management control of all operations, a disputes procedure which would eliminate all wildcat strikes and sabotage, and general acceptance of the new technology.

A few contracts were agreed to in time, and others, including the journalists', in a fortnight's period of grace that was offered when the closure took place. The main mechanical unions refused all compromise.

Under British law, it is extremely difficult to fire anyone except en masse. The departing employees are entitled to varying periods of notice, running from a week or two for junior secretaries to two or three months for senior staff – including, in this case, the most obdurate of the printers.

Journalists, having signed the new contract, will be kept on the payroll. At first The Times' journalists rejected the contract, although it was quite generous monetarily. They wanted to demonstrate their discontent at the way management had handled the affair, particularly in threatening to sack them.

They also made some specific demands, which management, hurt and horrified at the rejection, promptly conceded. Behind it all was the feeling that the print unions, by ruthless militancy and immoderate greed, have always done better for their members than congenitally moderate journalists, whose incomes have suffered badly because of the paper's unprofitability.

The journalists on the Financial Times (no relation) are on the verge of striking for the same reason – management refuses to give them a bonus for bringing out a German edition, to which they will contribute, while giving one to the print unions, who will contribute nothing.

It is all rather perverse of the Times' journalists to object to their management's policy because, after all, they have wanted the paper's production rationalized and modernized for years. The Sunday Times' journalists accepted their proposed contract when it was first offered.

Despite their professional interest in rationalization, a majority on both papers, including most editors, are horrified at any suggestion that the editorial side of the business might be tightened up. They are quite content to leave things the way they are: The Sunday Times sent a man to Jonestown, and it occurred to nobody that he might also file for The Times.

At the moment, however, the question is how long the papers can survive a closure.

Top management does not expect it to last more than three months, but the unions are determined people and the printers, at least, have their backs to the wall. Even The Times might find it difficult to reopen after six months, and somewhere along the line journalists are going to get tired of being paid to do nothing and are going to start leaving.

On its last night, The Times, foreseeing a long suspension, took pity on its readers and printed the solution to the last crossword. Usually the solutions appear the following day. One of the clues in that last puzzle was "overthrow top group." The answer: Upset.

Source: The Guardian, February 4, 1979.

Questions
1. Briefly explain the following:
   a. The folly of giving Dane-geld.
   b. The problems that can result from 'the division of labour'.
   c. The problems of introducing new technology.
   d. The difficulties of running a 'multi-union' plant.
   e. The particular economic problems that result from running a daily newspaper.
2. What were the main problems of producing *The Times*?
3. Argue the case that weak management exploits the consumer.
4. Why did *The Times* choose to act at the end of 1978?
5. What were the conditions that *The Times* management stood out for?
6. Why did this dispute typify the problems of British industry in the late 1970s?
7. Who benefited and who lost from the confrontation before production was resumed in November 1979?

C. Essay Questions

C1 Do you believe that collective bargaining might be improved with a tighter legal structure or greater psychological understanding?

C2 Do you believe that collective bargaining should be conducted at national or local level?

C3 Discuss the pros and cons of a 'comparability board'.

C4 To what extent is collective bargaining not so much about sharing wealth as about sharing power?

Chapter 10

Leadership in Practice

Synopsis: *The present chapter completes our discussion of leadership by looking at 'working models' of leadership in practice. We have chosen four contrasting examples: the works supervisor, the shop steward, the manager and the board of directors of a limited company.*

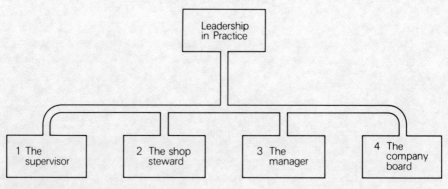

Fig. 10.1 Leadership in Practice

10.1 The Supervisor

'Supervisor' or 'foreman' is of special interest as a leadership role for the following reasons:

a. It is a *formal* leadership position and yet success in the role obviously depends more on *informal* acceptance by the group, and less on the status and authority granted by the firm.

b. As it is the first line of management, the post receives the brunt of conflicts which often result from attempting to unify the diverse objectives ot the men (us) and management (them).
c. Nowadays it is often an ill-defined role. It has lost much of its old directive meaning with the introduction of new human factor emphases (which are often poorly understood). To make matters worse, status and take-home pay are not always much better than those of the men the supervisor is supposed to control.
d. Supervisors are a very large group in business and they can have a considerable impact on industrial efficiency.

10.1.1 The Supervisor's Function

The role is often introduced to release the manager from a series of routine duties (but not responsibilities) which fall within his ambit. If one considers a manager as making, acting on and reviewing decisions which involve the activities of men moving towards a set objective, the supervisor tends to assist in the more routine executive areas of this role. However, like any leader, he has to fulfil the task and 'human' needs of his dependants.

Task Oriented Functions
His task duties might include:
a. The interpretation of plans for action sent down from higher management.
b. Planning production to satisfy these plans. This may mean co-ordinating labour, machines and resources to produce the right goods at the right time and at the right price.
c. During the productive phase he will need to assist workers, check progress and inspect the product.
d. He must deal with the many emergencies which will arise. These may be technical or human. For example, there may be shortages of material or equipment, machines may break down, space may be unavailable when required, or there may be absenteeism, disputes or problems of discipline.
e. Lastly, he ought to report back relevant information, often by completing forms, to his superiors so that they are in a good position to manage the business.

Person Oriented Functions
His 'human' duties might include the following:
a. Clarifying and explaining the objectives so that both individuals and the group see their real contribution.
b. In so far as he holds authority, to issue rewards and punishments.

c. Being an 'exemplar' – setting the general tone and mode of conduct for the department.
d. Providing an environment where the achievement of each individual is important and recognised (appropriate forms of target setting and job enlargement may be useful here).
e. Following from the above, he should train and support his men so that they grow in skill and confidence.

It is the human area duties which have been underplayed in the past and this is one of the reasons why the trade unions have had to provide for such needs. *The result has often been a split of leadership between the supervisor and the* **shop steward.**

10.1.2 **Some Problems Inherent in the Supervisor's Role**
A. Selection and Promotion
He is usually selected from within the firm, or even the same department and thus knows the task well. Ideally he might have already been the informal leader of the group concerned and can continue to hold this role while also wearing the cloak of formal authority. Yet it is easy to see the conflict which can result. The supervisor may be seen to have moved from 'us' to 'them' and to possess the kind of authority and status which some of the shop floor despise. He may thus become alienated from the group and find it difficult to provide for both the company's needs and those of the workers. The dilemma is of course made worse when supervisors are selected from workers who were previously only on the fringe of the informal work group and not well accepted.

Various methods of selection have been tried by different organisations to overcome some of these difficulties. However, there does seem to be a tendency to promote a person (a) who has been successful within a technical area, or (b) who has been with a firm a long time, or (c) who has shown sympathy with management's ideals. These attributes may bear little or no relationship to the requirements for productive and harmonious supervision. A potential supervisor should be thought capable of managing a group (often partly a matter of temperament and adaptability), and needs to possess the necessary administrative abilities. Usually the person can then be trained to become a good supervisor.

Within industry, many of the most suitable candidates decline to accept the supervisor's role. This may be for several reasons:
a. That the fixed wage, although in theory above that of the workers, in practice often means less in take-home-pay because of overtime or special piece-rate working. (On the other hand many do take the job because there is greater security and greater consistency of payment.)
b. More sensitive workers are extremely conscious of the conflict between 'them' and 'us'. They see it as a betrayal to move to the other camp with its different objectives. They also realise that it would be difficult to

continue the social and cultural ties which have been the basis of their life on the shop floor.

c. This last point is particularly important when one realises how hard it is for a supervisor to climb much further up the management ladder. Accordingly, a person is not going to be tempted to change his attitudes or friends in the false hope of becoming a 'manager'.

d. Other reasons for declining promotion to supervisor are an unwillingness to accept the necessary responsibility, not being in agreement with management's objectives, or having some fundamental political objection.

B. Formal Authority

Although occupying the lowest formal leadership position, the supervisor does have some of management's authoritative powers. Too often these powers are not clearly defined, or understood, in relationship to the new supervisor's changing responsibility.

In the past, the supervisor's role often provided a suitable opportunity to practise relatively autocratic supervisory methods as advocated by Frederick Taylor. Nowadays, with the emphasis moving more towards a supportive and integrative function, more democratic methods have often been found applicable. In essence, this means being a leader with the minimum of formal authority. This can be harmonious for both management and workers; but there are circumstances when the approach does not succeed and where there is a clash between some informal leader and the supervisor, thus throwing the supervisor back on to formal disciplinary measures.

Inevitably, the incompetence of particular supervisors explains many conflicts that occur in organisations, but middle and senior management must take their share of the blame. Many talk of human management methods and yet do not support the looser framework and authority which result. How can the supervisor lead when he is often not involved in decision making in areas which affect his department, when he is not given the information and terms on which to act? Too often middle management close their eyes to the supervisor's problems; and even with open eyes they could not see much since their offices are so far from the centre of the action.

To make matters worse, a fundamental conflict is still prevalent in British industries in which the objectives of workers and management are still sadly divergent. In the nineteenth and early twentieth century, managers were dominant, and labour often found it in their best interest to see that management objectives were reasonably fulfilled. But the balance of power has now shifted towards the employees. They have greater financial security, and are no longer prepared to sacrifice themselves as instruments of production, regardless of their own individual needs. In short, they feel the need for participative democracy so that they can have a fair voice in the running of the firm.

The supervisor is effectively trapped between the two sides and is bound to find difficulty in appeasing both of them while the conflict continues. It is largely up to senior management to intervene and find suitable ways of overcoming the problems of their own firms.

10.2 The Shop Steward

In this section we consider the unions' front-line leaders, the shop stewards. (At some point you may wish to revise the material on the function and organisation of trade unions in the previous chapter.) In many ways the shop steward is analogous to the supervisor and yet there are fundamental differences.

a. The shop steward is elected by the group of union members, within a department or small plant, to be their representative. The members choose a leader who they feel can best represent their interests in the circumstances. Thus the shop steward possesses his/her role in response to the wishes of the group (or at least the wishes of those who voted). The position is officially ratified by the union's local branch officer. This local official is the lowest-paid officer of the union and is the shop steward's immediate boss. It is through the shop steward that the official communicates union policy to members and receives back information on the members' pay, hours, conditions and such like.

b. The shop steward will also seek recognition from management, since without this a useful job cannot be done. Today most managements will accept the wish of the workers and allow the shop steward to be their representative – although there are companies with a small union membership which still ignore any union leader as a matter of policy.

c. The shop steward continues to be an employee of the firm. Normal work is done and normal wages received. Union duties are extras. Yet for the other workers he/she *is* the union. It is through the steward that they receive most of their information on union affairs; it is the steward who deals with the majority of the members' needs (all but their larger grievances). Even when affairs are taken out of his or her hands by the paid union branch officer, regional officer, or even the President of the union, it is the shop steward who reports the findings back to the members and seeks their agreement.

d. There are some 450 trade unions and between 150,000 and 200,000 shop stewards up and down the country. The shop stewards represent about 13 million trade union members (out of a total workforce of about 26 million). The job brings some status and recognition to the holder while it provides an outlet for enterprise and responsibility. But it also holds many trials and tribulations and consumes much time both inside and outside working hours.

10.2.1 The Functions of the Shop Steward
The shop steward's functions are ill-defined in many union rule books and such lack of definition leads to job complications. Generally, they might

include some or all of the following (tradition and local circumstances deciding the precise nature and importance of each):

Task Oriented Functions

a. Shop stewards are responsible for gaining new members wherever possible. If there is a **closed shop** they must check both the credentials and union cards of all workers.
b. They collect, or supervise the collection via the firm of members' weekly dues. These they forward to the branch office.
c. They negotiate with management on behalf of their members. The breadth of these negotiations varies. In small organisations where decisions are decentralised negotiation may be substantial. Often there is a basic agreement negotiated at national level between the leaders of the union and the leaders of the employers' association. This agreement then becomes the basis on which local bargaining takes place. The shop steward will seek to exploit any special factors in the situation which could increase benefits to the local workforce: the nature of the job, the productivity of the workers, the profitability of the firm; even the bargaining strength of the union and the skills of the negotiator may be taken into account. These local negotiations are often piecemeal and can be never-ending.
d. Whether the agreement is locally or nationally negotiated, the shop steward is responsible for seeing that it is carried out by both management and workers. This inevitably means a constant involvement in grievances, some petty, some major, since the shop steward must protect the interests of both workers and the union.
e. The shop steward is responsible for communicating union policy to the members, and maintaining their loyalty to the union.
f. Lastly, the steward is also responsible for communicating some elements of management policy to the workers and providing union interpretation of that policy, although much comes through the supervisor.

Person Oriented Functions

Like all leaders, shop stewards must look after the problems of the group and of the individuals within the group. These problems will be different according to the people involved and the particular situation. Responsibility often spreads far beyond factory affairs and into the lives of the members outside work. The shop steward's activity in this area seldom hits the headlines but many members have reason to be extremely grateful. Too often the supervisor, the person who holds formal responsibility for such factors, is less able to assist here than the union's own elected representative.

10.2.2 **Some Difficulties in the Role**

a. Job Definition and Responsibility. As we have said, the job definition can be far from clear and may be continuously evolving. This lays the holder open to the same problem as the supervisor: it is a key position but its nature is uncertain. The uncertainty is increased by a conflict of allegiance. The steward is responsible to the union members who elected him as well as to the wider union, and the wishes of both often do not coincide. Moreover, he has to accommodate to existing agreements negotiated between the union and the firm and carry all this out within normal terms of employment as a worker for that firm. It is hardly surprising that conflict arises.

b. Authority. The shop steward's unofficial authority clearly comes from the backing of the workers. Official authority, often ill-defined, comes through the union and is normally, although not always, recognised by management. Thus, as we have just noted, there can be conflict between directives from the union at national level and the wishes of the members at local level, a conflict which often ends in an 'unofficial' strike. (An unofficial strike is one called by the shop steward without official union consent; a shop steward is not entitled to call an 'official' strike.) Even the least militant shop steward may easily end up in a situation which virtually forces him/her to lead such a strike, and the opportunities for a militant leader are only too obvious.

c. The Election. The shop steward is elected for a relatively short term of office. This varies from a few months to a couple of years. Often elections are uncontested but sometimes there will be challengers. It is in times of challenge that the existing shop steward may feel under pressure to demonstrate his/her worth. The result may be a series of rather short-term arguments with the management in an attempt to improve his image, although the arguments themselves may achieve little to help the long-term interests of the members.

d. Co-operation and Conflict. Both of these exist in inter-union affairs. History has dictated that many enterprises have a number of unions each representing different groups. Officially each union will normally encourage its shop stewards to co-operate with their opposite numbers from other unions. For example, where joint negotiations are undertaken there is normally a factory **convenor**, the senior shop steward who negotiates with top management. The convenor is elected by all the shop stewards in the firm and many affairs are left entirely in his/her hands.

Since different unions may adopt different strategies, inter-union battles are inevitable. In addition, each union protects its own interests in cases like redundancy, differential pay rises and 'who-does-what?' disputes (demarcation disputes). The shop steward is caught in a situation of conflict which too often harms both the general interest of the workers, the unions and the management.

Because the interest of the worker appears so diametrically opposed to management, there is bound to be extra conflict. The difficulty for the shop steward is to set a tone which actually benefits the workforce.

e. Communication Pressures. All leaders spend a considerable time in communicating and the shop steward is no exception. The steward needs the fullest skills of communication to discuss complex issues, often in situations of considerable stress, with people of divergent status, interest and outlook. Yet the task commonly falls to men and women who have had few educational opportunities and inadequate training for their role.

As if this were not sufficient, the presence of long **scalar chains of command** provides problems. These chains exist both within management and within the official union structure. It is no wonder that the shop steward can feel compelled to act independently or on mere rumour.

f. Rewards. There are rewards from status, recognition and achievement for those who master the job, both from the unions and from management. A good shop steward is a good mini-manager. Often shop stewards are offered promotion to foreman level, which some accept, while others prefer to work their way up the union hierarchy.

g. Assistance for the Steward. The Employment Protection Act of 1975 has given the shop steward a great deal of extra assistance. For example, whether a company approves or not, they must give time off for a shop steward to undergo training in aspects of industrial relations relevant to his/her duties, safety, etc. The TUC have also started, in conjunction with many individual unions, shop steward training programmes and these are beginning to have an impact. Further, some managements will not even provide the steward with the most elementary physical resources to aid communication. There is often nowhere quiet to talk or write and no access to a telephone, nor are company facilities available for a minor meeting. However, progressive managements, aware of communication difficulties, assist shop stewards in this area.

Unless there is harmony and trust between men and management, the factory will not be a satisfying place for work. As a direct result, the long-term achievements of the firm will usually be limited. The shop steward has a large responsibility in such relationships, but is often ill-equipped to meet the complexities and conflicts of the role, especially if given minimal support either by management or by the union. In particular, management seem blind to the fact that they get the shop stewards they deserve. The day may come when management considers the shop steward as an instrument for improving the total work environment rather than as a focus of discontent.

10.3 The Manager

The term 'manager' is really very general. Although in common language a distinction is typically recognised between 'manager' and 'supervisor' or 'foreman', it will be clear from the earlier section that the supervisor is very much a manager even though his/her area of responsibility may be rather circumscribed. However, for our discussion we will take 'manager' as meaning at least one rung up the ladder from supervisor.

10.3.1 The Functions of the Manager

If being a manager means anything at all it means being a leader. In fact management and leadership skills are commonly spoken and written about in the same breath. As in the case of the supervisor and the shop steward, the manager's domain of responsibility is twofold.

a. Task Related Functions

i. Planning. The manager must be able to select appropriate objectives through seeing future requirements and consulting with those affected. In addition – and this is the harder part – he or she must choose the right policies and programmes for gaining these objectives, usually within the broad framework set by higher management. Again consultation is available, but within his/her own sphere the manager is the principal decision maker, and must stand or fall by these decisions.

ii. Organising. This means building up a structure of human and other resources so as to achieve, within existing constraints, the agreed objectives, and *then* making sure they are achieved. To this end, the various activities have to be grouped and assigned to take into account limitations imposed by time pressures, kind of skill available, plant layout, materials and suchlike.

iii. Staffing. It is the manager's task to man – and keep manned – the job functions within the part of the organisation being covered. He or she must be capable of building an integrated team, the members of which, ideally, are capable of managing themselves and of assessing their own performance in relation to the agreed objectives.

iv. Information. The manager is also responsible for controlling and reviewing the activities within his responsibility area. He/she should set up suitable information systems which can provide key data so that practices and policies can be altered where they are inefficient or poorly directed; such information is also needed to keep in balance the different responsibility areas within an organisation and to help plan for the future.

v. Awareness. Increasingly it is becoming necessary for managers to look beyond their own job function and have some working knowledge of what their colleagues are doing. It is noteworthy that high-level management training programmes pursue diversity of experience and skill as one of their major aims. Such a 'breadth' approach develops the perspective needed for the manager to rethink and innovate. While ten years ago a manager could let 'experts' deal with computers, nowadays an ambitious young manager knows he/she had better find out for himself. A manager also needs to develop some awareness of how the organisation works and competes against similar organisations within the context of a national and even international economy.

b. Person Related Functions

i. Motivation. The manager must supervise and motivate subordinates. This means first ensuring that all subordinates have a reasonable understanding of why the company is in business, the nature of the enterprise, the company history and traditions, and general objectives and policies. Second, the subordinate must learn the organisational structure and the job skills of the people with whom he/she must co-ordinate, what the organisation requires and equally what he/she may reasonably require of the employer. Job definition, delegation, training and both financial and non-financial motivational methods are all called in to play. Horizontal co-ordination with those over whom the manager has no control is at least as important as vertical co-ordination. It is from colleagues with complementary jobs that managers and subordinates alike obtain both task-based and emotional-based support.

ii. Praise and Discipline. The manager must also know how to nurse along a subordinate who is being placed under too much pressure, how to regroup so as to contain or bypass any team member who sets undesirable examples, and how to warn and dismiss subordinates as well as praise and promote them. A manager must have the empathy or sensitivity to cope with emotional reactions that are bound to occur when people work together in a team, and the social skills to execute the necessary remedies quickly before symptoms become too evident.

10.3.2 What Does a Manager in Fact Do?

When we get down to an hour-by-hour or even minute-by-minute observation of managers at work it turns out that the 'leadership' models we were discussing in Chapter 5 are too global to allow us to come to terms with what we actually find. Every manager has a role to play in the fulfilment of company objectives, and the principal company objective is to realise reasonable benefits (in profits and prestige) at minimum cost (in time and money). A manager's productivity is therefore an important index of how effective he/she is. Indices of productivity will depend obviously on the sphere of work, but include such things as level of sales, number of units produced/rejected, number of customer complaints, number of man hours lost/saved.

The working day seems hectic at both the lower and higher levels of management. For example, foremen in one study averaged about thirty separate activities per hour, while in another small study, top executives spent half their time on activities lasting nine minutes or less. Management is evidently a fast-moving business, and it is perhaps not surprising that new holders of posts suffer from stress and strain until basic experience is acquired. Routine use of formalised decision-making procedures such as those discussed in Chapter 12 are for time reasons simply not practicable except for major decisions – unless of course the *discipline* implied by such formalised procedures (which is a large part of their point) can be carried round in the manager's head.

Although practical management models do concern themselves with 'time spent with subordinates' little or nothing is said about time spent with opposite numbers in other departments, professional contacts, and with their own superiors: in fact, around half the time of top executives in the study just quoted was spent mixing with such non-subordinates, and a rather similar breakdown was found in a study which looked at foremen. Rather little time is spent with written memoranda; around 70 per cent of the manager's total time is spent in talking, and this talking is mainly of the information-exchange type with very little giving of instructions, again something of a surprise. We may be excused for wondering if this is the same leadership that the theorists in Chapter 5 were talking about.

10.4 The Board of a Limited Company

The Board is that group of people to whom the owners of the business, the shareholders, have delegated the task of looking after their interests. In the case of a public company this task is delegated to at least two people. Boards vary greatly in size and, although in large companies the average is around a dozen, it is not uncommon to find boards of five or thirty members (there is a slight correlation with the size of the firm and the size of the Board). These boards also vary greatly in age of their members. In general they are made up of elder statesmen but there has more recently been a move by some boards to reduce age.

As a great generalisation, the Board is made up of middle-class persons who have risen through the executive roles of management. Relatively few are paid by results nor do many have any substantial shareholding in the company they direct. Thus they often have little clear motivation to press for the shareholders' interests to the exclusion of their own.

Over two-thirds are full-time executive directors, which means that they work in the company as senior management, planning, organising and controlling some major activity. So, as members of the Board they are policy makers, overall decision makers and controllers, while as managers they have specific responsibilities within their departments for implementation. The remaining third are outside directors, mainly men (there are in fact few women board members) who are considered to have special expertise in one area or another, useful to the company, and who can use their independent judgement, on behalf of the shareholders, in the directing of the concern.

An idea of the make-up of the average Board in 1980, based on a survey of 200 large companies, is shown in the table below:

Number per board	11	Professionally qualified	32%
Proportion of full-time executives	69%	Previously employed in another company	52%
Average age	56	Holding over £20,000 of shares in company	32%
		Family connections with the company	15%

The job is becoming far more complex than of old. First, the size of firms and their international spread is increasing. Secondly, the Board no longer has *just* the clear legal responsibility to look after the well-being of the shareholders; it has vaguer, but no less obvious, responsibilities to the workers employed, the sections of society affected by its activities (pollution, regional employment), the consumer (quality, reliability) and the state (wage levels, exporting, international monetary movement).

10.4.1 How is the Board Elected and Rewarded?

Each member of the Board is elected for a given span, often three years, by the shareholders. This is normally done at the Annual General Meeting. About a third of the Board is elected each year to allow for continuity. Most adults are eligible, the commonest category to be excluded being the undischarged bankrupt. Nomination must be by two shareholders (usually members of the Board). The shareholders are then eligible to vote according to their voting rights (commonly one vote per share). If elected, there is an insistence in many Articles of Association that the new member buys, and continues to hold, a nominal holding of the company's shares. He must also declare any special interests he has in the company or in its activities.

In practice, it is very rare that this nominating and voting procedure is anything more than a formality. Very few shareholders will know the individuals concerned and hence they tend to accept the chairman's advice. Further, it is unusual if the abilities and usefulness of a man can be assessed by the outsider when all the Board meetings are in private and their decisions are collective. Only on the rare occasion when a board is split or a scapegoat has to be found does a member fail to be voted on after his nomination. Thus the member may well continue to serve until he is forced to retire, according to the company's articles, perhaps at seventy. However, his job is not as secure as it used to be. Company takeovers usually result in board 'reshuffles', while consistently poor company performance may lead to a 'new broom'.

The salaries of the Board are carefully controlled. They are clearly in a position of trust and not allowed to use their offices for personal profit or advantage – other than their agreed salary. Any new level is commonly suggested by outside consultants whose advice may be accepted by the chairman. The scales of payment and the relative distribution must be stated in the annual report of the company.

10.4.2 The Board's Task

The Board has the legal responsibility of safeguarding the long-term interests of the shareholders. It must formulate company policy and practise overall control of the organisation to achieve these ends. Hugh Parker sees five basic functions which he believes the Board should perform if this is to be achieved.

i.   Establishing the long-term objectives of the company and the basic strategies by which these are to be obtained.

ii. Defining the specific policies (finance, personnel, marketing and the like) to be followed when implementing the company's strategies.

iii. Deciding the organisation structure of the company's line management and making appointments to fill key positions.

iv. Developing management planning and control systems appropriate to the organisational structure of the company, and using these systems effectively to ensure control, at all times, over the results produced by executive management.

v.   Taking decisions on matters either that the Articles of Association reserve to the Board (e.g. payment of dividends, disposal of corporate assets, appointments to the Board) or that the Board in its own discretion decides not to delegate (e.g. capital projects above a certain amount, diversification into new business).

vi. To provide shareholders with an annual report on activities, progress, profits, problems and future plans.

These decisions will be made at Board meetings, which usually take place at regular intervals, the minutes of each meeting being carefully kept so that decisions may be on record.

You will see that the Board is concerned with the strategic decisions which are the key to the firm's success or failure. Key decisions may be judged by their impact on the company through their magnitude, the length of the commitment entailed, the inflexibility of action once started and the importance of the decision on people. The Board should not concern itself with tactical decisions – indeed it should attempt to lay down a policy which increases the number of decisions to be taken by executive management. In this way, it can delegate the maximum number of tasks to the executive whose job it is to run the company and conserve its own time and energy for the other vital functions. (See Chapter 7 for further discussion of delegation.)

10.4.3 The Difficulties of the Board's Role

a. The Fulfilment of Their Role. First, many boards find it difficult to concentrate on their directing role. Although it is the role of the chairman to see that both the agenda and the discussion are well focussed, too often their discussions move from strategic matters to unimportant detail. Second, many boards find it hard to lay down a clear company policy following their deliberations. Their decisions are *ad hoc* and provide no guidelines for the future on which senior management can act. Without a policy framework it is impossible for subsequent decisions to be delegated from the Board to senior management, and this can result in frustration lower down and consequently still more work for the Board.

Third, it is genuinely hard for a board to plan, in any meaningful way, sufficiently far ahead. The gestation period for a new product (length of time between the original idea and decision implementation) has generally increased over the present century; to introduce a new product may now take about five years when in the past it might have been possible in six months. This increase arises from the possibility of carrying out far more research and planning than was either possible or thought necessary thirty years ago. Planning is of course more difficult when the Board either asks for and/or is given insufficient information on which to plan. In addition, the outside directors may not be properly versed in the technicalities and possibilities of their company's particular market situation.

b. Information. The quality of board operation cannot be greater than the quality of the information it works with. Many boards do not know enough about either the plans or activities of those below them: they become out of touch. Hence they have lost control of activities for which they are *legally* responsible. Putting in an 'integrated system' from general integrated sub-objectives through to effective control is vital. They can then discover what management proposes to do, what it has done, and then (hopefully) have the will and ability to challenge deviations.

c. Divided Loyalty. There are two aspects of divided loyalty which clearly produce problems. First, as we have said, many members are executive and therefore operate as managers in the company which, as Board members, they are 'directing'. Thus they need to make decisions concerning their own departments and have to control and comment on departmental performance. Board members, in these circumstances, have to fight hard not to be just departmental watchdogs. This dilemma is one reason for the balancing presence of some outside directors.

Secondly, because of the *small* personal shareholdings which most directors have in their company, there can arise cases when decisions reflect their own personal interests and not those of their masters, the shareholders, or of the company employees.

d. Divided Responsibility. The legal requirements of the directors to safeguard the shareholders' assets are clearly (and perhaps alarmingly) established through the Companies Acts, the Articles of Association and additional Stock Exchange requirements. What is not so clear is the position they should adopt when considering the other parties. What are the ethical problems in deciding to withdraw from or continue in South Africa?

e. The Election of the Board. For reasons previously mentioned the shareholders actually have remarkably little say in who runs their own company. Further, the Board very soon becomes virtually self-perpetuating. Some shareholders feel that they should know more, possibly by even having one Board member elected specially to gain information and give advice to the shareholders.

f. Efficiency. It is the Board's responsibility to gain efficiency from their shareholders' company. However, this is hard to judge in the short term as many of their key decisions will take years to work through, by which time most present Board members will have retired. Attempts to tie efficiency (as judged through long-term results) to factors like the size of the Board, average age, professionalism, proportion of executive members to non-executive, have been inconclusive.

● In the present chapter we have covered many practical facets of leadership and management from both sides of the industrial fence. In doing so we have assembled the last components of people in groups. We can now look further at how people actually make decisions.

Work Section

A. Revision Questions

A1 What might be the human functions of a supervisor's job?

A2 How might the job of many supervisors be made more effective?

A3 Outline the difficulties present in the role of supervisor.

A4 Outline how a shop steward is chosen.

A5 Outline the shop steward's dual role in meeting both task and personal needs of union members.

A6 Describe the conflicts inherent in the role of many shop stewards.

A7 Name the main functions of a middle manager.

A8 How do managers in fact seem to spend their time?

A9 How is the Board of a public company elected?

A10 Describe the typical composition of a board of directors.

A11 Name the major roles and responsibilities of the Board.

A12 What kinds of difficulties are frequently encountered by a company board in trying to carry out its task?

B. Exercises/Case Studies

B1 Case Study: '*The Tale of One Foreman*'

'16 machines, 12 covermakers, 10 servicemen and a continuous flow of materials' – that was the recipe for at least 1,000 tyres a shift. Halfway through one shift, however, the senior foreman barked, 'About time you got the whip out, ain't it? There's only 200 on the clock.' He had just returned from a meeting and did not realise that nine machines had broken down, three servicemen were absent, and the supply of raw materials to two more machines had dried up.

Though there was nothing in writing, the foreman was officially charged with the overall running of his section on his shift. He was responsible as management and to management for everything which happened within this time and space. This responsibility included output, costs, quality, deployment of labour, planning, maintenance, housekeeping, safety, industrial relations, general personnel problems, the communication of management policy, and coordination both with other shifts and with other sections linked by the incoming and outgoing flow of work. He decided and acted on everything from a power failure to a lost screw, and from a strike threat to cloth-eared Charlie sleeping through his alarm.

This 'job description' was all very good in theory. But, in practice, the question 'what could the foreman have done?' still has to be asked in relation to specific incidents like the one outlined above. The fore- man's responsibility was broad, if not very high, yet the degree of his control was minimal. How could the foreman have prevented the loss of output and chaotic circumstances which had arisen? What could he have done to reduce further loss? The foreman was not the master; he was at the mercy of several different factors.

The first was *men*. Production workers on the section pleased them- selves whether they worked or not, and, if they worked, how much they produced. They were paid an individual piecework rate, and geared their effort and overall behaviour to the take-home pay that suited them; even though the average output was 130 and the maximum achieved 160, one maker produced 100 tyres each shift, no more and no less, if he had a clear run, and there was nothing the foreman could do to influence this amount. Similarly, four days' pay was as good as five for some, and the absenteeism rate was consistently higher on the Friday night-shift. Nothing against the lads; it was the obvious thing to do; but the foreman could not take the same course, nor could he do anything about it.

Casual absenteeism was particularly high among servicemen. It was their job to feed component parts (e.g. beads, fabric, treads) to the cover- makers (i.e. tyre assemblers). This absenteeism partially reflected their youth and bacherlordom; it seemed, more important, to arise because of rather than in spite of their relatively underpaid and underprivileged position. The poor foreman was saddled with externally imposed dif- ferentials between covermakers and servicemen, both in the level and form of payment (servicemen were paid a flat rate); this increased rather than reduced his problems. The differentials were supposed to provide an incentive for servicemen to be good boys and so eventually become covermakers; but their disincentive effect was so great that no amount of cajoling and persuasion by the foreman could con them into loving (often even doing) their jobs.

On the criterion of dispensability, servicemen's pay should have been higher (one serviceman's absence affected the output of several cover- makers). It was in practice so much lower, and the short-term opportunity for individuals to raise or even influence its level so much more limited, that their hangdog pessimism was understandable and apparently in- superable.

The second form of control on the foreman was *machines*. The planned obsolescence of covermaking machines seemed high, and their planned maintenance non-existent. There were breakdowns galore (Monday morning invariably hit the jackpot), and although as many machine options as possible were kept open, the tyres lost while fitters finished their tea or *Titbits* hardly bore counting. The foreman was responsible for maximum machine/man utilization, yet his influence on machinery purchases was inconsequential. His authority over maintenance staff was also nil. They reported up a specialist functional line; and, if the foreman approached them to fix a machine, were as liable to give him two fingers as two hands.

The third factor which limited the scope of the foreman was the supply of *materials*. A good third of the foreman's time was spent (a) sorting out poor quality which should have been pre-rejected and (b) chasing materials which had not arrived on schedule. Supply departments were scattered throughout the factory and, as phones were seldom answered, journeys of marathon length were required to arrange for priority scheduling or delivery, and to negotiate with foremen of other production shops who were after the same component. A milometer was never attached to foremen's feet, but a conservative estimate of ground covered was half-a-mile an hour on an eight hour shift.

The final form of control on the foreman was his *management*. The first one up was Frank, the senior foreman responsible for coordinating the three shifts on his section. The main thing Frank could never figure out was that everything which went wrong was the fault of the 'other shift'. Three shifts rotating round the clock were hard enough to keep track of; he never did find the 'other' one.

Frank treated shift foremen as he expected them to treat the lads; his 'get the whip out' approach was reminiscent of Mr 'unter, otherwise known as Misery, in Robert Tressell's *The Ragged Trousered Philanthropists*: 'a reign of terror ... prevailed on all the "jobs" ... no man felt safe for a moment; at the most unexpected times Misery would arrive and rush like a whirlwind all over the "job".... '

Frank could not wave the sack threat as menacingly as Misery; but he adopted identical attitudes and assumed no less unwaveringly that right and authority were on his side. Frank, on the other hand, cannot be blamed for his approach; he only behaved towards his minions as did his bosses towards him. Communication from senior management was poor and consultation non-existent; policy was ordained from above and woe unto him who asked any questions or attempted to contribute to its formulation.

When the department manager saw fit to call a meeting, this was held at a moment's notice, with the foreman's overriding responsibility to drop everything regardless taken for granted. Similarly a foreman's opportunity to plan ahead was limited by the notice of change he was given. Management spent far longer reaching a decision than was allowed between its communication and implementation. The foreman was constantly getting landed with the 'ten commandments' which took effect yesterday. His work could only be *ad hoc*; and last-minute management was all too often whitewashed as deadbeat supervision. It seemed a strange coincidence that things invariably went better on night shift when the gaffers were home in bed.

If senior foremen and department managers were bad, then the senior company management was worse. There seemed to be a direct correlation between a company manager's visit to the shop and reduction in output. For a week before one of 'God's cousins' was expected, half the production workers would be spitting and polishing their machines and workspaces. As the basic material was rubber, the factory was usually as black as the hole of Calcutta; but when one of the company's many 'Sirs' was due, it could have been an advertisement for soap flakes. The only thorn in Frank's flesh was that, as often as not, the visits were cancelled at the last minute.

The foreman was therefore hounded on all sides by his men and their monetary reward, his machines and materials, and his management at all levels. His position looked and felt like a four-sided trap. These four forces – management, men, machines, and materials – were all exerting pressure on the foreman; but each force acted independently. The 'system' seemed like a monstrous mechanism breathing down the foreman's neck. But there was no system as such, because the separate elements were in no way interactive with each other. Men, machines, materials and managers all bore down on the foreman independently, and divergently. The foreman's job was to integrate different inputs to his section and to reconcile their conflicting demands. In times past the foreman had the status and authority, as well as the responsibility, for coping with and even managing this vortex of apparently accidental happenings. Now, all he had left was the responsibility.

The foreman therefore had an impossible job; the more smoothly the 'system' worked, the easier his job was. But it never did work. His *status quo* was trying to see the wood of future planning for the trees of everyday (or every minute) problems. He spent his life correcting mistakes and sorting out messes. He often did not know where they originated, but, as the universal scapegoat who received no praise, only degrees of blame, he knew well enough who would carry the can.

Source: Patrick Sills, *Management Today*, March, 1972.

Questions

a. How might middle management help this supervisor's situation?
b. How might senior management assist the situation?
c. How might Frank stop 'buck passing' between the shifts?
d. Comment on Frank's style of leadership and his attitude to the job.
e. Why have a foreman – why not let the shop steward do the job?

B2 The managing director is appointed by the Board to carry out their policy. This appointment will be for a fixed number of years, usually at least three, to allow time for some of his actions to bear fruit. He is responsible to the Board through its chairman and is now often co-opted on to the Board. Just as the Board has to collectively act as the entrepreneur of the organisation so the managing director is the commissar or man of action, who interprets the Board's decisions and sees that they are carried out by the line managers (some of whom, in other hats, will also be serving on the Board).

The company can be seen to pivot around the managing director. He is the vital link man between the shareholders' representatives (the Board), those executing the policy either as management or men and those on whom both of these parties ultimately depend (the consumer). Although the Board are ultimately responsible for the company, the managing director handles the problems arising from their policy and his own actions; these problems can be internal or external as shown in Fig. 10.2.

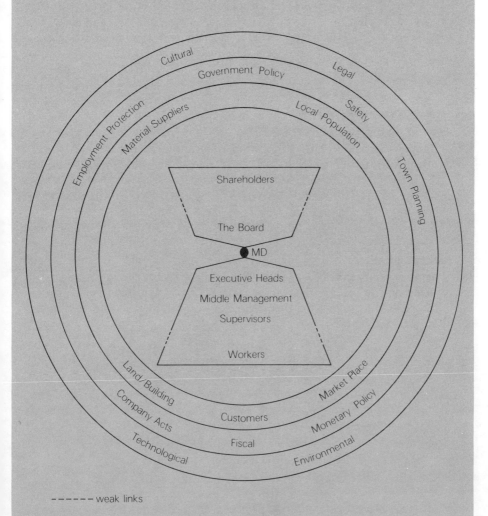

— — — — — weak links

Fig. 10.2

Questions
   a. Using illustrations from business and education (warden, principal, headmaster), compare the task and problems of a managing director with those of the chairman of the board of directors.
   b. Why do you feel a managing director's job is said to be getting more complex and exacting?
B3 Think of two individuals you have known whom you would describe as successful leaders. Write a short description of each, and then answer the following questions.
   a. What did they have in common?
   b. In what did they differ?
   c. Were there any special features of their situations that should be taken into account?
   d. Were there any special features of their task that need to be considered?

C. Essay Questions

C1 What makes a good manager?
C2 Should management strive to avoid frustrating situations?
C3 Given your understanding of a middle manager's role, how do you feel such a person should be selected?
C4 Compare and contrast the problems of leadership facing a supervisor with those facing either a head boy/girl or a shop steward.
C5 How does a manager's job vary according to the level in the hierarchy at which he/she is operating?
C6 Some people say that a manager's job is decision making while others argue it is organising and motivating others. What do you feel?
C7 What do you feel are the functions of the board of directors? If worker directors were to join the Board, how do you feel they should be selected and elected?

Chapter 11

Human Information Processing

Synopsis   *In this chapter we stay with the individual decision maker as typified by the profiles in the previous chapter and show how the whole range of constraints operates on him as he handles incoming information. We show how information from people and events in the outside world is subject to selective sampling immediately it is perceived. This selectively reduced information is then passed on for analysing as the person examines possible solutions from memory of similar situations in the past. But for the present chapter we start with the view that every individual in an organisation can be regarded as a 'human information processor'. There are, however, limitations to individual efficiency, and some of the distortions individuals superimpose on the original information are enough to cause us concern. Before embarking on this chapter, the reader is recommended to familiarise himself with the main ideas of the general decision model in Chapter 1.*

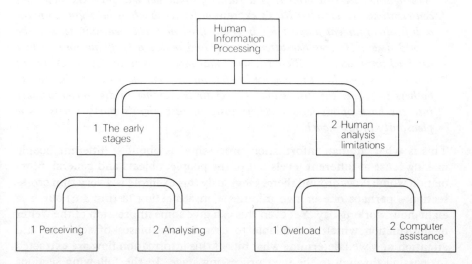

Fig. 11.1: Human Information Processing.

11.1 First and Second Stages

11.1.1 The Perceiving Stage

We are continuously exposed to a stream of information which requires little or no action or reaction from us. A radio in the background gives out the latest world news. Colleagues at the next table evaluate company performance. Traffic and people pass the window. Other information we have to search out in books, files and telephone conversations. Consider the following scenario:

> *Bill, Rita and Richard run a publishing organisation. Today they are having one of their weekly meetings, and Bill is addressing the two others. Rita is obviously listening to his words, and considering the way he makes occasional emphasis by moving his head slightly. Being bright, she follows and even anticipates his argument easily. At the same time she notices that when Bill smiles his teeth appear rather uneven. She is also half-watching Richard and noting that he is looking at her: her attention to Bill's voice slips as she recalls a brief incident the other week. A laugh from Bill pulls back her full attention once again. . . . Bill himself is a rather formal person, but very able and conscientious: he watches Rita's expression for feedback as he begins to make a difficult argument about why diversification into new ventures needs to be slowed down. He sees her attention slip and makes a laughing joke to pull her back into line. . . . Richard, somewhat moody as usual, is watching the two of them; he has thoroughly briefed himself on the issues so he hardly bothers to follow the discussion. The chair is starting to dig uncomfortably into the back of his legs, and the taste of last night's party persists unpleasantly in his mouth.*

This is what 'human information processing' is about – different people making sense at different levels out of the people, objects and general information which flows around them. Obviously this example is a very thin cross-section – perhaps one or two minutes – in a meeting lasting an hour in a eight-hour working day. Yet even this can give some impression of the welter of information which is available to us and how biases of selection and attention may well determine what bits of this information flow are extracted for passing through to the next processing stage. In the following sections we shall talk about two major characteristics of the perceiving stage: (a) selection and attention; (b) prediction and integration, and then go on to discuss the importance of differences between people's perceptions of the same facts.

a. Selection and Attention

Essentially, the flow of information arriving at the senses from the outside world is massive and varied. Some sort of filtering process must allow us to extract selectively what we want from it at any given time. You are probably familiar with your own ability at parties to maintain one conversation yet tune into one or even two other conversations apparently at the same time. Thus attention can be seen first as a steering mechanism locking on to information sources that seem promising and then as a selecting mechanism which only allows through things of importance. What are these 'things of importance'?

The first is *any novel occurrence or change*: in the immediate present our attention, and therefore our perception, is attracted by something novel – a flash of light or a noise makes us turn our heads quickly *unless* of course we are in a busy factory where the same noise may have no effect and where it may well be a sudden silence which attracts the attention. Therefore perception is geared to novelty or *change* in the information flow. This is really very economical since there is little point in keeping on registering the fact that things are the same. We 'get used to' the noise level on an assembly line, or the pressure from tight-fitting clothes, or the delicious smells that hit us when we first walk into a restaurant. We no longer remark on or complain about these things because we no longer ordinarily attend to them – unless someone again 'draws our attention' to them. Equally, we can get used to people: only when they do something unexpected (like 'answering back' or asking for promotion) do we sit up and 'pay attention'. So then, the first way of defining these 'things of importance' that are accepted into the input or perceiving stage is in terms of novel events or change.

The second is *information carrying personal significance*. The personal relevance of a particular bit of information can also determine whether it will be picked up or not. One's own name has a way of breaking through even when one is not particularly attending to a conversation. Personal (individual) constraints such as interests and needs also steer our perception. For example, a bank manager walking down the street may primarily notice the affluence of the shoppers, and how the stores that bank with him are faring relative to those that bank with his rivals. An architect walking down the same street might be primarily aware of the quality of the buildings. So the factor which generally orients our attention and therefore our perception in different directions is what is relevant, significant, interesting and important for us as individuals.

b. Prediction and Integration

Perception does not just use the information arriving at the ear or eye at this very moment. I *predict* a red blob in the distance to be the bus I am waiting for, or when I am waiting cold at the station in the dark every pair of head-lights I perceive as the car that is coming to pick me up. Life would be difficult or absurd if this 'guessing' aspect of perception did not in fact operate: instead of being satisfied with a side view of, say, a chair as actually being a chair, we would have to count the legs before sitting down! This is precisely why in our general decision model arrows are shown feeding into perception from the whole range of individual constraints: we have particular kinds of knowledge, attitudes, anxieties and a whole range of constraints which actually *shape* the kind of perceptions we have. Moreover, many of the perceptions then feed back through our actions to reinforce those very constraints. An example will help here. Because we have prejudiced attitudes this *causes* us to have certain distorted perceptions about, for example, 'males', 'Chinese', 'youngsters', or 'bank managers', and these selective perceptions feed the very prejudices that gave rise to them, so that the prejudice becomes strengthened. Although the predictive element in perception *can* let us down it is usually sufficiently dependable for us to make sense of the world. A cough outside the door, a look on someone's face, a disarray of clothes on the floor, ashtrays at a meeting piled high with cigarette ends – all these lead us to make inferences, i.e. forward or backward predictions, about what has happened or what is going to happen.

Differences Between People in Selecting the Same Information
If people initially have different perceptions of the same person, event, or problem, then it follows that thereafter they are processing *different information*. Yet varying perceptions of the same facts is the rule rather than the exception. Understanding this fundamental point is the key to understanding *why* different people make different decisions, as well as to understanding the problems of communication and of group decision making as discussed in Chapters 13 and 14. Let us go through some examples.

Perhaps a works manager may regard himself as 'dedicated and fair-minded', while those under him see him as 'too concerned with work problems, and always sitting on the fence in discussions'. The chairman of the company might take a different view of his works manager, the wife and children other different views, and so on. We all see not only people but events and situations quite differently. The classic example is a two-car collision: one event with very diverse perceptions of what actually happened by the drivers involved, not to mention the interpretations of bystanders.

Or consider the case of a firm's employees who were asked what they thought was the most important problem facing the new chairman. Over 80 per cent of sale executives named a problem in sales whereas under 30 per cent of other staff picked out a sales problem. Clearly the sales staff were blinkered by their own particular concerns (although of course, they could have been the only ones right). The fact that people perceive differently is also important in committee situations: a good committee member will be able to consider and make allowances for all the various influences, including prejudices, which make other members perceive events, and therefore behave, in a particular fashion.

11.1.2 The Analysis Stage

Information that has been selectively accepted through the perception 'gate' is now subject to reflection and analysis. The least structured kind of thinking occurs when we relax and let information, as it were, wash over us, letting the mind wander loose and perhaps day-dreaming. A tighter form of thinking, close to what we mean by 'analysis', occurs when we are trying to form ideas about new experiences and in particular trying to determine the significance of information coming through.

a. Problem Solving and Memory

Memory has quite a crucial role in determining whether problem-solving activity meets success or failure. Our immediate 'holding capacity' for incoming information is especially important since it determines how efficiently we can 'stack' information without loss or distortion. For example, the main reason it is difficult to multiply three-digit numbers in the head (like 174×136) is not a calculation difficulty, but a holding difficulty. You start, $6 \times 4 = 24$ and then you must make the 4 stick in the right place while you carry the 2, but by the time you come to the last operation in the sequence it has become quite difficult to remember what came before. Now you *can* stretch your holding capacity for seconds or minutes, as long as you 'run over' the material in your head: and of course if you run over it enough times it eventually sticks and becomes part of more permanent memory. For the decision maker, difficulties in 'holding memory' present themselves in various forms. For example, the smaller this holding capacity, the less able a person is to accept information coming into the analysis stage while he works on the analysis of information *already* accepted. In other words he is subject to information **overload** with the dire results discussed later in this chapter.

More durable memory is also important for information processing. Most obviously durable memory includes what we have previously been calling knowledge and skills: we store the details of significant experiences so that we are less likely to make the same mistakes again. All of our 'common sense' knowledge can be regarded as part of our memory bank, as well as the profusion of 'facts' that we acquire during education.

Various kinds of forgetting and distortion occur during the analysis stage. These are:

1. *Condensation* – important slabs of material are dropped (like the reasons why a particular action is being proposed). Such condensation can easily make the decision appear outrageous.
2. *Invention* – when people cannot remember too clearly all the points they do not hesitate to fill in missing material, although this may be sheer fabrication. This is the raw material of rumour.

3. *Magnification* – sometimes a curious name or fact sticks in the memory because of its very unusualness rather than its importance. This piece of information may persist as we reflect on the whole and take on increasing relative importance as other material drops out.

b. Rules for Solving Problems

Let us now examine how problem analysis draws on memory. Probably no problem we encounter as adults is ever entirely new: we have usually seen something a bit like it before, and therefore have some memory of what we did last time and how we did it and what the outcome was – in other words we have at least some rudimentary knowledge and skill and know what sort of rules to follow in approaching the new problem. We may be able to use our recall of related situations to get to the heart of the problem fairly quickly, or at least indulge in some reasonably sophisticated trial and error.

Indeed, one way of looking at problem solving is in terms of 'following rules' based on one's own or other's experience. These rules can be of two kinds: (i) rules that if followed guarantee the correct solutions; and (ii) rules that are more in the nature of general hints and have no guarantee of a correct solution. Most of life's problems have already been solved by others before us. Books have been written on how to swim, cross the road or ride a bicycle. Our parents tell us how to wash and behave at the dinner table. These 'behaviour rules' are now part of our permanent memory. Such rules that if followed *guarantee* the required outcome are called **algorithms**. However, nobody has yet developed algorithms for perfect industrial relations, for brilliant product development or for breathtaking scientific discovery. We can think out and write down plans of action and they *may* work – but we no longer have the guarantee. Such 'unguaranteed' plans of action are called *heuristics*, where you 'bootstrap' yourself from one phase of the problem to the next on the basis of a set formula. The only written-down aspect is the framework or the basis of what has helped others in the past (e.g. for industrial relations, try not to favour one side/try to be fair to everybody publicly). And as we saw in the work section of Chapter 4, while there is no algorithm which if followed will guarantee recall of learned material, there is a set of heuristics which will take you some of the way at least.

But heuristics too can be inefficient. Moreover, unlike algorithms, they can be downright wrong. For example, much research and development time is spent barking up wrong trees, especially where new technology is involved. But as we gain experience our problem-solving strategies or heuristics tend to be more successful – a phenomenon that has been called 'learning to learn'. One important thing we have to learn as we generate these untried strategies is to avoid unstated assumptions. How often it is that one declares a set problem insoluble – until the obvious is pointed out! Too often we accept the structure of the problem as stated by the questioner whereas the solution may require a complete turning of the problem on its head or a denial of the very terms in which the problem is stated. For example,

'How can we raise support to prevent our organisation being taken over?' may not be answerable precisely as stated. Perhaps the question should have been 'How can we *arrange* things so that they will not *want* to take us over?' Many puzzle-corner problems where the solution turns out to be so annoyingly simple depend on a pretty safe assumption that the reader will employ his own unjustified assumptions. We give you some of these problems in the work section to sharpen your brains on. In practice, the real way to make progress in open-ended problem situations is to question *everything*. This applies especially to the 'self-evident'. For example, if it is self-evident that your firm's main aim is to maximise profits, you can alter this premise then draw out the consequences which follow. Most provocative is to start from the premise that the firm's true objective is to *minimise* profits. Now, this might strike you as quite mad, but it does concentrate the mind wonderfully and leads you into recognising circumstances in which the statement could be true. The whole point of the exercise is to develop a fluid reasoning approach which does not accept unchecked assumptions. It is such a fluid or 'creative' approach to problem analysis that has allowed industry in recent years to look increasingly for ways of recycling or finding untapped markets for so-called 'waste products'.

It is tempting to conclude from the above that analysis of *any* new problem is only a matter of creative flair. But this would be a mistake since different kinds of problem require different kinds of analysis. The problem illustrations above involve seeking new solutions or inventing new products where the emphasis is on creativity. But what about a problem of excessive rejects on a manufacturing line? Here there is less premium on creative flair: the successful problem analyst will be the one who can be not only imaginative but also methodical and systematic in breaking down the problem. Such a breakdown would include: (1) an exhaustive specification of problem symptoms and how the present unsatisfactory state differs from the desired state; (2) a definition of the boundaries of the problem and what is special about situations where the problem does *not* exist; (3) specification of changes which have taken place that *could* be the cause of the problem and how these can be progressively eliminated as causes.

Take yet another kind of problem. Suppose a supervisor comes to you because the works manager has asked him to take responsibility for an additional assembly line. The supervisor concerned is undoubtedly the best man to take it on, but he is already sufficiently stretched. The works manager suggests that one of the more routine assembly lines be taken out of his charge so as to redress the work load, but this seems unreasonable to the supervisor since has has got to know the men well and it is only because of this that the line is trouble-free. Positions on both sides are starting to harden, and the union representative is waiting on the sidelines. Now industrial relations problems, even such as this rather simple one, typically require not so much creative flair or methodical analysis as listening and interpretative skills so that one can understand both the content of what the person is saying and also make inferences about underlying reasons for his saying it. Also needed is considerable social skill in eventually presenting solutions in such a way as to be acceptable to both sides. None of these qualities is necessarily possessed by the 'creative' or 'methodical' problem solver, yet problems involving people are probably more serious than those facing technology since they are at the heart of national strikes and international misunderstanding.

11.2 Human Analysis Limitations

People are inefficient analysers of information. In this section we look at processing problems due to memory loss, distortion and overload.

11.2.1 Information Overload

If too much information is received at one time – there is a jamming of the processing machinery. This happens on that first driving lesson, when we are coping with all the switches, dials, levers, handles and pedals that appear to sprout from nowhere. To give a more dramatic example, a commander who has just landed his troops on the beach under fire is quite likely being bombarded with more information than flak, and at a variety of levels: casualty figures, ammunition levels, intelligence from patrols, advice from brigade headquarters. How should he weight these fragments of information to shape up a decision on whether to move forward, dig in or withdraw?

One particular consequence of overload stress we mentioned in Chapter 4 is a tunnelling effect in the sense that the human processor closes down the aperture so as to concentrate on rather few pieces of information. In this way he avoids overload stress – but he also prevents himself picking up perhaps crucial information from an unattended source. Moreover, as we shall see in the next chapter, when the individual decision maker is faced with information overload he moves away from a criterion of 'the best possible solution' to one of accepting 'any reasonable solution' or even snatching blindly at any 'solution' at all. Considerations such as these make 'stupid' decisions more understandable.

Information underload is the converse problem. We can imagine some thoroughly tedious task such as the job of a quality control assistant who has to keep an eye on the conveyor belt for the one misshapen sausage or burnt cornflake in a million which must not reach the customer, or the plight of an office clerk who has endlessly to collate sheets or stick on labels. Little wonder that attention wanders, so that when the one-in-a-million error does pop up it is actually missed! In these examples the consequences would not be catastrophic, but a much more serious underload problem is faced in tracking satellites where, because there is no status change for long periods, observers tend to make errors and are not efficient for periods much above half an hour at a time.

Here are some more examples of bias and distortion that occur during the analysis stage:

i. People need to warm up to the task before they can begin to evaluate information properly. Conversely, when they are tired or bored significant information is allowed to slip through.

ii. Information tends to be dichotomised into 'good' *vs* 'bad' or 'for' *vs* 'against' a given position: the 'shades of grey' in between are not used properly.

iii. New information tends to be given too much importance relative to information already discussed.

iv. People overestimate the likelihood of outcomes favourable to themselves and conversely underestimate on unfavourable outcomes.

v. Too much importance is attached to contributions from prestigious people or sources – status swamps a truly objective evaluation.

All in all, decision makers usually spend far too long waiting for information which they are not in the end going to use efficiently. They also as a generalisation spend too long on information analysis. And the longer they spend analysing, the more difficult it becomes for them to respond to changes in the status of the problem and in its relationship to adjacent problem areas – they grow blinkers. Generally, as we shall see in the next chapter, decision makers are unable to develop more than a few decision criteria and they tend to simplify the decision situation by concentrating on only the most striking features or on their 'favourite' features. There is disturbing evidence, moreover, that an action is often determined in advance and the information selected and criteria adjusted so as to support that predetermined decision....

11.2.2 Computer Assistance

It might be expected that several if not all of the deficiencies of man as an information processor might be remedied by automating all or part of the processing. Computers can handle very large quantities of data. They have no perceptual distortions. They do not attach more importance to information at the beginning or in the middle. They don't avoid unpleasant information or form decisions too quickly or too slowly. Yet there are two provisos:

i. The analyst must use the appropriate method for the problem in hand.

ii. The decision maker must be willing to accept the computer's decision, i.e. accept a less active role or even reject his own 'feel' for the correct solution when this is out of line with the computer decision.

And indeed there are potential difficulties here. Bank managers, for example, may feel their control is usurped by the computer if credit facilities are given to customers on the basis of a 'risk factor' supplied by the computer. The effect is to downgrade the self-image of the managers to something like head of section rather than manager of a bank. Another revealing comment is provided by General Electric who state that sometimes in order to gain acceptance for the system they have found they must deliberately build in a human decision element even though it would be possible to run without it.

It seems from available studies that computers do lead to a more extensive analysis of available information, possible solutions and their outcomes. There is also scope for better integration of decision making within an organisation, and central data banking can allow the computer to learn and improve on previous decisions in a way which is just not practicable for an individual or even a group within an organisation. A less passive and more satisfying way of using computers for the manager is not as a rather baffling yes–no machine but as an ancillary to his own computing capacity where he provides the creative input by asking the computer to work out the consequences of different decision sequences: this enormously increases the decision maker's horizons, clarifies the decision structure, and accordingly allows him to ask questions he might not otherwise have thought of – especially if he can 'converse' directly with the computer (on-line). 'On-line' decision making allows the manager in principle to seek out new information, to be reminded of possibilities and to explore likely outcomes, so that the computer is involved in both information search and integration as well as in the actual decision. The best solution is clearly to let computers do the things people are worst at and leave people to do the things computers are worst at.

Work Section

A. Revision Questions

A1 What are the various stages in the decision-making model?

A2 Give three examples of how (a) individual, (b) external constraints operate on the perception and analysis stages. (Use different examples from those in the chapter.)

A3 In your own words, give a 200-word summary of how the model works as a whole.

A4 Name two major characteristics of the perceiving stage.

A5 Name two 'things of importance' that can attract our attention in conversation.

A6 Why is 'prediction' in perception both useful and yet dangerous?

A7 Why do we commonly perceive so differently from each other?

A8 Why is differential perception of information so potentially destructive to good decision making?

A9 Why is memory so important in problem solving?

A10 Explain the difference between algorithmic and heuristic problem solving.

A11 Why don't we always use algorithmic methods?

A12 What skills is it claimed that an 'industrial relations' problem-solver needs?

A13 Give two examples of information distortion and two of information overloading.

A14 Why can 'underload' also be a problem?

A15 When would you not use computers in information processing?

B. Exercises/Case Studies

B1 What sorts of information distortion can arise from:
   a. Telephone conversations?
   b. Use of conference interpreters?

B2 What is your strategy in an overload situation where you have left too little time to prepare for an examination or are asked to prepare for a difficult meeting at short notice?

B3 Carry out the following exercise to check what was referred to in the chapter as holding memory. Read out a list of words (about 15) to a friend at one word per second and ask him to recall them. Does he recall more from the beginning, middle or end of the list? Why could this be?

B4 We discuss the first stage of information processing as a selective process where the selection itself is determined by the overall psychological make-up (constraints) of the particular individual. Write down one or two main features about *each* of the following aspects of your own psychological make-up and against each propose some of the ways *your* particular perception is made selective because of each feature:

    Abilities   Intelligence
    Interests   Needs, motives
    Personality   Beliefs and attitudes

B5 Try out the following problems with a partner, both of you talking continuously so that you can monitor each other's approach to a solution. If a tape recorder is available so much the better since you can reflect back with understanding on the various blind alleys you entered. (Don't assume that your verbal description has anything other than a loose connection with what is actually going on in your head – in particular, many steps may be short-circuited.)

a. Brainteaser Involving an Actual Task

Place a pound note on the table then place a large milk bottle upside down in the middle of the note. Your task is to get the pound note from underneath the upside-down bottle *without* knocking the bottle over or allowing anything to touch the bottle – except of course for the paper note and the table itself. Discuss some possible solutions with your partner, or jot ideas down if you are working by yourself so that you can follow development towards a solution. Do you find successive blind alleys are closer to a solution? Do you work it out logically step by step or is there a sudden flash of understanding in which the obvious hits you in the face?

b. The Doodlebug Problem

The Conditions. Joe Doodlebug is a strange sort of bug. He can and cannot do the following things:

i.   He can jump only in four directions, north, south, east and west. He cannot jump diagonally (e.g. southeast, northwest).
ii. Once he starts in any direction, that is north, south, east or west, he must jump four times in that direction before he can switch to another direction.
iii. He can only jump, not crawl, fly or walk.
iv. He can jump very large distances or very small distances, but not less than one inch per jump.
v.   Joe cannot turn around.

The Situation. Joe has been jumping all over the place getting some exercise when his master places a pile of food three feet directly west of him. Joe notices that the pile of food is a little larger than he. As soon as Joe sees all this food he stops dead in his tracks facing north. After all his exercise

Joe is very hungry and wants to get the food as quickly as he possibly can. Joe examines the situation and then says, 'Darn it, I'll have to jump four times to get the food.'

Question. Joe Doodlebug was a smart bug and he was dead right in his conclusions. Why do you suppose Joe Doodlebug had to take four jumps, no more and no less to reach the food?

C. Essay Questions

C1 Write an essay on the biases, distortions and other pitfalls encountered in the human information processing pathway.
C2 Argue the case for and against using computers as a major adjunct to information processing.
C3 What is an individual's correct information load?

Chapter 12

Making the Decision

Synopsis: *In arriving at the decision stage itself we have of course reached a landmark in the book. We open in a general vein with basic ideas about the decision-making characteristics of 'economic man' and of 'psychological man'. We then move on to look at examples of 'rules' that form the basis of decision making. Beginning with the simplest rules, we then look at a 'gambling' rule before going on to more orthodox rules concerning the maximisation of either profit or utility. Our fifth example concerns the so-called 'satisficing' principle, and finally we examine how it pays the manufacturer to help construct decision rules on the customer's behalf. We end with a short section on decisions over time.*

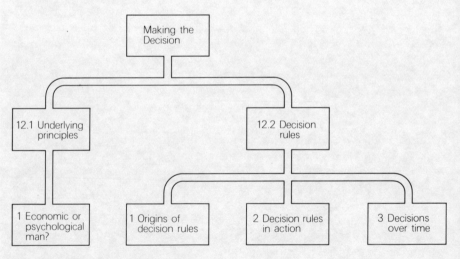

Fig. 12.1: Making the Decision.

12.1 The Underlying Principles

Once we start looking properly at people and decisions we discover that a good deal of common ground exists among the disciplines of economics, business studies, mathematics and psychology. We are all looking down our microscopes at man the decision maker. Since we have already discussed how differences in interests and experience give rise to differences in perception, it may come as less of a surprise to discover that the economist, the management scientist, the mathematician and the psychologist all perceive rather different things at the bottom of their individual microscopes.

12.1.1 Economic or Psychological Man?

The theoretical economist sees under his microscope a producer or consumer of goods whose two main characteristics are: (a) that he is completely informed (in other words he knows all courses of action open to him and what the consequences of each choice would be); and (b) that he is rational. In particular, **economic man** always chooses the most attractive option, the one most financially beneficial to him as he sees it. Since economic man is totally informed and totally rational, theories about his decision making are called *theories of riskless choice*. Obviously economic man is only an ideal –a bit like the physicist's 'frictionless bearing' that does not exist in reality. People are simply not entirely rational, nor are they completely informed either in terms of what outcomes will follow from particular courses of action, or even in terms of what range of possible choices is open to them in the first place. Uncertainty is much more typical of decision making than is certainty, and because of this, alternative theories of 'risky choice' have been developed which recognise the intrinsic uncertainty.

But it would be a terrible mistake to suppose that since all-knowing, all-rational economic man obviously is a fiction, that economists from Jeremy Bentham onwards were stupid to have based so much theory on his supposed existence. The point is that real man operates *sufficiently* rationally to make forecasting at a general level reasonably accurate. Models of decision making that accept intrinsic uncertainty – what we called above theories of risky choice – have more power since they can predict with more accuracy how people ought to behave in a wider range of situations.

12.2 Decision Rules

In order to *understand* a decision, we have to know the criteria or rules on which it was based. If we encounter what is on the face of it a very peculiar choice but are then told it was based simply on a wild guess under pressure of the moment then we are able in some sense to understand the 'decision process' that occurred. Similarly, if we know that a businessman's main strategy is to maximise profit, then we can both understand his past decisions and help him on future ones.

12.2.1 Origins of Decision Rules

You will recall that in our general decision model, the individual and external constraints are depicted as operating not only on the perceiving and analysing stages but also on the deciding stage itself. In effect, many **decision rules** are *imposed* on us via these constraints. The law, for example, prevents you from driving on the wrong side of the road or at more than 70 m.p.h. The law also says you cannot loiter or steal or attack your fellow man, and so on, and in placing these boundaries on permissible behaviour it is clearly an important shaping influence on the kinds of decisions that can be taken. Company law is an obvious major constraint on decision rules that can emerge concerning such things as share dealing or manufacturing standards.

We know that well before we become adults decision rules were already being imposed on us. In the family setting, we gradually 'internalise' thousands of rules such as 'Always look both ways before crossing the road', 'Never take sweets from a stranger.' These rules may be directly imposed or we may copy what our parents or brothers and sisters do, through one of the kinds of learning we talked about in Chapter 4. And, of course, our own first-hand experiences also give rise to rules which guide the decisions we take: 'Don't trust people who smile too much,' 'Never ask your superior for an awkward favour on Monday mornings.' One useful decision rule we learn early on at school is 'Always raise your hand when the teacher asks the class a question.' This is a good rule because: (a) the chances are that you probably will not be asked; (b) if teacher does not ask she will nevertheless be impressed by the fact your hand is up; (c) if you are asked there is always a chance that you can come up with at least a partly correct answer; (d) even if you get it wrong, teacher will be impressed by the fact that you are a trier.

Turning from decision rules of 'external' origin to those of 'internal' origin, you can probably work out for yourself a number of examples where individual constraints either determine or at least influence the formation of different decision rules for different people. For some of us, our motivational make-up requires us to consider only those possible decisions which show us in a favourable light. For other persons this rule may be displaced by one based on ethical or humanitarian considerations. Again, different people will view certain decision rules as 'too conservative' or 'too risky' depending on the kinds of ability or personalities that they possess.

It is worth making the point that many of the decision rules we use we are in fact unaware of. Our conscious daily existence may be no more than the tip of a psychological iceberg, with most of the decision rules that guide our outward behaviour lying below the surface. You may not be aware that you try to please Mr B rather than Mr A even though Mr A controls your career prospects and Mr B does not. You may not be aware that you favour physically attractive job applicants even when their credentials are not the best of the short-listed candidates. Not only may you not be aware of using implicit decision rules, but even if queried you might not agree you were using them. And if you did agree, you might not be able to explain exactly why you were doing so....

12.2.2 Decision Rules in Action

In this section we shall look at some examples of decision rules in more detail and follow through their implications for the decision itself.

While there are large individual differences, many decision makers are cautious on easy decisions but prepared to take a gamble on difficult ones. This fits in with what we were saying in earlier chapters about how under stress or when faced with a decision of insuperable complexity, people snatch at almost anything and call it a decision. There is also considerable irrationality about the way easier tasks get attended to first while the more difficult ones get put off and then suffer through lack of time to come to a proper decision. Generally, people prefer to spend more time than necessary on routine work and spend too little time on more abstract planning. In fact as we shall see in this section, irrationality and poor information processing are the hallmarks of human decision making.

1. Common-Sense Decision Rules

We include under this heading those informal 'rules of thumb' which are learned either on the job or from watching how a skilled person goes about his work. A machine operator may learn that a change in rhythm or pitch of his machine means overload so that the feed rate must be reduced. At a different level he may have a rule of thumb concerning how far he can 'push' his supervisor in various circumstances. However, 'common-sense' decision rules are not necessarily that easy to spot. Suppose you wish to appoint an assistant. Several people apply, but you cut the final choice to two candidates, Mr Bright and Miss Wise. You interview them and give each a score out of ten on what you decide are the relevant criteria, viz:

		Miss Wise	*Mr Bright*
A.	Knowledge of the industry	2	7
B.	Appearance and manner	5	9
C.	Referees' opinions	6	4
D.	Intelligence and initiative	9	7
E.	Typing/shorthand speeds	9	8

Now how do you use this information in deciding which one to appoint? You need a decision rule, and four such rules are possible in the present example:

a. Select the candidate with the highest total score (Mr Bright wins on this decision rule).
b. Choose the applicant who is superior on most items (Miss Wise wins here).
c. Instead of treating the items as equally important, *weight* them in some way. For example, for this particular job, Item A might be multiplied by 5, B by 4, C by 3, D by 2 and E by 1. This would make Miss Wise the better candidate. On the other hand, if the order of importance were the *reverse* then Mr Bright would be the winner.
d. You could come to decide on the basis of 'overriding criteria'. The fact that Mr Bright attended your old college might suddenly seem to be an all-important consideration, or Miss Wise's extraordinary beauty might make other criteria absurdly irrelevant.

2. The Gambler's Fallacy
Although we refer to this rule as the **gambler's fallacy**, it is actually a form of rule adopted by decision makers who have never been near a casino or a racecourse. It is not unusual for people to view chance as a sort of self-correcting process in the sense that if they toss a coin and it comes up tails, then on the next toss they will believe it more likely to come up heads (assuming a fair coin). Herein lies the fallacy. It is true that over very long runs – say thousands of coin tosses – the number of heads and tails will be very close. But over short runs within that overall sequence the head/tail ratio may be very biased indeed. Ten heads or tails in a row will in fact be quite common.

We can give our thumbs a rest, and see variations on the gambler's fallacy operating as a decision rule in more everyday situations. For example, events which have in fact a very low probability such as earthquakes or being struck by lightning are assigned probabilities which are generally too high. Conversely, high-probability events, such as the number of times it rains per year, tend to be underestimated. People also operate like gamblers in the sense that they overestimate the likelihood of events favourable to themselves. Chancellors of the Exchequer, for example, always seem to see economic recovery just around the corner. Conversely, people underestimate the likelihood of unfavourable events such as economic recessions, drops in share prices and the like. In more mundane settings, maintenance and service engineers often show disdain for systematic, algorithmic procedures which will guarantee successful trouble shooting. Instead they prefer to gamble on 'riskier' short cuts which are more often wrong and therefore time-wasting.

3. Maximising Profits or Maximising Utility?
Let us take another two-choice situation, this time an investment example where you can assign probabilities to different outcomes, probabilities based on market study plus past performance of the firms concerned. You have to choose between Option A and Option B. What should be your decision rule?

Option A		Option B	
Profit/Loss	Probability	Profit/Loss	Probability
+£10,000	0.7	+£5,000	0.5
−£6,000	0.3	−£1,000	0.5

You could go for Option A, deciding to risk the loss of £6,000 simply because of the 70 per cent chance of pulling off the big one, regarding Option B as too tame. Unless you have money to burn a safer way of working out the better option is to take account of all available information as follows:

Option A offers me:

$(0.7 \times £10,000) + (0.3 \times minus \ £6,000) = £5,000$

(this is known as the monetary value of choosing Option A)

Option B offers me:

$(0.5 \times £5,000) + (0.5 \times minus \ £1,000) = £2,000$

Therefore, *on the principle of maximising one's expected monetary gains*, in a commercial decision situation, one must clearly choose Option A. Nevertheless, you may be very uncomfortable indeed at the possibility of losing £6,000 – true, it's only three chances in ten and you are much more likely to pull off the £10,000 profit – but just supposing it did all go wrong, how could you face up? How could you even find £6,000 without going bankrupt? Even if the chances of disaster were only one in a hundred, to some people it would loom sufficiently large so as to 'derationalise' the purely economic decision. Indeed, if I were to offer you now £1,000 in crisp, new fivers in your pocket, with no strings, *or* the possibility of winning £2,000 on a heads or tails coin toss (i.e. a 50–50 chance) you would surely take the money and avoid the gamble. But supposing I made it £1,000 'definite' versus £50,000 on the coin toss?

What we are getting at is that although decisions in organisations and by individuals may on some occasions appear to be made on the basis of maximising purely monetary returns, it is likely that something closer to reality is achieved by looking at **utility**, or how the decision maker construes the options open to him and how he weights the various possible outcomes *in terms of their benefits for him or her*. For reasons such as this, it often becomes necessary to talk not so much about how much net profit a course of action would bring, as how 'desirable' would be the consequences of each course of action. This 'apparent desirability' of different outcomes is called their 'utility', it includes monetary gain but it also covers other kinds of gain such as pleasure, pride and satisfaction. Clearly, we are now no longer considering outcomes in any absolute sense, but outcomes *with respect to the person who actually makes the choice*.

Note that when we seek to 'maximise utility', we do it first for ourselves – personal utility – and next for the close group to which we belong, e.g. your getting promotion has definite utility for your family. Then and only then are we concerned about maximising utility for our firm or our clients. It follows that the more closely bound are the employees into the organisation the greater the overlap between personal and organisational utility. This may in effect be the main reason why small firms, or large firms which are heavily decentralised, seem to suffer less from management–labour frictions, since what is the best choice for the firm will tend to be the best choice for the individual employee, and *vice versa*.

4. A Conservative Decision Rule: 'Minimax'

When the market is sluggish or the government is indirectly discouraging reinvestment the decision maker may respond to these external constraints by being cautious. There can also be individual, psychological reasons for caution: the person may be a pessimist by nature or be over-reacting to a recent bad experience. In any event he may decide to adopt a strategy which allows him to minimise his maximum losses – the **'minimax'** strategy (sometimes called 'maximin', i.e. maximising one's minimum *gains*). The application of this strategy to our simple investment problem is straightforward: you enter the expected monetary values, both of which you have already calculated (or expected subjective utilities, if wished), into a matrix as follows:

	Option A	Option B
Profit	£7,000	£2,500
Loss	£2,000	£500

Since option B minimises the maximum loss (£500) this is the one chosen. You can see how this contrasts with the strategy of *maximising* expected monetary gain ('maximax') which we discussed as Rule 3.

5. Looking for Satisfactory Returns: the 'Satisficing' Principle

The economist H. A. Simon proposed replacing the omniscient rationality of economic man with a kind of rationality that is compatible with his limited access to information and limited computing capabilities. Now, instead of trying to 'maximise utility', he chooses the first possible action that 'satisfices' what he aims to achieve. In choosing a car, for example, he would, according to this principle, choose the first car that is 'good' or 'better than good' on his particular criteria, say, speed, economy and appearance. The first car which manages to 'satisfice' in the dimensions our purchaser considers relevant is bought. It is an economical decision rule since all possible attributes of all possible cars do *not* have to be considered.

On the other hand one has the impression that many consumers would *not* stop searching once they had found something just satisfactory; in fact having a choice to fall back on might well have the effect of encouraging a bit of adventurous looking around. In other words, following a satisficing decision rule would be helpful in getting people to a stage where they could *attempt* to maximise personal utility. There is nevertheless a ring of truth about the satisficing principle, perhaps because it is the decision maker's equivalent of the doing-just-enough-work-to-keep-one's-job approach that one so often finds in faceless, large organisations. A manager who all the time uses satisficing as his main decision rule, i.e. not only when the information load is too much for him to handle, will be the kind of manager who is content to coast along looking more for security than for achievement.

6. *Creating the Consumer's Decision Rules*

The strategy in marketing must be to make the consumer believe that in buying your product he is not just satisficing but he is indeed maximising his subjective utility. To return to the case of buying a car, it may, for example, pay the manufacturer to inflate the price for the 'standard' model so that everyone will buy the 'de luxe' version and thereby appear to be getting the bargain (maximising subjective utility). This strategy will be aided if the standard model is always 'out of stock', i.e. does not exist, for practical purposes. Note that in order to produce maximum confusion in the purchaser the extras should be integrally related to the main product being purchased, partly because if you are buying a car you want to be offered free fog and reversing lights and not a free table lamp for your drawing-room, and partly because non-related items, although still 'bargains', can be more easily dissociated in the decision maker's appraisal from the thing he is *supposed* to be buying. This general ploy of harping on the giveaway price of extras, or so much 'off', without referring to the base price at all is found in book-club promotions (any 5 books for 10p!) and in the 'free' sets of saucepans given away by the gas and electricity boards in exchange for merely buying a cooker.

12.2.3 **Decisions Over Time**

In spite of the convenience of a 'static' general decision-making model for the purpose of exposition, it is essential to remember the dynamic *changing* structure of the decision situation. This quality of changeability implies two things:

i. We have to represent the decision as a sequential staged process. This can be through the construction of what are called **decision trees**, or alternatively **critical paths**, where each event and each subsequent sub-decision is mapped out in the proper sequence.

ii. We have to represent the fact that the information on which possible decisions are based is itself being updated or added to, so that the advisability of alternative courses of action may well vary during the total decision period. This updating can be carried out mathematically using Bayes' Theorem. The reader who is interested in quantitative changes in the decision structure over time should consult *Statistics and Decision Making* by John Harris which is published in the present series.

Summary. This has been a key chapter in the unfolding argument, since we have started to come to terms with the structure of the decision itself. We have seen that though essentially based on a subjective kind of rationality, the decisions that different people reach vary in quality because the constraints that operate are different and because in any case different decision criteria are employed. This basic approach is now easily extendable to cover the related topics of communication between people and group decision making which we meet in the next two chapters.

Work Section

A. Revision Questions

A1 What are the differences between economic man and psychological man?

A2 Explain the difference between 'normative' and 'descriptive' models of decision making.

A3 What is meant by the term 'personal (or subjective) utility'?

A4 Where do the decision rules we use come from?

A5 What is meant by the term 'decision rule'?

A6 How does the so-called 'gambler's fallacy' relate to ordinary decision making?

A7 Explain how monetary values are converted into utility values.

A8 Explain the concept of utility in an organisational context.

A9 Contrast the minimax and the maximax decision rules.

A10 Explain the difference between maximising and satisficing.

A11 Why do you feel that people become more conservative in their decisions as problem complexity increases?

B. Exercises/Case Studies

B1 Commodity Consultants Ltd

Introduction

Commodity Consultants Ltd (CCL) is a small independent firm of economic consultants specialising in primary raw materials. The company was set up in 1969 by two brothers, Michael and Stephen Williams. They had concluded that there was an opportunity for an independent consultancy able to advise governments and international companies on the economic aspects of the production and consumption of primary raw materials, especially metals and minerals.

The services now provided by CCL cover a wide range. They include short- and long-term price and market forecasts for industries dealing with commodities like copper, zinc, lead, nickel and market studies for a great variety of products, e.g. potash in Europe, antimony oxide in the USA, lead scrap in Italy.

It was recognised from the start that most of the company's business would come from outside the UK and, in particular, from the USA and Canada. Consequently, in 1971 Michael Williams opened a branch office in New York. As managing director, he kept himself in London and placed Stephen Williams in New York in charge of promoting sales throughout America. As a result of this move and together with some hard selling from the main office, the company's revenue had increased steadily. For the financial year ending 30 June 1980 it was expected to be about £450,000 with over 60 per cent of this coming from sales made through the New York office.

The Company's Conflicting Problems

Michael Williams had set himself a number of objectives for CCL. He recognised he would not be able to compete with large consultancy organisations, nor indeed to carry out studies for governments and international companies who had large economics departments of their own, unless the quality of work produced by CCL was of an exceptionally high standard. To gain this quality, and offer a unique service, he used simulation models, computer storage and econometrics (the statistical analysis of economic data – usually with the aid of a computer, in order to estimate the relationships between factors such as the demand for and supply of primary metal. Naturally, Michael wanted the company to grow and to make a profit but, more than that, he was keen that CCL should develop a worldwide reputation as an organisation that produced high calibre work which showed not only deep understanding of the industry under study but also offered creative solutions and new perspectives.

Given these general objectives, he was originally faced with two main alternative strategies, i.e. blanket coverage or specialisation. Specialisation would allow him to concentrate his expertise on a limited number of industries so that, with only a small staff, a very detailed knowledge of these industries could be built up. This investment in knowledge could then be applied to different studies carried out for a wide variety of companies and governments involved in those industries, thereby yielding a handsome financial return. This should make CCL well known and respected but it had to be acknowledged that the work would become repetitive and lacking in intellectual stimulation. It could also be that the company would be very vulnerable to the fortunes and judgement of the industries which it chose.

The alternative strategy was for CCL to seek work in a wide range of primary raw material industries. This would certainly be stimulating and less risky but would probably lead to less profit. There was always a learning period when the company carried out a study involving an unfamiliar industry – e.g. background reading material and previous reports had to be located, basic data analysed and contacts established in the area. All this took time and was therefore expensive.

Which of the policies he should adopt was decided by the personal desires of the knowledgeable and creative executives employed by the firm. They were of broadly two different types. First, three men who had extensive industrial experience in particular products –the industry experts – and, secondly, five capable economists and econometricians who could provide the special input to CCL's studies which made them unique and valuable. Both of these types of expert proved not only hard to recruit and expensive to pay but needed a constant intellectual stimulation if they were to be satisfied with their work and remain with the firm.

The personnel involved in the company at present are as follows:

1 Managing Director (Michael Williams)
1 Finance Director (Brian Gilbert)
8 Senior Consultants
8 Junior Consultants
1 Librarian
7 Secretaries and Typists

26

(In addition, 4 members of the company including Stephen Williams are employed in New York.)

Contract Proposal

Three days ago, on 27 June 1980, the Moroccan Government asked CCL to quote a price for a study on the market for their salt in Europe, North Africa and West Africa. Michael Williams examined the specification and estimated the amount of work which would be needed. He calculated it would take one of the senior consultants three months, provided he had one of the junior consultants to help him over that period, and another junior consultant for the first month only. No computer time would be involved but it would be necessary to make two visits to Europe and one to North and West Africa – the estimated total cost for these visits was £1,750 for travel, accommodation and subsistence.

Michael passed these specifications and estimations to his colleague, Brian Gilbert, who was the finance director. He asked him to estimate the cost of carrying out the study if it was conducted in the autumn of 1980. Brian then made his calculations on the basis of the budgeted figures for the second half of the financial year 1980 and these are given on page 192.

From past experience Brian knew that virtually all of his own and Michael's time would be spent on administration, general promotion or selling, with no time left for direct participation in a study. The salaries of all the other office staff, as indeed London office overheads and expenses of the New York office, could also be regarded as general overheads that must be covered by the revenue from Projects. On the other hand, the senior and junior consultants' time, and hence salaries, must be attributed directly to the projects they worked on. All consultants he regarded as working 225 days each year, after holidays, weekends and illness had been taken into account.

Another Financial Decision

With the end of the company's financial year on 30 June, Brian knows he has another contentious issue on his hands – the valuations of work in progress. He has already been given a provisional analysis of the status of uncompleted studies and from his own files he draws up the following summary:

Study	Price of study to each client (£)	No. of clients	Estimated degree of completion %	Consultant man days to 30 June Sen.	Jun.	Direct Costs Travel (£)	Computer (£)
Copper in Peru	18,500	1	50	12	20		
Long-term aluminium	7,500	5	30	105	37		625
Lead scrap in USA	2,500	10	40	15	45	2,300	700
Market for phosphates	5,000	7	75	87	53	1,600	

Budget Figures for half-year period 1 July–31 December 1980

Salaries
Managing and Finance Directors (2)	12,000
Senior Consultants (8)	33,000
Junior Consultants (8)	16,000
Secretaries, Typists and Librarian (8)	13,000

	74,000
Travel	10,000 *(1)*
Computer	14,000 *(1)*

Office Overheads
Rent, Rates, Gas, Electricity, etc.	14,000
Telephone and Telex	10,500
Postage	6,000
Printing	7,500
Office's Supplies	7,500
Entertainment	2,500
Other	5,000

	53,000
New York Office Expenses	25,000

	£176,000

(1) Note: Half the budgeted estimate for general travel and computer expenses was not directly attributable to individual projects.

Using the consultant daily fee rate for Jan.–June 1980, of £140 for senior consultants and £65 for junior consultants respectively, Brian can work out the direct costs of the studies to date. He feels that this figure should be the value of work in progress. Michael, however, argues that the study should be valued according to the proportion completed and the final price expected.

Questions
a. Why should firms who have long specialised in a commodity, or commodities, wish to employ the services of CCL?
b. Comment on Michael William's objectives for CCL and the strategies he appears to be following.
c. *The Moroccan Study*. Consider the direct costs, and adding a reasonable share of CCL's overheads, calculate a price that could be charged if an estimated 20 per cent profit margin was required and the study was conducted in the autumn of 1980. State any other major assumptions that you make.
d. Discuss other general factors and marketing strategies which might suggest that the quotation price sent to the Moroccan Government differed from the price referred to in question (c) above.
e. Considering the various decision rules discussed in the chapter, state which are being used by Michael Williams and which might be applicable for him to consider.

C. Essay Questions

C1 What decision rules of thumb might (a) a salesman, (b) a secretary, (c) a buyer be expected to pick up from experience?

C2 What do you think it is about people that makes them underestimate or overestimate probabilities in the ways outlined in the 'gambler's fallacy' discussion?

C3 Do you think that the so-called satisficing principle is very prevalent in industry or does it represent merely another jaundiced academic viewpoint?

C4 If managers at all levels take the decisions, what rules of decision making might be employed by the managing director which would be different from those commonly used by his subordinates?

C5 'Decision making is the art of the possible and not the optimising of the apparent alternatives.' Discuss.

C6 'Success in business comes from judgement and not from any form of logical decision analysis.' Discuss.

Chapter 13

Communicating Information

Synopsis: *The topic of communication has special importance at this point in the book, since it allows us to move from the case of the individual decision maker to the case of several individuals in a group reaching a decision together. In the opening section of this chapter we look at communication between two people. We recognise the biases and limitations of the human communicator, examine the problems of transmission itself, and deal with difficulties in the listener. We note that often information is conveyed as much by the way people say things as by what they actually say, and we show how non speech behaviour allows the speaker to 'control' the person, or people, he is talking to. We extend this discussion to communication in groups, examining Robert Bales' scheme which identifies and analyses members' contributions in terms of the group or the task. From groups we move to information handling in organisations, considering the work Alex Bavelas carried out on how quality of decisions is affected by different communication structures. The chapter ends by looking in more detail at the general problems of horizontal and vertical information flow.*

Plan of the chapter: *This is illustrated in Fig. 13.1.*

13.1 The Nature of Communication

Communication is fundamental to our existence. It allows us to satisfy basic friendship needs; it enables us to live intricate family lives, and particularly relevant to our theme, it is the life-blood of organisations.

There have been a series of spectacular advances in man's ability to communicate with speed and accuracy over wide geographical areas to huge masses of people, and there is an ever-increasing amount of research and writing on the subject of communication. Yet despite this intense activity and the great leap forward, the communication gap among different individuals, and among groups, seems to be increasing.

Communication can be divided into the following elements. First, there must be a communicator, who normally takes the initial action. Secondly, there is the delivering of certain pieces of information – what we might call transmission. Thirdly, the message comes to a receiver. And lastly (not to be forgotten), the originator of the message must be aware how accurate his

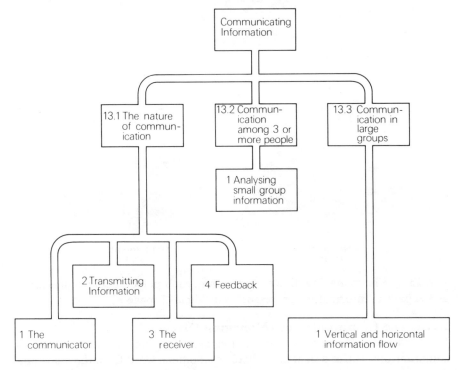

Fig. 13.1: Communicating Information

communication has been through 'feedback' from the listener or receiver. Harold Leavitt has defined a communicator as 'One who shoots information to hit a target and who gets feedback to know that the target has been hit.' Figure 13.2 provides a basic communication model which sets the framework for this chapter. Communication is about how people link or relate to each other, and this boils down to how they handle and pass on information. This is why our communication model is no more than a version of the familiar general decision model, with the output of one person forming the input of another. Particular points about the model will be expounded by using the example of a managing director (communicator) relating to a departmental head (receiver).

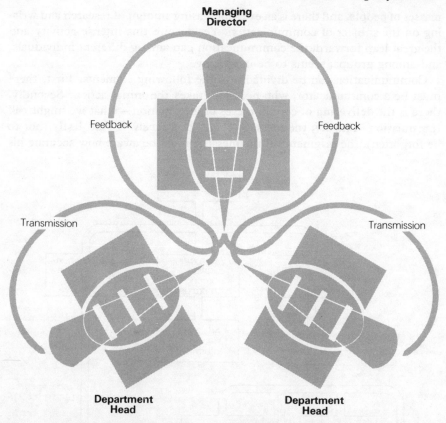

Fig. 13.2: The managing director's meeting, each person being represented as a separate 'information processor' (see Fig. 1.2, page 8)

13.1.1 The Communicator (Managing Director)

First, it is as well to check that our managing director is the right one to communicate. Is this a situation where an unofficial word from the managing director's secretary might be more appropriate? Would it be better to send the message through another formal head or through a shop steward?

Next, he must now clarify the purpose of any communication. What is it that he wants to happen – to placate, to change attitudes, to motivate, or what? Until our managing director has clarified this purpose or objective there is no chance of useful communication. The absence of such planned thinking is the most fundamental barrier to successful communication.

Third, the person or persons to receive the communication should be clarified. If too many are told then it is wasting everybody's time: if vital people are not told then the formal communication will not succeed (although the grapevine might help if luck is on the managing director's side).

And last, the timing of the communication must be decided from several points of view. Will it be necessary to preserve secrecy over the affair and hence only allow information out at the eleventh hour? Alternatively, is the organisation so large that extra time will be needed to let the formal system transmit the information through to the furthest ends? At what juncture is the communication likely to be most successful in creating the desired change? It is important that the minimum time, money, resources and energy are spent in gaining the maximum impact on the recipient.

13.1.2 Transmitting Information

It makes sense to regard transmission as being made up of two elements as communication always operates on two simultaneous channels. On Channel 1, if you like, we have the *content* of what the speaker is saying and this contains most information. But on Channel 2, we also listen to the *way* he says it, his facial expressions and gestures or even (if written) his style or writing and sense of timing. We will look at each of these channels separately.

A. Content (Channel 1)

Most communicators, whether in writing or in speech, spend more time considering the content than they do the manner of delivery. Yet, surprisingly, most people's efficiency is low. Here are some common errors:

a. The information may be transmitted in a language which is incomprehensible. The managing director may use words and phrases which are not in the normal vocabulary of the manager or he may use technical language which for him is an everyday shorthand but to the receiver can be double-Dutch.

b. Secondly, the message content may be perfectly comprehensible in its different parts but its *purpose* may not be at all clear to the departmental manager. 'Why is he telling me this? I've heard it all before.' This shows an inability to assist the receiver in filtering and ordering information.

c. Next there is the constant problem of poor presentation. The managing director may mumble or joke over important points, or, in written communications, he may write so vaguely that the message is ambiguous. After long discussions he may fail to convince when a crisp memo with a simple diagram could have made his point better.

d. When there is failure of the managing director to assess the information load. He may be going too fast and leaving his audience hazy and muddled – perhaps because he fails to interpret, or even look for, feedback from his listener(s). Or the problem may be underload where the crushing predictability of the speaker's words produces suppressed yawns in the audience. All communication must have interest, life and use the natural humour inherent in the situation. Sir Ernest Gower's simple rule in his *The Complete Plain Words* is worth noting: 'Be simple, be short, be human, be correct.'

e. Lastly, our transmission needs to take into account the need to persuade the listener or reader. It is not sufficient for a manufacturer to say on a can of paint, 'Do not shake,' if we simply interpret this as a labour-saving gesture: we may wish to give it a good old-fashioned shake anyway. We need to be told *why* we should not shake, or 'open other end,' or 'not place in direct sunlight even when empty'. It is the purpose that gives us the spur to act rather than the simple information.

B. *The Way It is Said (Channel 2)*

Channel 2 can operate in written communication, but is at its most important with verbal exchanges. Indeed, in discussion it is often the *way* people say things which communicates more than *what* they say. For example, have you ever sat waiting for an interview along with another applicant? There is some effort at conversation, but neither of you is listening much to content, only to what voice, gestures and posture reveal about the quality of the opposition. Fig. 13.3 shows simple examples of how we read certain information from postures, although we can pick up information at a much more subtle level than this.

It is clear that **body language,** *how* you communicate, is crucial in determining *what* you communicate. How you stand, where you stand with respect to the other person, the amount of body tension, the amount of gesture and above all the facial expressions you use are all part of this language. The use of the smile is an interesting single illustration. Smiling or chuckling is

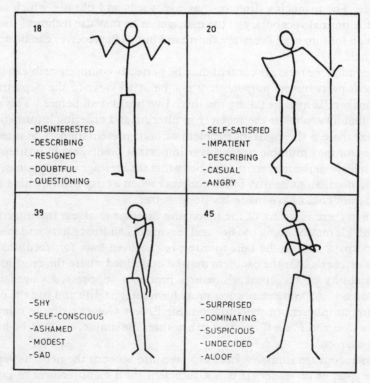

Fig. 13.3

a socially acceptable 'camouflage' permitting all manner of excesses – for example between opponents in an argument. Insults may flow freely provided both parties keep smiling. The more vicious or intimate the attack the wider the smile. The offending party will of course beam back an even bigger smile partly to confirm that he can keep cool and partly to relax himself and control the quaver in his voice as he replies. But above the smile his eyes may be signalling, 'You've got me hooked.'

This leads us to the situation where the content and the gesture are totally conflicting in their message. You will have noticed this phenomenon in social gatherings where one can partly ignore the content of what is being said – be it about the weather, politics, babies or television – and mainly tune in to the facial expressions. These expressions may be saying, 'I am tired,' 'I find you interesting,' 'I am bored,' 'I have drunk too much,' 'Something is worrying me.' Social gatherings are one thing, but for efficient communication conflicting messages are clearly to be avoided.

C. Other General Transmission Problems

The wrong means of communication may be adopted, like the use of the telephone when a more direct and personally satisfying discussion may have greater impact. External stresses such as uncomfortable heat, cold or noise levels may cause failure to hear or attend to the message. Internal stresses such as fear, anxiety, headaches have similar consequences. A familiar problem for executives these days is 'jet lag' – the cumulative effect of sleep deficit combined with work strain and the need for rapid psychological reorientation.

13.1.3 The Receiver (The Departmental Head)

And so we can move in Fig. 13.2 to the receiver who is accepting an incomplete, partially inappropriate and much distorted transmission, which then has to make its way in turn through the warrens of his information processing pathway before he decides on his own actions. Many of the problems we have already considered in 13.1.1. but there are a few others which are best looked at from this end.

First, there are all the traditional problems of perception. Has he the background to understand the message? Can she appreciate the purpose as much as the content? Can he filter and remember the key points rather than absorbing the trivialities? Can she link the new information with her existing experience? Is he open to understanding or do his own prejudices about the communicator blind him to the message?

While perception is important, it is the analysis and resulting action which show whether the communication has been successful. Often we do know exactly our boss's intentions and because of this find ways of avoiding the action he would like! In other words, if the communicator has not produced an environment in which there is trust and motivation then it will be small consolation that perception of his intentions has been clear. This clearly echoes the points we were making about management–union communication difficulties in the collective bargaining situation (Chapter 9).

13.1.4 Feedback

Feedback is important for two reasons. We have already seen that the communicator is basically inefficient in the way that he accepts, analyses and then transmits most of his information. It is only by understanding how well the receiver perceives the communication that he is able to adjust towards more effective communication. If the receiver does not pick up the message then all the communicator's thoughts and actions are of no practical benefit. Equally, if the receiver does not act then again no effective communication has taken place. It is thus through feedback that the communicator can gauge success and know whether to try another approach. In the case of many management information systems there will be a mechanism to modify the input so that it gradually gets nearer to the optimum as a result of information feedback.

Secondly, at the micro level we use feedback to maintain and control verbal exchanges. If a speaker realises that his audience is becoming inattentive or bored then he will often increase his vocal decibels, adopt a new approach or modulate his voice more vigorously in an attempt to regain 'control'. Equally, a speaker will look away from the other person when he is making a fairly long statement but glance at him so as to check from time to time that the listener is still attentive. As he comes to the end of his argument he will again make eye-contact as a signal that the other may ask his question or give his point of view. Without such an acceptable mechanism normal communication would be difficult, and it is a fact that this easy rhythm is not found between strangers who have not yet fully learned exactly how each expresses these 'stop' and 'start' cues.

Our effectiveness as communicators is greatly dependent on our ability to respond to feedback with sensitivity and speed. Skilled negotiators in industrial relations are able to sense areas of difficulty *before* they are explicitly broached and can therefore skirt round them.

Another valuable aspect of feedback is what we might call *live listening*. Perhaps surprisingly, skilled communicators are typically good *listeners*. Being a good listener is a sign of maturity and professionalism, and we may learn a great deal about ourselves if we really listen to others. It is often we who will need to make a complete or partial change and not the other party. The implications of this in industrial relations, to take only one example, will be obvious.

Live listening is not just 'saying nothing', but rather trying to gain understanding of the other's communication with a genuine respect and interest. Thus it is attempting to understand the full implications of the message and to gauge its significance. If one of the parties really listens he will quickly find the other tends to do the same and so the element of conflict and the

In the communicator

Biased choice of information to be transmitted
Not believable as a person
Objectives unclear
Failure to define audience appropriately
Failure to interpret feedback correctly

In the message transmission

Message poorly structured or too technical
No reasons or assumptions explained
Wrongly paced for audience
Poorly timed
Conveys conflicting non-verbal message
Presence of noise or distractors

In the receiver

Biased acceptance of information
Low interest or motivation level
Poor background knowledge
Specific dislike of communicator or his message
Failure to give appropriate feedback.

Fig. 13.4: Reasons Why Communication Can Fail (Summary)

weapons of status, intellectual snobbery or superior knowledge, become reduced.

13.2 Communication Among 3 or More People

The critical influence of adding another person to the simplest two-person communication chain is evident from examples such as the behaviour of a young couple with and without a chaperone, or the influence of the presence of a teacher on the easy spontaneity of a conversation between two students. 'Channel control' is much more difficult among three people than two, although awkward silences are slightly more easily managed since there is now someone else whose fault it could be! Non-verbal control through facial expression and gesture must be more difficult since it is unlikely that your two listeners will agree equally with what you are saying or be equally adept in picking up points as you make them. In the face of different feedback from the two listeners you will of course behave differently to each as far as you can, but the totality of your control has been weakened. It can be seen that as the number of listeners increases to four, five and more, the possibility of control with any degree of refinement is progressively lost, and we gradually approach a 'public speaking' kind of situation where the appeal is diffuse in order, hopefully, to encompass every listener, and the non-verbal gestures and expressions become stylised, and exaggerated.

13.2.1 Analysing Small-Group Communication: the Bales Method

Most small-group research has consisted of getting five or six people around a table in a 'laboratory' type situation and there has been too little concern with naturalistic observation of what small community groups actually do in practice. Communication in a small group is in any case often of the two-person type – A addresses B – but always of course in the moderating presence of other people. Much work on small groups has been done by Robert F. Bales. The research is of great intrinsic interest because of the importance of committees and consultative groups in business activity. Bales limited his work to a special type of group given a particular type of task:

i.   The group was small.
ii. There was to be no formal leader.
iii. Each task was a small problem which the group really wanted to solve (i.e. they were highly motivated towards a common objective).
iv. The problem could only be solved when: (a) its real nature was clear; (b) alternative solutions had been isolated; (c) one of these had been selected.

Bales was concerned with the different types of interaction among group members which either helped or hindered problem solution. He separated contributions from members into those which were task oriented and those which were directed at emotional support. A scoring system was developed based on the categories in Fig. 13.5. Every contribution fits one of these categories, and thereby earns a tally mark. At the end of a meeting a bar chart is constructed representing the number of tallies in each category. This has been done in Fig. 13.5 and shows the different profiles obtained by a group that rated itself 'satisfied' as against a 'dissatisfied' group that was unhappy about how it was being run. It need hardly be stated that any observer needs some practice before group discussions can be easily categorised. One of the greatest difficulties is that, as we saw in the previous section, speech is only one element of communication; gesture and other non-speech behaviour really ought to be categorised as well.

More generally, the amount that members contribute seems related to group size. The larger the group the more there is a tendency for a few to say a great deal and for many to say virtually nothing. Remarks tend to be addressed one person to another following a sort of pecking order, the highest contributor being addressed by the next highest, and so on. These high contributors are also the initiators of ideas. At the low contributor end there are only a few comments and these are mainly passed among the low contributors themselves. The informal leader tends to be generally liked and the most

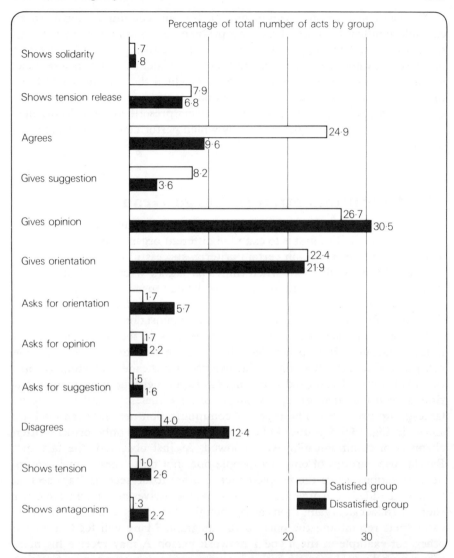

Fig. 13.5: Distribution of interaction by categories within a satisfied and a dissatisfied group. (Based on data from Bales, 1952). From E. P. Hollander, *Principles and Methods of Social Psychology* – 2nd Ed. 1971, page 482, Oxford U. Press.

talkative member of the group. In contrast, the formal leader (unless he is one and the same person) becomes commonly the *least liked* person in the group. While he scores high in productivity, this often comes to feel like 'control' to others in the group and control is disliked. More is said about such matters in the next chapter on group decision making.

We may conclude this section on small-group communication with an example familiar to most of us: the problem of communication between teacher and student. Typically there is a gulf between the teacher's terms of reference, values and objectives and those of students. Teachers also make assumptions about the student as a 'learner' which the student has to learn to comply with. Too rarely is there genuine communication: questions are typically narrowly conceived with the answers prescribed. Nor do teachers make explicit to students the criteria by which performance will be accepted or rejected.

13.3 Communication in Large Groups

There are two ways that communication in large groups or organisations might be studied. The first is to examine different organisations and attempt to see what makes them, on certain criteria, successful or unsuccessful. In practice, this is usually done when things have gone wrong. Industrial relations are sour or a strike has occurred, or labour turnover is too high. The problem in these cases is how to isolate the responsible factor(s) considering the incredible complexity of large dynamic organisations.

A second approach is to leave the complexities of the real situation and to try to isolate certain principles which can be seen to operate in simple controlled situations. It was Alex Bavelas who had the idea of testing hypotheses in this way. He started work in 1948 experimenting on **communication nets** using small groups which were nevertheless intended to model large-group processes. The types of communication nets he examined are shown in Fig. 13.6. Groups of five people were used and only formal written channels of communication were allowed. As just observed, the fact that Bavelas used groups of only five people does not make these 'small-group' demonstrations, since the people concerned are to be seen as (say) section heads embedded in an organisational matrix, themselves being fed from other sources. In fact an organisation can be thought of as an aggregate of communication nets resembling the ones in the diagram. Many will feed into each other, for example in the Type I network person A may receive his main inputs via a Type II network within his own section, whereas person C within *his* own section may be at the centre of a Type IV network. Thus networks are arranged in both a hierarchical and overlapping manner within a given organisation, and any given person may well have membership of several of these networks at different levels in the hierarchy. It is *especially important* to appreciate that each of the small circles representing a person in the Fig. 13.6 networks really needs to be magnified so as to show the detail found in Fig. 13.2. In other words, each person who is a node in the communication network is very much a biased perceiver and analyser of the incoming message, and similarly biased about deciding what should be passed on.

Bavelas gave the different nets a series of problems varying in complexity

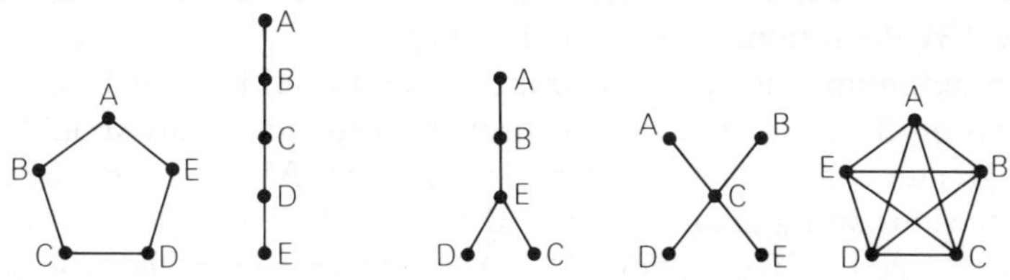

	Type I	Type II	Type III	Type IV	Type V
Leader	Any	Probably C	Probably E	Usually C	Any
Speed of learning a procedure	Relatively slow			Quick	Slow
Speed of solution	Relatively slow	Slow		Quick	Slow
Mistakes not corrected; flexibility to change	Quite good	Weak		Often inflexible	
Originality of ideas, eg, for brainstorming				Low	High
Number of messages sent	Fairly large			Small	Large
Satisfaction/morale	Usually good	Not high		C often high; remainder low	All equal

Fig. 13.6

and originality of solution required. Quality of performance and member satisfaction were then scored for the different nets. The diagrams and tables in Fig. 13.6 summarise his findings, which are also taken up in the next section.

13.3.1 The General Problems of Vertical and Horizontal Information Flow

a. Formal Channels

In many organisations there has long been a tendency for a whole series of links to be joined vertically in a manner similar to Bavelas's networks II and III, especially since, once upon a time, communication was designed only to move down in the form of orders backed by the necessary authority. However, linear networks are subject to serious limitations:

i.   If the chain is too long the speed of communication will be very slow.

ii. If any member of the chain is absent, or there is a block for 'personal' reasons, communication completely fails to operate.

iii. It will be easy for errors to arise and there are no means of checking.
iv. By definition, there is no feedback.

In communication terms an improvement would clearly be to make the information flow *two*-way, i.e. to provide feedback. This should mean there is a greater chance that information will reach A so that he may make the right decision, and a greater chance that those below will really understand and then take the right action. Also A would know whether the communication had been successfully received.

However there are problems with two-way linear networks:

a. Waiting for upward information flow or feedback leads to slower decision making. In practice A and E at the two ends of the chain often become so frustrated that they deal direct (e.g. a managing director directly consulting with the works' convenor or shop steward). It is easy to see what this means for other men in the chain – they are by-passed. They have apparently lost responsibility, and often fail to pick up information relevant to their job.

b. It is common for only selective information to be sent up. Men will not split on their peers so that the boss, who can reward and punish those below, tends to be fed only with 'good' information.

c. Those at the bottom are often not provided with enough basic awareness to really know what information is important, when it is important, and for whom.

d. Different levels in vertical linear networks usually imply different social status and different educational background; these must provide substantial communication barriers.

e. The less the trust that is held for immediate superiors the less accurately juniors will communicate problem-type information. Again, lower-status persons who aspire to move upwards will use regulation of communication flow as a means of gaining power and control.

f. Juniors are usually career-dependent on their immediate superiors and therefore do not like to give information or ask advice which in any way casts doubt on their own work competence. Since the anxiety in the relationship lies mainly with the junior there is relatively more inhibition of communication in the upward direction. Similarly, while junior managers may hold on to upcoming information in order, as we saw, to give themselves power or distort it to put themselves in a more favourable light, a senior does not ordinarily have equivalent power needs with respect to his juniors in the organisation. Thus upward flow is again affected more than downward flow.

Laboratory model studies of communication in organisations also show that low-prestige members spend a lot of their time and energy trying to impress high-prestige members, i.e. in distortions of one kind or another. Such distortions can include the 'overlooking' of blatant errors from above since the junior feels his standing would be threatened if he made corrective comments.

b. *Informal Channels For the Flow of Information: the Grapevine*

As we have already noted in Chapter 7, official organisation charts describe at best only some part of the true information network. They do not indicate, for example, that the marketing director cannot tolerate the personnel director and obtains all his necessary personnel information from neighbourly visits to his deputy, who also doesn't get on too well with his senior. Nor do such charts describe the coffee-break communication networks through which gossip – the zest of an organisation – is passed freely from mouth to mouth. Studies have shown how civil servants in a government department needing expert information approached their friends in the same department rather than supervisors or available experts, since in either case they felt they would appear incompetent. A 'helping contract' therefore developed between pairs of friends.

The vertical scalar system is insufficient in itself. Within any formal organisation it is necessary to gain co-operation between departments in order to optimise decisions for the whole company. Most formal organisations will have some element of horizontal communication but it is common for this to be ill-developed or of low efficiency. Some of the reasons are clear:

i. With any horizontal communication there are problems of uncertainty in authority and status.

ii. Different departments often do not understand the tasks and problems of others.

iii. The outlook of personnel in the different departments can be so different that there are 'personality clashes' (production with marketing: staff with line, and so on).

In general information flow seems to work most efficiently in organisations (i) where status is a function of earned respect and not simply 'ascribed', (ii) where a formal organisational chart is rather hard to draw, and (iii) where the number of levels of management, i.e. nodes in the communication chain, are few.

This chapter has been quite densely packed with information. Taking one human information processing system by itself provides a good deal to discuss; when we then interface two or more systems and study how they 'communicate' the complexity is bound to increase. But in establishing a communications link among several human processors we have taken a vital step which allows us to look at the major topic of *group* decision making in the next chapter.

Work Section

A. Revision Questions

A1   What are the main features of communication?

A2   What factors might a possible communicator consider before the message is delivered?

A3   Name the two types of transmission.

A4   What are some common mistakes in spoken communication?

A5   Why is feedback so important? ·

A6   According to the Bales scheme, what different types of comments are made by group members when discussing an issue?

A7   How may group leaders be popular or unpopular?

A8   What did Bavelas show with his network experiments?

A9   Name some problems with vertical linear communication in a large organisation.

A10 Why is upward-flowing information slower and subject to more distortion than downward-flowing?

A11 What value has 'the grapevine'?

A12 Why is very careful listening an essential ingredient of communication?

A13 Who controls communication, the source or the receiver?

B. Exercise/Case Studies

B1   On the point in 13.2.1 about the teacher–student communication gap, what specific advice could you give an ineffective teacher on the use of feedback and live listening? What general advice might you glean from the rest of this chapter to help a teacher who is failing to communicate?

B2   Consider the distortion of information through selective perception and memory loss as it is passed from one person to another. Read a story to one person and then let this be passed on in, say, five separate communications with individuals who have not previously heard the message. The message may be written down (or tape recorded) in an attempt to demonstrate why it changes. The rest of the group may also witness each separate communication and make their own diagnosis.

B3   The chairman of a Northern hardware distributor found, on looking at management recruitment, that the personnel director took on few graduates. The chairman felt this was wrong as his large company now needed good brains and more sophisticated personnel. The problem was that the personnel director, although an extremely capable man, had risen without much formal education and saw university as a dubious way of spending three years. As a means of making his views known, the chairman commented quite casually, over lunch with his fellow directors, that he thought the company needed more graduates in management positions. None of the directors made any comment.

Question: In what circumstances do you feel that this style of communication might be successful? What would you have done if you had been the chairman?

B4 A Communications Survey?

Mr George Pim is industrial relations manager of a manufacturing firm. The firm employs 2,000 people. Mr Pim is convinced that communications within the organisation are not effective, and that rumour, gossip and misunderstanding are resulting in depressed morale.

On this basis, he has asked permission to pay for a communications survey by the industrial relations department of a nearby university. He suggests that the problem is one faced by many other firms, and that the university team can bring its experience to bear in detecting weaknesses in the communication structure.

The managing director of the firm is sharply opposed to the suggestion. He says that Mr Pim should be able to recognise deficiencies and weaknesses without outside help. He insists that social scientists in a university cannot be of help in a practical problem like this and would have no real interest in it. He says that the problem is not a scientific problem anyway, that all it takes is applied common sense. He also argues that installation of a public address system would be a better use of the money.

Question: Write, in 300 words, Mr Pim's reply to the managing director – the one he sent rather than the first effort he tore up and threw away.

B5 An American-based multi-national has just taken the decision to close down one of its four plants in the United Kingdom. You are in charge of the plant affected which, at various levels, employs nearly 400 people.

State carefully how you might communicate this to all the parties involved.

C. Essay Questions

C1 Comment on: (a) the advantages; and (b) the disadvantages of three of the following types of communication:
   i. The letter.
   ii. The noticeboard.
   iii. The telephone.
   iv. The Company report.
   v. An architect's plans.
   vi. A computer print-out.

C2 Classify the types of communication that your organisation uses. Analyse the effectiveness of your systems for each type. (May be tackled in groups.)

C3 With particular reference to communication, explain how a conciliator helping the parties in an industrial dispute can sometimes bring the two sides together.

C4 What is the formal communication system of an organisation attempting to achieve?

C5 In less than 300 words state precisely why really skilled communicators need a full command of language.

Chapter 14

Decisions in Groups

Synopsis: *It is true to say that choosing among possible courses of action usually involves communication among a number of people. Indeed, at one extreme the person appearing to make the decision may be no more than the signatory to something worked out by junior managers or civil servants over a period of many months. It is to these decision-making teams or groups that we turn our attention in this chapter. To some extent the idea of individuals or groups is a false dichotomy, since the individual and group components in the decision process are in fact interwoven: the individual relies on his group back-up at different stages for testing out ideas and the group depends on its individuals to come to the fore and determine the direction the group should take, again at different stages in the decision process.*

The single most important activity that goes on in a decision-making group is the communication of information from one member to another, with each member being an information receiver and sender hampered by all the limitations described in the previous chapter. The more you can keep in mind the idea of the person as a perceiving-analysing-deciding 'unit' surrounded by other such units the more effectively you will understand the points to be made in the present chapter.

We begin by discussing what happens in terms of group processes during a single meeting and then over many months of meetings as expectations and norms develop among the members. We go on to ask whether groups or individuals make the best decision makers, and you will see that on a range of different criteria there is no ready-made answer.

Plan of the chapter: *This is illustrated in Fig. 14.1.*

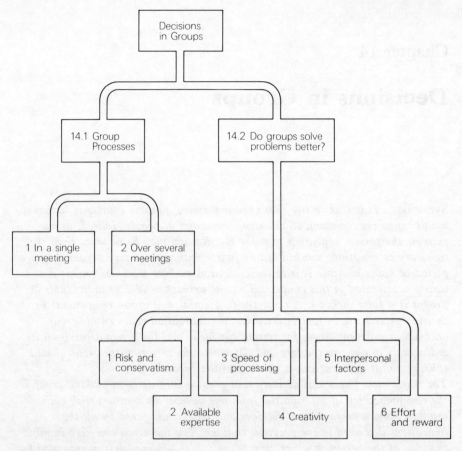

Fig. 14.1: Decisions in Groups

14.1 Group Processes

There are two levels of group process that can be observed in committees
and other small-to-medium size groups which are set up with some task in
mind. The first level concerns what goes on within a single session as members
move through the agenda. The second process level concerns the evolution
of the group over many sessions including a time span of perhaps months
or even years.

14.1.1 Processes Within a Single Meeting

a. The Structure of the Problem Has First to be Identified and Agreed. The
classical observations of Robert Bales (see 13.2.1) point to this initial fact-
finding phase in which the main characteristics of the problem are identified.
People request, supply and exchange information without necessarily any

wish at this stage to select information favourable to their own views – perhaps because these views themselves are often only beginning to be formed. Information will be available in abundance and the problem of the chairman is to direct the problem solving process by encouraging concise input of relevant information. The group will almost always be a more efficient information resource than the individual decision maker, and the simple fact of having more than one person increases the probability of a correct solution being available. Weak chairmen allow discussion to go 'all round the houses', and this is one of the sources of the view that committees never decide anything. Dissatisfaction with committees also arises from members who are by nature low contributors since unless the group works to allow them to express their viewpoints frustration easily leads to disillusionment.

b. The Second Phase of the Meeting is When Members Begin Putting Forward Suggestions. Conflicts, negative feelings and tension naturally arise at this time. This phase is characterised by the asking for and giving of opinions, evaluations, analyses and expressions of feeling. Some signs of dominance or deference emerge as well as agreement or disagreement, co-operation or rejection, among different members.

c. Finally there is a Resolution Phase. Here the dominating views are gradually accepted by dissenting members and a group decision emerges. Some evaluation does continue, but this last phase is mainly marked by the acceptance or rejection of directions and suggestions, by manifest support of various kinds among coalitions, and by tension build-up and release (laughing, joking) as agreement is finally reached all round.

14.1.2 Processes Occurring over Several Meetings
Rather like the people who make them up, groups mature and develop over time. Some of the main identifiable states in this development are as follows:

a. Forming. The individual members of the group seek to merge their individual identities. They talk about such things as the purpose of the *group*, what it should be called, who will belong to it, the leadership pattern and how long it will last.

b. Setting Norms. The group needs to establish the norms or standards of practice which we talked about in Chapter 6: when and how the group should meet, how decisions are to be made; what kind of behaviour is expected. At this stage individual members will often experiment by seeking out new ways and new methods.

c. Conflict. Most groups go through a stage where the originally agreed objectives and norms somehow come under strain and are challenged. The hidden needs of the individuals will now emerge and a certain amount of interpersonal hostility is generated. If the leader handles the situation properly, a revised and more appropriate set of objectives can be set. This stage is often important in testing the degree of frankness and trust within the group.

d. Maturity. Only when the three previous stages have been completed can the group be said to have reached 'maturity' so that proper output and productivity can be expected. Some groups mature quickly while others take much longer; it depends on how homogeneous and complementary is the mix of skills and temperaments that the members bring into the group.

14.2 Do Groups Solve Problems Better Than Individuals?

First, what are the criteria for being 'better'? Do we mean 'better' in terms of producing more and better quality, or better in terms of more motivating and satisfying to the members? In the following sections we will identify some of the pros and cons of group vs. individual problem solving.

14.2.1 Groups Can Be Less Conservative Than Individuals

You may remember that individual decision making is often characterised by an unwillingness to back more adventurous or 'riskier' courses of action. We can amplify this point here. Supposing we were to ask three or four colleagues to work through some specimen problems quite individually in their own offices to get some idea of the levels of risk each accepted. Then we bring the small group together around a table and ask them to work through the same problems – but this time with a view to obtaining something close to group agreement on acceptable risk levels. Lastly, we again send them off to their individual offices to reconsider their individual decisions in the light of the various group decisions (with which they would not always have been in complete agreement). A general finding would be that:

a. Group decisions are often 'riskier' (i.e. accept lower odds of success) than individual decisions.

b. Individual decisions *after* the group discussion are also often riskier than the original individual decision.

How Can We Explain How This Risky Shift in Decision Making Comes About? The first thing to be clear about is that **risky shift** does not always occur in group decision making. It can and does happen that believers in riskier courses of action are concerned about looking foolish and therefore soft-pedal their views. Again, some people may promote risky solutions on some issues but be relatively conservative on others. Or it can happen that prestigious members of a group are also cautious minded and lead the group into decisions which in fact leave many members dissatisfied. Therefore, consensus *can* occur on a middle-of-the-road course of action, but it is more likely to occur at a somewhat more risky level than a consideration of members' views *before* the meeting would lead one to expect.

You may recall here the work of Solomon Asch (Chapter 6) who showed in his problem on matching lengths of lines that the pressures on a person to conform are so strong that often he or she is prepared to give an answer which is known to be wrong, i.e. they are pushed into accepting an extreme or risky position. The basic idea is that if the group says something is okay, or must be done, then the individual feels able to indulge.

While risky shift is interesting because we tend to think of group consensus as always being the average of individual opinion, we must not assume that more daring decisions are necessarily *better* decisions. In fact, daring decisions can be the result of the very same conservative information processing of which we previously accused the individual decision maker. An illustration will make this clearer.

> *The sales promotion team of an overseas car manufacturer had plans to mop up the UK market. Everything went wrong. The dealers did not provide the local backing necessary to the national campaign; home manufacturers were not caught by surprise; stocks of new vehicles were not shipped in promptly enough, and the overseas manufacturer's market-intelligence made several fundamental miscalculations about British car buyers. Not only did sales not leap ahead, but there was a fall on the previous year's levels, as well as heavy incidental losses due to dealers' not accepting late stock. After many senior heads had rolled, the owners of the remaining heads wondered how such a disaster could have been allowed to happen, since it should have been obvious to anyone that the operation could never have come off.*

Irving Janis (on whose analysis the above scenario is based) has argued that senior decision makers can become victims of what he calls **groupthink**. This refers to an insidious process by which decision makers, although they may be remarkably insightful people with unparalleled access to information, time after time convince one another that an emerging shaky plan is sound, that all the important facts are being considered and that criticisms are unjustified. Individuals who are not personally convinced tend to remain silent or to soft-pedal their objections. Collectively, the members of the group reach a decision to which few might have subscribed had each relied on his own critical judgement.

But how and why does it work? Janis suggests that when people are strongly motivated to establish consensus, overt disagreements are avoided, the facts that might reduce support for the emerging majority view are suppressed and faulty assumptions not questioned. As sentiment in favour of the operation grows, dissenters are subtly and politely dissuaded from pressing their contrary opinions, and certain members of the group begin acting as self-appointed mindguards who protect their associates from unwelcome ideas. Thus participants hear arguments on only *one* side of the question and potential dissenters come to believe that nobody else shares their doubts! In the face of such 'unanimous agreement', all members of the group eventually approve the plan.

We may make the following inferences from Janis's important work:
a. The quality of a group's decision need not be determined by the knowledge

possessed by each individual member, since information not communicated or not listened to, even though of major importance, can have no
influence on decisions taken.
b. Facts or ideas expressed by high-status persons are, as we noted earlier,
disproportionately influential.
c. Too quick a movement towards consensus is a bad thing since it freezes
the direction of thinking and makes consideration of other alternatives
seem like a time-wasting discourtesy to other participants.
d. There needs to be a guaranteed channel by which minority or dissenting
views are allowed proper presentation. Ideally an outsider without vested
interests but with the relevant skills and experience is needed to monitor
developments in the decision-making process. One of his duties might be
to make participants think through the consequences of making wrong
appraisals at each juncture, possibly by having people assign probabilities
to outcomes and drawing out the full decision tree as discussed in Chapter
12. Formalisation of this kind makes people dwell on the full implications
of different moves at each choice point and it allows 'dissent' to occur
without the need for personality clashes.

14.2.2 Available Expertise
a. For Groups. The array of personal expertise is more likely to accommodate
the problem in hand, particularly when it is across a wide technical area. The
information available will be richer, in more depth and, if the personality
mix in the group is right, more likely to be given appropriate weighting. Provided again the personal factors are right – and here leadership is so important
– a group will be able to handle greater amounts of information, decide better
how to weight various inputs, and tolerate input ambiguity and irrelevant
information more easily.

b. Against Groups. If groups are too large there will be too much competition
for speaking time and some members may switch off and opt out in spite
of the efforts of the chairman. Equally, some people can only give of their
best in the relative intimacy of a group of say three or four and beyond that
size they simply clam up.

14.2.3 Speed of Processing
a. For Groups. One obvious advantage of groups is that the problem can be
broken down into sections and the sections hived off to different specialists
for prompt action. Working parties may also deal with sub-tasks if the group
is willing and the chairman may act on minor matters to hurry things along.

b. Against Groups. Groups are often slower than individuals. Getting people
together for regular meetings is a thankless task: often crucial members have
to be absent because 'something comes up', and frequent, fully attended
meetings are difficult. There is nothing like the flexibility of the individual,
who can work on the train, after dinner or indeed at any time until he reaches

a solution. Within a meeting there is no more common experience than a slow-moving agenda as a chairman fails to keep people to the point and or to inject pace into the proceedings. Other sources of delay are the time it takes for the slowest members to understand the point in hand, the time it takes to deal with matters only tangential to the point in hand, and the time it takes to bring the most reluctant members into the group agreement. And, of course, the simple process of discussing something in a group can inflate its importance and cause a polarisation of opinions out of all proportion to the significance of the matter. People who know little or nothing about the real issues involved seem especially prone to becoming excited about details. For this reason, fundamental, detailed discussion is best done by smaller groups of experts who then present working papers to the main group.

14.2.4 Creativity

a. For Groups. Group membership produces a higher level of interest in finding solutions. A certain competitive element may serve to sharpen wits and lift the individual's performance, provided he is within the general ability range, and provided the group is welcoming. This is well illustrated by so-called brainstorming groups which seem to work best when the members can choose whom they are going to 'storm' with and when the activity is used as a warm-up for later individual problem solving. Any group is better able to detect errors of fact since members overall have access to wider information than the individual, and can also be more objective about such information.

b. Against Groups. On the other hand, the presence of others can be inhibitory so that 'impossible' ideas never get aired. The most creative people tend to work best alone, with occasional recourse to close colleagues, and can be effectively switched off by a group setting (however, the ideas of mediocre individuals may be improved by the group situation!). Groups may also lack flexibility in following the same line of thinking for too long, whereas the individual is more able to dart in and out of the problem and attack it from all sides.

14.2.5 Interpersonal Factors

a. For Groups. The greater the degree of liking among the members the more effort they make towards integrated decision-making activity. People who are similar in status and attitudes, form stable, stress-free and more enduring groups: similarity promotes general satisfaction while dissimilarity leads to more conflict – although this conflict could well be productive (see the earlier discussion of 'groupthink'). Compatibility of members becomes more crucial as the task becomes more complex.

b. Against Groups. Many good ideas die because they are not listened to (e.g. when they come from a low-status member) or not properly expounded (when they come from a member unable to show dominance because nervous).

Status problems or dislike between members prevents information sharing and co-operation, and dominant but ill-informed members may push the group into a bad decision. Note, however, that once a group has had one or two meetings, it is perceived competence in the group setting that determines who is listened to rather than ascribed status from outside the group. A divisional head amongst section heads can only obtain certain mileage out of his status unless that status is reinforced by demonstrated competence and expertise within the group itself. In general, mixing people of widely different status does not help since it gives rise to inhibitions in both directions. Mixing people of different personalities can also lead to interpersonal difficulties although the fact that people of different personalities tackle the same problems in different ways could increase the group's problem-solving potential.

In practice, committees are usually chosen by outsiders such as departmental heads, on the basis of who can be spared as much as on ability or personality matching. Little wonder that factions, coalitions and apathy so often characterise real-life committees. The best example of ability and compatibility screening is probably provided by the selection of space crews where not just fitting the individual to the job, but also fitting the individual to the team for the job has to be taken very seriously. A shouting match in space between crew and ground control could cost millions of dollars and a good deal of international embarrassment.

Of course, individuals will also use the group for their own selfish personal needs, thereby introducing distortions into the decision-making process. Needs to protect one's own interests, to be dominant, to impress others, to score points or cover up errors are typical examples.

As always, the chairman can achieve a great deal by emphasising the co-operative nature of the task and defusing crises arising from the personal needs of invidual members. Yet it is hardly possible to satisfy all the individual and group objectives at the same time. There has to be some 'trade off', and in order to achieve the best *combined* result the individual has got to sacrifice some of his own needs.

14.2.6 Effort and Reward

a. For Groups. A team represents a mosaic of skills, and members can cover for or bring out the skills of any individual. Thus as a member of a team you can achieve more than you could do alone. And as we saw in Chapter 6, working with a group of good people can inspire the individual to greater efforts. In this sense, the group gives you greater access to reward and often a stronger *feeling* of being rewarded amidst the general shared exhilaration. The experience also has the effect of binding the group closer together.

b. Against Groups. However, unless it is self-evident, group reward does not tell individuals whether their specific contribution was important or negligible in determining success and hence they do not know whether to repeat the same contribution or role on the next occasion. When a sales team receives an accolade from the managing director, some members may feel they have contributed more than others and that this is not being recognised. Future team effort can then be adversely influenced. The problem is worse when a figurehead leader who contributed nothing is the person who actually receives the handshake and praise. There is evidence that people work less hard in a group situation than when they are problem solving alone. One study made a literal test of 'pulling one's weight' by asking young men, either alone or in groups of varying size, to pull as hard as they could on a rope. Theoretically, two people should have pulled twice as hard as one, whereas in fact they pulled slightly less at 1.9 times as hard: the largest discrepancy was in groups of eight which pulled only four times as hard as one person. This seems to reflect the feelings one has about people who like to be carried by others and who are helped by the camouflage the group provides. Diffusion of responsibility also means that a given individual does not have to sweat over whether he is doing the right thing, and this can lead to lazy decision making.

14.2.7 General
In spite of the fact that we have emerged overall with more factors against groups as decision makers than for them, the prevailing view is that small, well-chosen teams can ordinarily do a better job than the individual can. What is more, groups are more likely to be listened to – the decision of a committee or working party is more difficult to contest than the decision of an individual – and through the action that follows will have more enduring influence as a decision-making precedent. This fact alone may be sufficient to justify team rather than individual-based decisions in many situations.

For Groups	Against Groups
Less conservative	Competition for speaking time
More expertise	Slowest members limit efficiency
Can break down problems	Creative members inhibited
Lifts performance	Status prevents information-sharing
More productive	People work less hard
More influential	Reward misses individual contributions

Fig. 14.2: Summary of advantages/disadvantages of group decision making

Work Section

A. Revision Questions

A1 Describe the processes that can be observed between the opening and the closing of a meeting.

A2 Why is it that the decisions of groups are often riskier than those of individuals?

A3 Describe a procedure you might use to bring about acceptance of new technology in a work group.

A4 Is 'groupthink' desirable or undesirable?

A5 Why does the 'personality mix in the group' (14.2.2) affect how well information is processed by that group?

A6 Why do you think some people can only give of their best in a very small group?

A7 What reasons are there for the common tendency of group discussions to spend more time off the point than on it?

A8 Give five reasons why, on balance, groups are more 'creative' in problem solving than individuals.

A9 Give five reasons why individuals may be more efficient than groups.

A10 Why can group decision making often lead to superior implementation than can individual decision making?

A11 Give examples of cases where a group solving problems could be improved by personality clashes.

A12 Why is it that 'compatibility' becomes more important as the problem becomes more complex?

A13 Explain why a group, relative to an individual decision maker, might be more or less inclined to follow a 'satisficing' rule?

B. Exercises/Case Studies

B1 **Group Exercise: The NASA Moon Survival Problem**
Directions: You are members of a space crew originally scheduled to rendezvous with a mother ship on the lighted surface of the moon. Because of mechanical difficulties, however, your ship was forced to land at a spot some 200 miles from the rendezvous point. During reentry and landing, much of the equipment aboard was damaged and, since survival depends on reaching the mother ship, the most critical items available must be chosen for the 200-mile trip. Below are listed the 13 items left

intact and undamaged after landing. Your group task is to rank order them in terms of their importance for your crew in allowing them to reach the rendezvous point. Place the number 1 by the most important item, the number 2 by the second most important and so on through number 13, the least important.

Box of matches
Food concentrate
50 feet of nylon rope
Parachute silk
Portable heating unit
Two .45-calibre pistols
One case dehydrated|milk
Two 100-lb tanks of oxygen
Stellar map (of the moon's constellation)
Magnetic compass
5 gallons of water
First aid kit containing injection needles
Solar-powered FM receiver-transmitter

Are any of the processes in your group discussion similar to those discussed in 14.2?
Source: Jay Hall and W. H. Watson. 'The Effects of a Normative Intervention on Group Decision-Making Performance', *Human Relations*, Vol. 23, No. 4 (Plenum Publishing Corporation, August, 1970), pp. 299–317. The directions and the items to be ranked in importance are presented in the Appendix of the article, pp. 316–17. The NASA Moon Survival Problem was developed by Jay Hall in 1963.

B2 The risky shift phenomenon was actually demonstrated with management students and has subsequently been shown to have broad application throughout the business world at all levels and in many different settings.

There are five possible explanations or part-explanations of why group decisions can be more risky than the average of members' views considered individually:

a. Hearing a more extreme view than one's own actually discussed and evaluated makes it become at least a possibility.

b. In the absence of information individuals act in a way that is unnaturally conservative, whereas providing information by group discussion allows some relaxation to a slightly more open-minded position.

c. Public commitment by the showing of hands provides clear evidence of a shift in the group norm so that change is now not only possible but also desirable.

d. The desire to be compliant and reach early consensus with one's friends and colleagues can lead to blinkered problem analysis.

e. The fact that the group provides camouflage for personal accountability means that the individual is more prepared to chance his arm.

Question: Order these explanations from what you see as the most likely to the least likely and provide notes justifying the order you have chosen.

B3 An electrical engineer who is married and has one child, has been working for a large electronics firm since he left univeristy. He is now 30 and he could expect a job with the electronics firm for the rest of his life; the job would provide a modest salary and liberal pension benefits on retirement. He could not expect any great increase in salary nor substantial retirement benefits.

While on a management training course he is offered a job with a small, newly formed company which has a highly uncertain future. The job is better paid already and would offer possibilities of a financial stake in the ownership of the company if it survived through the first few years.

Questions

a. You are advising this young man. List, independently, the *lowest* probability that you would consider acceptable to make it worthwhile to take the new job. $\frac{10}{10}$ (a certainty that the firm would become successful); $\frac{9}{10}$; $\frac{8}{10}$, etc.

b. Now join with five or six other members who have also made this independent decision. Discuss the matter until a risk level is agreed by all members of the group and compare this consensus view with previous individual acceptance levels. Do not attempt any majority vote or arrive at any numerical averaging.

C. Essay Questions

C1 'The boss tells me we are all to work together as a team,' complained Joe Green to his wife when he returned home from his first day on the new job. 'I suppose I'll never get to do anything my way.' Is there a problem here? How can you reconcile these views?

C2 Does conflict between people improve or interfere with the quality of decisions?

C3 'Group judgement is fiction. If delegation has been carried out properly, one man and not a group has the obligation for making any particular decision. If this man wants the advice of others, he can get it by conversing with them or through staff and control reports. Forming a committee is a sure way to get men to abrogate their responsibilities and is a costly and time-consuming use of executive time.' How would you reply to this statement?

C4 A product manager of a food company explained that all major decisions on the group of breakfast foods he was 'responsible' for were made not by him but by a product management committee. He was chairman of the committee that included vice-presidents in charge of the production, sales, and research departments. What advantages do you see to such an arrangement? What potential drawbacks?

C5 In what ways are 'collective bargaining' and 'group decision making' similar and dissimilar?

Chapter 15

Implementation and Change

Synopsis: *In this chapter we complete our presentation of the general decision model by looking at the stages following the taking of the decision. A decision is not taken in one gulp: it has to be tested, perhaps through test marketing or simulation studies, and then in all probability adjusted accordingly. This decision – test – revision sequence may be repeated several times before doubts gradually give way to a sense of commitment. At commitment we have 'gone public' and the decision is now for practical purposes irreversible. There is an increased feeling of confidence in the choice we have made, and a simultaneous devaluation of what had been earlier plausible alternative choices. From commitment we now move in the general decision model to implementation, noting that the consequences of implementation can as often be unexpected and unplanned as planned. Concerning* methods *of implementing change in the organisation, we discuss the principle of changing opinions, attitudes and behaviour, then describe two techniques for implementing these changes: the use of an outside consultant and training programmes. The final topic area in this chapter is also the last component in the general decision model: feedback. It emphasises the crucial importance of feedback in shaping the future efforts of decision makers and shows why feedback from a labour force can so often be negative. We end thoughtfully by asking whether resistance to change in an organisation might have positive aspects.*

Plan of the chapter. *This is illustrated in Fig. 15.1.*

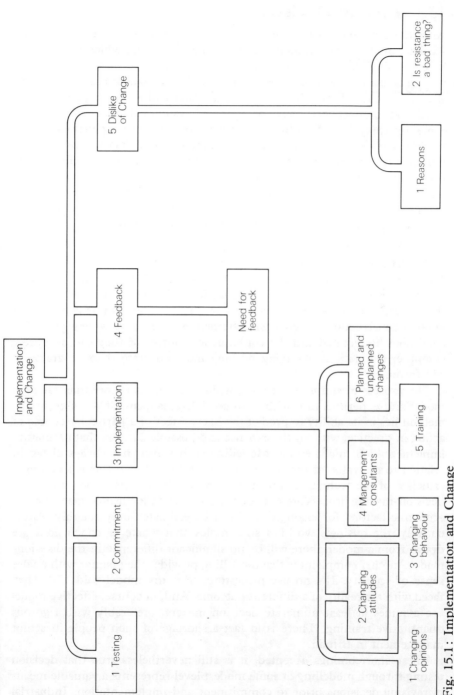

Fig. 15.1: Implementation and Change

15.1 Testing Decisions

After the decision has been taken there is a period – which may be only seconds, but is more commonly days or longer – during which the decision is reversible. The hand is moving towards the lever but has not yet pulled it.... The banns have not yet been read.... The agreement has not yet actually been signed. Between the time of decision and actual implementation it is the fate of most decisions to be 'unmade' to some extent as *decision testing* comes into play. This 'test loop' – as it is represented in the general decision model – acts back on the decision and reshapes it as necessary. Thus by examining a test market or a scale model we can determine the viability of the original decision. In practice this sequence of decision – test –adjust – decision – test – adjust can take place many times before commitment to final details takes place. In the following section we shall look briefly at an example of the decision test loop in action, through simulation studies.

15.1.1 Simulation with Models

Models are, in effect, methods of representing the real world in a way that allows for experimentation and investigation. The different types of model that we can choose facilitate different approaches. They can be actual wood or metal constructions tested in wind tunnels or water tanks, where simulated conditions are created and the consequences noted, or they can be purely computer simulations involving nothing more concrete than programmes and formulae.

The process of simulation testing is, in principle, no more than taking a model and experimenting with it to see what happens. The value of the method lies in its ability to predict the likely effect of a particular course of action in practice, without the expense and possible dangers that premature implementation might entail. Modelling is, however, not always cheap in relation to the value of the results that are achieved, and this is a common criticism of the technique. Further, many of the factors which affect the decision-making process are outside the control of the businessman (macroeconomic factors, for example) and can be estimated only roughly. Alternatively, the business world is so complex that whatever conclusions are drawn from a model, there will be no significant difference in the decisions made. Another complaint is that modelling provides the planner with a false sense of security. It's no use protesting, 'But my model said...,' when faced with the reality of a different outcome. And, of course, effective model use assumes at least numerate decision makers, preferably with rigorous quantitative training. There is in fact a shortage of such people in senior management in Britain.

These shortcomings accepted, it is still nevertheless true that decision testing through modelling at some modest level represents a valuable means of revising decisions prior to commitment and implementation. Industrial market research is another very common example, sounding out potential customers and using the information obtained to develop a model of the kind of product they want. A beautifully conceived machine tool represents a very poor investment if it fails to meet the latest specifications of the people who are supposed to buy it.

15.2 Commitment to Decisions

As testing draws to a close and the time for implementation approaches there may still be vacillation, but this is gradually replaced by a hardening of the decision state until we reach a point called *commitment*. At this point you can no longer reverse your decision without, say, heavy financial penalties or international embarrassment – you are committed even though costs may soar to absurd heights!

Consider the following example. Suppose you have two equally attractive options in your business: to go for small orders and faster payments, or to go for bigger orders with slower returns. You consider all the information laid before you, such as it is, and then make what turns out to be a difficult decision. Your decision is as yet only tentative – it can be revoked. You 'test' the decision by discussing it with other businessmen, and you go into a phase of wondering if you are doing the right thing. But as soon as you *commit* yourself – for example, by making a public statement – you then find yourself dwelling on all the advantages of your choice together with the disadvantages of the alternative choice. The consequence of this strange psychological bolstering-up exercise, and one we have all experienced, is that two alternative choices which a few hours or even minutes earlier had been juggled very closely as *real* alternatives suddenly become polar opposites as you hear yourself saying to a colleague, 'Of course the long-term approach was full of pitfalls; world prices are just too unstable for that kind of commitment.' If you had chosen the alternative then you would have been uttering the opposite rationalisation. For difficult decisions, genuine doubt, although discomforting and tension producing, seems a necessary prelude to commitment. But once we have made the commitment, doubt is no longer something we have to live with so we attack it by boosting the virtues of our particular choice and simultaneously demeaning the alternative course of action. Moreover, we actually defend ourselves against post-decision information which shows how marvellous the other choice would have been: if we search around for a 'best buy', finally deciding that Brown's is the best, we get very cross with someone who comes along and says we could have got it cheaper at Smith's, although beforehand, of course, we would have been extremely grateful for that same information.

15.2.1 Factors Influencing Commitment
a. Volition. There is no commitment to a decision made under duress or in unnatural circumstances: free choice (or what a person feels is free choice) is essential.

b. Interlock with Contingent Decisions. There will be more commitment when the decision taking initiates a whole chain of subsequent commitments: the effort of 'undeciding' the whole chain is so formidable that the person would rather go along with a poor decision – perhaps even a wrong decision – than attempt to unmake it.

c. 'Publicness' of Decision. If the person is publicly seen (e.g. by other committee members or through a newspaper report) to have taken the decision and to be personally responsible for it there will be considerable commitment to carry it through.

d. Irrevocability. If it is impossible to change a decision then you may as well have total commitment to it. A common example is mistaken long-term planning which gives us a bridge we do not need, or wrongly pressing the button which aborts a space launch.

e. Importance to the Person. If your prestige or your future career is at stake on the decision, you may display almost religious commitment to it. But for decisions about, say, which card to play in poker, you may more easily laugh and admit to a blunder since the personal or financial stakes are usually trivial.

Following commitment the decision maker shuts off conflicting information and an awful lot of counterindicative information is needed to change his mind, partly because of the polarisation process we have noted and partly because commitment is a *personal* thing and needs defending as such. Of course to the outsider who knows the true value of a new piece of information this cavalier dismissal seems highly irrational; we saw in Chapter 14 in talking about 'groupthink' how dangerous such a clamp-down on new information can be.

15.3 Implementation

Once we have some form of commitment we can turn to putting the decision into practice. Implementing any significant decision requires *communication skills* to make sure that the right people have the right information at the right time, *social skills* to ensure these people are properly prepared to receive the idea of change without feeling undue anxiety, and of course *technical skills* to make sure that the recommended changes, be they in assembly line layout or in organisational reporting practices, are in fact correctly executed.

15.3.1 Changing Opinions

Having made the decision, *how* do we implement the required changes in the people affected? The decision may require simply changes in people's ways of looking at things (opinions), or it may require changes in behaviour as when automation is introduced into a firm which had been getting by with traditional methods. Taking the first case first, the most impressive contribution to the psychology of changing people's opinions has been due to Carl

Hovland and his fellow psychologists at Yale in the 1950s. For example, they found that a message is more effective if it is counter to the self-interests of the speaker: a senior manager putting forward a fair-play-for-the unions argument will be more convincing that a senior union official arguing the same theme. The prestige of the speaker was also found to be a very important factor in determining the *extent* of opinion change in the audience.

A question that often crosses one's mind in trying to present a persuasive argument is whether it is better to present a little of the opposing view or stick to a single-minded presentation of one's own case. Hovland tried out the alternatives on soldiers towards the end of the Second World War. Employing an argument to the effect that the war with Japan would be much more drawn out than generally thought, one group received only reasons why the war would be protracted (one-sided approach) while a second group were in addition given *some* reasons for thinking it could in fact be a much shorter war (two-sided approach). The **one-sided persuasion** was more effective on the relatively uneducated and on those soldiers who already believed some protraction of the war was inevitable. The two-sided approach was more effective on those who were initially of the opposite view, and the better educated soldiers. Changes were also rather longer lasting. Thus, in so far as we can generalise from this kind of finding to the realms of business, knowing your target audience is very important in determining what approach to take.

Since, as we have just noted, intelligence levels come into the propaganda equation, you might expect that personality also must be taken into account. Hovland found that the more persuasible people are those who have feelings of personal inadequacy and who are very conformist in their social behaviour.

15.3.2 Changing Attitudes

Although well-fixed attitudes do not change nearly as readily as casual opinions, they can and do change. Some attitudes change by themselves simply through age and experience: heavy spending teenagers become thrifty savers when they marry; shopfloor staff who are promoted over the years gradually change their attitude to 'management'.

A good start in trying to change attitudes is to try to understand why the attitude is in fact held. For example, if a manager holds certain attitudes towards the workforce because by holding them he gains the approval of his superiors, it is going to be rather hard to 'change the attitude'. A more useful approach would be to offer better or easier ways of earning the same, or more, respect and approval – in ways which are incompatible with the original attitude. Another way of bringing about change is to make holding the attitude no longer rewarding, perhaps by making the point of view unfashionable. However, the more central an attitude – the more locked into a basic belief – the more difficult it is to change it. Similarly, if the attitude under focus is one of a similar set then the rest of the attitudes in that set will act to prevent change. For example, anyone who dislikes *all* sports (general attitude) will be harder to get to a football match than someone who only dislikes one other sport. Think of a single attitude as a jigsaw piece that slides easily on the table but which moves less and less readily as more additional pieces are fitted into it (the rest of the set).

Another factor which makes attitudes relatively immovable is the fact that they may be held not just by the person himself but also by his family and by the people he goes around with. He is part of a 'social jigsaw', and if he changes his attitude he risks ridicule by these people. It follows that in addition to aiming at a person's underlying belief system, another approach would be to alter the views of people he likes and goes around with (rather difficult) or (easier) to alter his view so that he wants to identify with a different group that has views more in line with your target attitude. Just making a foreman into an executive immediately shifts his frame of reference so the necessary changes in attitudes will to some extent automatically follow. Still in the work situation, two individuals or groups with conflicting attitudes towards each other can have their conflict reduced through the creation of a co-operative work situation. The mutual prejudices held by British and immigrant workers tend to smooth out when they are working at a bench together, especially if they are part of the same team where the output and job satisfaction of each member is interdependent with that of the others.

Another tactic in bringing about attitude change is to invoke some overriding value or attitude: for example, a person can be persuaded to take on a part-time job as a salesman or collector not by any appeal to the worth of the job as such, but by pointing out that these few hours enable him to buy the things he would like to give his family. Similarly, people have been persuaded to kill 'for the good of the country'.

15.3.3 Changing Behaviour

As often as not when we ask the question 'Can we change their attitudes?', what we really mean is 'Can we get them to act differently?'. For example, manufacturers are much more concerned about whether the public buy their goods than whether they have positive attitudes towards them. We said in Chapter 6 that the links between attitude and behaviour are not always strong. Most people have strongly positive attitudes to Oxfam appeals but very few send any money. The point is that attitudes do give rise to **intentions**, but these intentions are by no means always fulfilled: we see a marvellous gadget we simply 'must have' advertised in the Sunday colour supplements and we intend to fill in the coupon and post it off with a cheque immediately after breakfast. But we rarely do this. Carl Hovland, whom we met earlier when talking about opinion change, also investigated behaviour change through the use of emotional appeals. The theme was 'dental hygiene'. One group of people were subjected to an approach emphasising the painful and cosmetic consequences of tooth decay and diseased gums. The second group received a less severe version of the same approach, while a third group covered the same ground using a yet milder approach which did not press home the consequences of tooth decay. And it was this last 'mild fear' group which showed most changes in tooth brushing practices when questioned a week later. In fact, amount of change in behaviour *de*creased with amount of 'fear' in the original mesage. This may be because anxiety or repulsion acts as a distractor from the essential message, or, indeed, causes the listener to reject the package as a whole. Rather similar findings have emerged in studying the effects of road-safety propaganda where too much horror seems definitely counter-productive. But, as we said, a modicum of anxiety is helpful in bringing about behaviour change: the best procedure is to arouse anxiety, say about lung cancer, *then* follow this with practical advice on how to stop smoking, i.e. on resolving the anxiety. Doing it the other way round – information followed by depiction of the consequences of disregarding it – does not work well, probably because the original information is not well assimilated (since there was no anxiety) and when anxiety is subsequently aroused no way is offered of resolving it.

15.3.4 **The Management Consultant as a Force for Change**
Management consultants come in all shapes and sizes. Some are systems analysts or financial advisers who aim to bring about change by modifying the organisation as a structure. Another type more central to the theme of this book is the behavioural consultant who focuses on the personnel making up that structure. Solutions offered by consultants are often so simple as to have managers wonder, 'Why didn't we do it ourselves and put the fee into the staff fund?'

The single fact that allows the outside consultant to play his magical role is that he is indeed an *outsider*, not subject to the constraints imposed by employer–employee relations. As we saw when discussing 'groupthink' in Chapter 14, it is very difficult even for a fairly senior person to intervene in top-level decision making which he feels is taking the wrong direction. He is worried about the 1 per cent chance that he *may* be making a fool of himself, and the fact that the chairman will interpret his objections in terms of 'poor old Smith worrying again'. The net effect, as we saw, is that boards of directors can hypnotise themselves into a course of action which observers are powerless to prevent. It is therefore remarkable that a relatively young and inexperienced outsider may be needed to lead 'decision makers' into doing what they really suspected all along had to be done. Note that the behavioural consultant is not like the systems analyst or scientific consultant who simply feeds his skills into the organisation as and when required. He is a participator himself: he mixes with different personnel and work groups to talk to staff and get the 'feel' of problem areas both actual and latent. He will probably spend most of his time with top management who have the power to initiate change, offering a range of possible courses of action they could take in various areas of stress and dissatisfaction. He will try to show the consequences of each available choice, but it is up to the organisation to make its own choice.

It is interesting how an organisation buzzes when a consultant is around: there is a brave new feeling that at least the company is on the threshold of big changes and everyone perks up. In so far as the consultant is the agent of change he has to use this group willingness to act as soon as it starts to appear, since consultancy ideas shelved now will be very difficult to implement later when inertia has once more healed over.

15.3.5 Change Through Training
In the 1970s the government invested many millions of pounds in retraining programmes designed to increase flexibility of movement among different industries. At the level of sheer *technical* skill the programmes seemed fairly successful, although factors such as union resistance and the changing economic situation prevented full benefits being obtained. The problem with training programmes in *management* skills seems to be that although such programmes can be very uplifting for the participants at the time, once they return to familiar pastures they are awkward about applying new skills especially when their new-found sophistication provokes jibes from superiors and juniors alike. Trainees also discover that the return to the old working context tends to evoke in themselves the same old behaviours and that the constraints of reality have a different flavour from those of the role-playing situations they experienced in the training programme.

As is well recognised in psychotherapy, it is little use having a patient who says and does all the right things during therapy but who picks up the same problems immediately he gets home. Accordingly some attempt should be made to restructure the environment as well as the manager himself: in this way those around will be more prepared to receive the new behaviour and foster it. For this reason, group training which brings together all managers, rather than dealing with individuals, should have a better chance of succeeding. Nobody would think of training a football team as individuals and then bringing them together on the day and hoping it will go all right, but something like this is often expected from management. There may even be something to be said for training whole sections of an organisation en bloc in order that change is simultaneously transmitted as a common expectation to all members at all levels.

As would be expected, implementation problems such as these are most severe following 'human relations' training and least severe after purely technical training. It is anyway pretty unrealistic to expect too much from a short course. Perhaps the most that can be hoped for is a sensitisation of the trainee to other possible styles and solutions and for some marginal influence to be reflected in the everyday decisions he later makes.

15.3.6 Planned and Unplanned Changes
Implementing any decision has both planned and unplanned consequences – the latter cannot be avoided since we live in a world of changing con-

straints and imperfect information. Everyone is pleased by the planned move to a bright new headquarters building – at first. Then unforeseen consequences of the move gradually emerge. In the new set-up, the post room is no longer across the corridor from the sales office, which is now more 'efficiently' located. Thus an informal but highly efficient communication link between despatch and sales, which appeared nowhere on the organisational chart but evolved in such a way that the outflow from the firm depended on it, is lost. Other unplanned side-effects can be even more subtle, at the level of morale perhaps, and might never be diagnosed. Thus in aiming at one target problem – the obviously cramped accommodation – you have caused ripple effects in dependent systems.

The decision environment is rather like a bowl of greasy ball bearings: disturbing any one is bound to cause slippage in contingent decision structures which before were quite stable. Crises from unforeseen aspects of change arise not only internally but externally through economic forces. Fashion affects market demand, new technology makes your products obsolete, new legislation prevents you pumping waste into waterways. One-product companies are particularly vulnerable to change crises from external constraints. If you only make radio valves and the world wants transistors, you are in trouble; if you only make transistors and the market wants integrated circuits you are again in trouble. Yet a firm which had diversified at the earliest technologically opportune moment into the next generation of components, would have buffered itself against the tougher aspects of change and even benefited from it. Thus diversification is one major way in which the organisation can protect itself against the unplanned, the unexpected. Two other forms of organisational 'defence' against being caught out by change are: (i) maintaining active market intelligence and product development departments whose antennae listen forward into the future; (ii) providing substantial reserves so that brief crises can be ridden out while the company reorients itself.

These varied changes as a result of implementing decisions are found not only at the level of the organisation but at the level of its individual members. Some of these changes are of course planned either by the organisation, as in the case of training schemes, or by the individual himself, who may decide to take professional examinations, get married, take a weekend job, and so on. But of course many changes in one's personal constraints can again be unplanned. A sudden illness or death of a close member of the family will affect both the efficiency and the outlook of the person who makes decisions, and possibly cause him to rethink the values on which he previously made those decisions. Because we typically see our colleagues only at work we overlook the importance of events in their domestic lives as factors in their work efficiency.

15.4 Feedback

You have now signed the contract, pressed the button, or in some other way terminated the decision–test–commitment–implementation sequence. The consequences of your action will now feed back to modify the structure of the constraints which has operated on the decision in the first place. For example, supposing last year you decided to convert an unwanted warehouse into a new staff canteen: today you see your vision implemented, and you are as hungry for feedback as the staff are for their first lunch. The feedback consequences of your decision can be summarised as follows:

- virtual elimination of a major *problem* producing discontented employees;
- considerable improvement in staff morale and related *external constraints* with the result that future management–staff decision making will be generally facilitated;
- a boost for your own self-confidence and sense of importance in the firm with a consequent increase in liking for your own job (*personal contraints*).

It follows that this feedback aspect in the general decision model is an essential *motivator* for the decision maker, showing him what he has or has not achieved and accordingly setting his aspiration levels for future occasions.

15.4.1 Need for Feedback

Unless the decision maker is *told* either that he miscalculated or that he ought to have involved the catering manager at an earlier stage, or that many staff still prefer to use the snack bar, and so on, he will have no opportunity to learn from experience. His actions will still feed back to affect the initial problem and modify the external constraints surrounding that problem but they will not feed back to modify the man himself. Without feedback you cannot learn any skill – and this involves the skill of decision making. Nor can you learn whether you have solved the real problem or only a symptom. Nor can your own interest and motivation be sustained.

Participative planning is powerful because it maximises a constant feedback loop between those making the decision and those affected by the decision. Quantitative feedback is most effective since this tells you exactly what you have done right or wrong and how much adjustment is needed. Qualitative feedback in the form of praise (or abuse) is on balance less useful.

15.5 Dislike of Change

15.5.1 Reasons for Dislike

Change is unwelcome when we believe that personal needs previously being satisfied might be no longer satisfied in the new situation. The more central the need the more obstinate the person if he feels change will disturb it.

Thus any change which affects needs at the foundation of Maslow's hierarchy (Chapter 2) will strike at the very roots of our existence and will typically be vigorously opposed. Examples:

i.   Economic or financial reversals: we are all singularly selfish in this respect and will normally only consider our own situation rather than any group or national good. We also seem particularly prone to consider the short term rather than the long term.

ii. Increase in work effort or complexity: we all seem to have the idea that our present level of work is right and we naturally rebel against increases – unless we are financially well rewarded.

iii. Dislike of learning new job skills. Ironically, effort at 'job enrichment' can be received as unwelcome change. Supervisors are especially prone to feelings of having power taken from them and of being bypassed in organisational restructuring.

iv. Uncertainty: whenever change is in the wind people want to know what is happening. If official channels do not meet this need with planned information, the grapevine will start to hum and as uncertainty increases yet more fantastic 'information' is passed on.

v.   Change in social relationships or status: to the extent that people become 'bonded' into their work groups, they worry about splitting or reassigning the group or giving it another leader who may not be liked.

vi. General attitude of self and group. Our general attitude may be against change. This is unfortunately common in industry today where the unions and management distrust each other and will not accept change, especially if initiated from 'above'. The response to a new bonus scheme proposed by the managing director is quite different from the response to the same scheme proposed by a shop steward.

The employee can protect himself from what he sees as adverse change in a number of ways. First, he can attempt to renegotiate the effects of higher policy decisions which have spilled down to his level. For example, if a maintenance team is now to rob him of a valued sense of responsibility for his own machine he can pass his observations up through the organisational hierarchy or, if he well recognises the kinds of transmission distortions we discussed in Chapter 13, he may well go direct to the managing director himself. Secondly, he can bring the problem to the attention of the shop steward, who will then decide whether to make formal representation, and in what way. Thirdly, there is another group of responses which include working to rule, with or without union backing, non-cooperation, and ultimately withdrawal of labour. Finally, in extreme cases he can, individually or through his union, have recourse to the law: claims for unfair dismissal or compensation for industrial accidents are common examples.

15.5.2 Is Resistance to Change Necessarily a Bad Thing?

Sometimes one is labelled reactionary or even disloyal if one speaks out against change. But those who resist can have certain points in their favour:

a. Often those affected by the changes can see woolly thinking or even potential disaster and can press for greater precision.
b. They expose situations where there has been inadequate discussion and possibly a grievous shortage of information or poor communication, since those producing the change may have failed to clarify the purpose and the results which they hope will be achieved.
c. While the theoretical need for change may be relatively simple to see, what is often left poorly considered are the human consequences of actions. There may be an obligation to put in support and training programmes specifically aimed at meeting the individual needs of those to be affected by changes.

Work Section

A. Revision Questions

A1 Summarise the advantages and disadvantages of simulation using models.

A2 What characterises that state of mind in the decision maker we refer to as 'commitment'?

A3 How can 'unplanned' changes come about in a properly planned decision?

A4 List some useful principles from the psychological study of:
   a. Changing opinions.
   b. Changing attitudes.
   c. Changing behaviour.

A5 Why is it harder to change someone's behaviour than to change his opinion?

A6 Why can a management consultant be so potent an influence in bringing about organisational change?

A7 What are the limitations of management training programmes?

A8 Describe the functions of feedback for the decision maker.

A9 Why do people dislike decisions that require them to change their ways?

A10 Write out the complete series of stages in the general decision model between 'problem perception' and 'feedback'.

B. Exercises/Case Studies

B1 We emphasised the importance of the test loop before commitment to any final decision and used the example of simulation with real or mathematical models. Test marketing is another example of trying out a new product or marketing technique before commitment to a decision involving an expensive national campaign. Imagine you were in the position of mounting such an exercise. Write a case study showing how an early decision might show progressive changes as the decision – test – adjust sequence comes into repeated operation.

B2 You are the industrial relations adviser in a medium-sized chemicals firm which is facing inevitable changes as a result of being bought out by a larger international company. These changes are bound to include redundancies, staff redeployment, and changes in ways of doing things.

The managing director has had the foresight to ask you to prepare a pamphlet of principles, guidelines, pitfalls and similar considerations to be borne in mind when significant organisational changes have to be implemented. Write out a set of perhaps 10–20 points which you would eventually want to develop in producing your pamphlet. Search through the present chapter to find your points, but do not hesitate to have recourse to previous chapters as well.

B3 Fashion Ltd was started in the East End of London just after the Second World War. The firm was one of many making up garments for the middle section of the market. It has been successful because of sound working practices and good management–worker relations. As was normal, virtually all the workers were women.

In 1978 the lease of its old multi-storey building ran out and it was decided that this was the moment to move from London. After a short search, a new building on a trading estate in Harlow New Town (about 20 miles northeast of London) was found. The building was single-storey and the floor area would allow for some expansion in the years ahead. In Harlow as a whole there were found to be about 5,000 male manual jobs and only about 1,500 for women; these latter were largely in light assembly work and women were commonly employed as they were cheaper than men.

Early in 1979 the move was made and the firm had no difficulty in keeping ten of its most experienced seamstresses. The remainder of the labour force was recruited locally. The firm was able to recruit the 70 women they needed at the old London rate. This proved to be a low wage for females in employment in Harlow.

When they first moved in they kept the old system of production which the firm had used from its inception. The 80 women were organised in groups of four. Each group sat around a table which was large enough to hold sewing machines and material (see Fig. 15.2). The exact division of the work within each group was decided by its members (the senior operative being finally responsible for making a decision). It had been traditional for groups to complete each garment from scratch. The whole was overseen by one supervisor whose job was to hand out the tasks, check bonus rates and quality. She also helped new entrants.

This bonus rate was paid according to each group's output. If the girls disagreed with the supervisor, the production manager was called in and the girls were sometimes timed in action. The system was primitive but worked quite well with goodwill on both sides. In general, the pay was average for the garment trade but, as previously explained, a little low for Harlow. However, the girls seemed happy and their morale was high.

There were generally about three major designs in production at any one time and each design would be produced for from one to four days. It was necessary for each group to collect material and patterns from the Cloth Store and, on completion, to deliver them to the Finished

Goods Store. The output of each group was recorded each day on the notice-board near the entrance.

Thus production was running smoothly, but 1979 had been a bad year for sales. The economic climate had been difficult and there was less money being spent in the shops on clothes. Because of this, competition within the trade had increased and margins had been squeezed.

At the time of the move, early in 1979, a new production manager was appointed. He had agreed to keep the traditional system in the early days at the new works but now, at the end of the first year, he had become convinced that reorganisation was desirable. Basically, he saw the need for greater job specialisation which he considered would increase output per head by between 20 and 25 per cent. He suggested the following plan:

The factory should be organised in 3 main groups of 20 women each. Members of each group would specialise in particular jobs, the time cycle for which, would be between 60 and 70 seconds each. The division of work could be scientifically devised and controlled by himself and the supervisor. Such a scheme would need a reorganisation of work benches (which could easily be carried out) so that work flowed from one member to another.

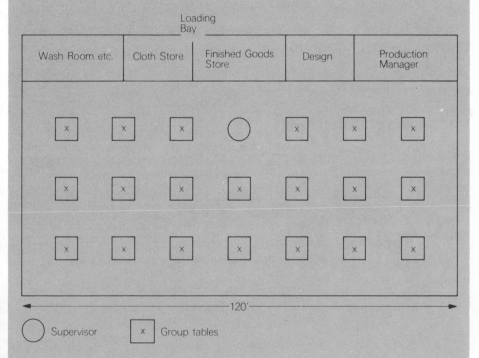

Fig. 15.2 Present Factory Layout at Harlow

In addition to the 3 major groups there would be up to 3 smaller groups of 4 each. These would be for training purposes, to do one-off jobs, and to stand in for members absent from the main groups.

He insisted that no extra physical work would be required by the women to produce the extra output: in fact, this might diminish slightly as a result of the superior organisation.

Questions

1. What are the apparent advantages of the present production and payment system?
2. Suggest a new factory layout which would be suitable for the new policy.
3. If you were the managing director, would you make the change? Give reasons.
4. Given the conditions of Fashion Ltd, what problems would you expect to arise during the changeover from the old to the new system?
5. The director has been concerned with the following matters and has asked for a report on each. Write, in 300 words, a short report on each.
   a. What criteria should be used in judging the methods and level of payments made to the workers?
   b. What are the main factors to be considered in deciding a future pricing policy for Fashion Ltd?
6. In the light of your knowledge about location comment on the factors mentioned.
7. What other factors might have been considered by a large shirt manufacturer who was planning to set up in the United Kingdom for the first time?

C. Essay Questions

C1 Why do you think that the link between what you, as an organisation, decide to do and what you actually do is often a weak one? Is this necessarily a bad thing?

C2 How would you set up a management training programme, taking into account difficulties mentioned in the chapter?

C3 How might you introduce a more favourable productivity scheme into an engineering department?

C4 Why do some people appear to welcome and encourage change, while some fight hard against it?

C5 What are the major advantages and limitations of using outside consultancies in making decisions affecting a firm?

Chapter 16

Future Decisions

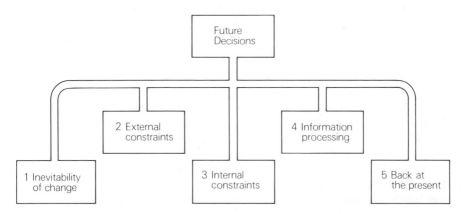

Fig. 16.1: Future Decisions

16.1 Inevitability of Change

This brief chapter is no more than a coda to the book as a whole. Painting future scenarios is always fraught with hazard and can be tedious if carried too far. In the following sections we would like to no more than catch the flavour of the changes that will be shooting us through the 1980s and into the century ahead.

Change links the past with the present and with the future. As I sit innocently drafting this page, manufacturers are making decisions about my range of work and leisure choices for the year ahead. The courts are passing judgements whose ripple effects will act as at least a marginal constraint on my own behaviour. Scientists and technologists who have given us nuclear energy, television and space travel in a mere hiccup of historical time are now bent on yet bigger changes. Change is occurring all the time, within us and around us: a point which has concerned us right from the opening chapter of this book. The rate and extent of this change of course varies. Sometimes it is so gentle as to be imperceptible, as in the case of growing older or gaining increasing job confidence; sometimes trivial as in the case of 'white collars' being given separate tables in the canteen; sometimes major as in the case of the introduction of new production methods, and sometimes violent, as in the case of worker revolutions.

Because we exist in this flux of continuous change, when we repeat today the same solutions as last year, last week or, strictly, even yesterday, it is being done within a *different* pattern of constraints. Of course many people *pretend* that things do not change. In their own heads they adopt the steady-state model: their decision making becomes a matter of habit rather than genuine rethinking. Such people will at the very least be making sub-optimal decisions and may even be courting danger. It sometimes takes catastrophes such as factory explosions or financial ruin to unfreeze such fixed decision habits. The very best decision makers take change by the scruff of the neck and make it work in thé direction they want. These are the great thinkers, social architects, statesmen and business entrepreneurs who shape the behaviour and even the thoughts of people throughout the civilised world. But even the humblest administrator must accept that values are changing – whether he planned it or not and whether he likes it or not – and that these changing values, both personal and external to him, must be reflected in the choices he makes. It is salutary to review our long-serving general decision model to see how the internal and external constraints, as well as the processing function itself, are all going to change in the coming years.

16.2 External Constraints

'Science and technology' in our general decision model will be *the* massive and changing constraint. It will give us a superb example of an external constraint imposing changes on the pattern of the individual's needs, skills and on his modes of processing information. Really, most of the problems arising in organisations are associated with deficiencies in the human processing of information. 'Should I tell X about this or keep quiet?' 'What is the proper span of control for a management team?' 'Should we centralise or decentralise our decisions?' The reciprocal problems of trust and control should become less when human decision making is computer-backed, since the scope for subordinates to make mistakes will be reduced. Expertise will instantly be available throughout the organisation so that the foreman (if he or she exists) will only call the works manager (if he or she exists) when some unprogrammed eventuality comes up or a malfunction develops which the system cannot itself repair. The functions of staff and line will come much closer together since there will no longer be a 'shop floor' in the present-day sense. While increasing computer control of dangerous or tedious work is obviously desirable in itself, it is bound to increase problems, first of overmanning and then of unemployment. As we said previously, 'solutions' never really solve anything: they merely present us with a different level of problem.

The skilled 'in danger' are those in the highly technologised industries where they may well be swallowed up by automation, but plumbers, farmers, surgeons, the executors of high-grade motor skills should find their jobs protected for longer, if this is what they want. But even here, for example, automatic planting and harvesting is around the corner, and the day may come when the patient who has already provisionally diagnosed himself using the home-based interactive medical computer now turns up at the 'hospital' and is automatically anaesthetised, operated on and returned to the post-op ward (still being monitored of course) all without the intervention of human hands – or human error.

Media will become much more pervasive. Readers will be able to call up on their home video screens a complete 'newspaper' of any date, or even certain pages, which they may wish to turn into full colour and photocopy. Exposure to propagandist material could become less voluntary than nowadays since agencies may be able to interrupt or automatically bypass the on–off switch for certain kinds of information. And of course the possibility of storing massive amounts of data about private citizens raises new ethical questions.

16.3 Internal Constraints

The character of human needs and motives has changed considerably from the first industrial revolution to the present, and we may expect the new technological revolution to bring about further change. Work is important not just because it satisfies economic needs, but also because it fulfils social needs such as to be liked and respected by others. People, however, are going to figure less and less in the world of work as automation takes over. They will stay at home, where social needs can be less readily satisfied. Intensive development of leisure groups where people can derive satisfaction from 'leisuring' together will remedy this. New technology also *creates* its own needs. The consumer who had to have televisions and washing machines simply because they had been invented will eventually have to have a domestic robot with at least as many programs as that of the Joneses next door. Thus technology opens up possibilities of experience which become a need, and this need has to be satisfied or people become frustrated and angry. Although we spoke about money as a special motivator, differentials may become less tied to money. Certainly the decline in physical handling of monies which has been taking place over many years through increasing use of cheques and credit cards can be expected to increase with the advent of computerised tills in supermarkets which can be linked not only to warehouse stock computers, but also to the bank computer, which will debit your account automatically without money cards or cheques changing hands. And why bother having a shop when you can call up any catalogue and price list on your home terminal, key-in the order and wait for automatic delivery? Perhaps the question of motivating man to work will eventually be turned upside down: in the same way that 'unemployed' has a negative ring about it, 'working' may take on a similar image since only the silly people will have to work – the clever ones will be 'leisuring'.

16.4 Information Processing and Decisions

The microelectronic revolution is a revolution in information handling. Since information is the raw material of decisions it follows that changes in range, style and presumably quality of decisions are also imminent. Access to information will become universal. Information systems such as Prestel are only the beginning. There is no reason why the information and the creative ideas of the best brains in the world could not be available for general access via a terminal in the office or home. Interaction with such computers would allow critical-path analysis for diagnosing illnesses. 'Incoming mail' would now be a queue of messages waiting to be called up. Writing a reply would also be a thing of the past – you dictate to your computer, which displays your 'letter' which you then voice-edit; you then press the 'Despatch' key and the letter is immediately passed and stored, to be called up by your addressee as he also sorts his 'incoming mail'.

Computers will free us from being tied to a desk: in the same way that the busy executive now dictates while driving home in the evening, it will be possible for senior executives to have interactive voice plus video control over any personnel, or any information, anywhere in their empire, anywhere in the world – from the side of their pools. Hence the migration of senior personnel to warmer climes – everywhere is central now, and actual travelling between places is unusual and rather old-fashioned.

In the realms of decision making itself, shareholders may no longer need boards of directors to look after all or, indeed, any of their interests. Interactive video links with the controlling manager, together with the possibility of mass tele-voting, will make for more direct and more sensitive control of the shareholders' own interests. Of course what works for shareholders can also be made to work for the unions and for customer firms. All may wish to have interactive links into the firm's decision-making processes, so that 'participative decision making' may have to occur on a much grander scale than implied by the term nowadays. Interactive television systems will also downgrade the role of members of parliament as people's representatives: the people will be told what issues are coming up, and they will key in their votes to be processed at the appropriate time by the parliamentary computer. With such interaction the issues themselves which are to be debated can be decided by the people – since the expertise once held by solicitors, doctors, university lecturers, and by all professionals is now banked with the central computer for use by all. Thus decision making will become more total, in the sense of taking into account more information, less subject to human biases and distortions of the kind we discussed in this book. It will also become more total in the sense of involving more people: this means greater participation by the staff in running the firm and by citizens in running the country. Free information flow is the very thing that breaks down mutual prejudices and allows people to realise that we are all much, much more similar than we are different. Dare we hope that the 'them' and 'us' problems of industry will then be resolved?

16.5 Meanwhile – Back at the Present

In this book we have taken the individual decision maker as our primary focus. Within the framework of a simple decison model we have assembled the component parts of his psychological make-up and observed how he operates as information processor and ultimately as decision maker. But we have always been mindful of the real-world constraints that limit his choices, constraints arising from the wishes of other people such as colleagues and superiors, politicians, lawyers, policemen, and so on. No decision maker is an island, and our reference context has always been as much social and sociological as strictly individual. We have found it essential to consider organisational as well as individual needs; organisational as well as individual attitudes; organisational as well as personal change, and indeed organisational as well as individual decision making. And along the way we have picked up context information on such topics as organisational structures, and the nature and role of the trades unions. At the end of all this, the reader should have developed some basic feel for the decision-making environment.

You may well have started this book hoping and expecting that all was about to be revealed. So it has been – or a large amount anyway. But, you protest, precisely how does it help me do any better with the wretched people I have to work with in real life? Here are some attempts at an answer.

a. In the same way that no management training scheme can actually be there in the office with you when the crisis erupts, neither can any book reach out and provide formula solutions that will guarantee *you* favourable outcomes in your unique decision situations. Really the answer to the question, 'What do I do when . . . ?' is simply: 'Make the best decision possible.' What your best decision is will be unique to you and the situation you find yourself in, no matter how many techniques you have at your disposal.

b. Most important, if you have read the book with reasonable care *and* attempted at least some of the 'B' questions in the Work Sections, your sensitivity to the nature of how people decide things will have been considerably improved. The net result of this is that a large number of questions that you previously had will *no longer exist* since they have become absorbed into your new level of common sense in the area of decision making.

c. As with any activity, being well limbered up in the constituent skills that make for a good decision maker is going to improve your performance.

During the time you have been involved with this book, or with the course of which it may be a part, you may have found yourself beginning to watch people or read newspaper accounts more from the decision maker's standpoint. If you *have* begun to wonder on these lines then we have achieved something.

Glossary

ACAS: The Arbitration, Conciliation and Advisory Service. A statutory body run independently of Government, set up in 1975 to assist all parties in industry to reach individual or collective agreements. It may also be requested by Government to carry out investigations into industrial relations affairs.

Affiliation: A major personal need to be with other people.

Algorithm: In problem solving, a rule which if followed guarantees a successful outcome.

Arbitration: A decision reached by an outside party to a dispute over how the argument should be settled. May be voluntary or compulsory, i.e. legally binding.

Arousal Level: Level of activity of the nervous system which defines whether the person is alert or drowsy, and therefore his level of efficiency.

Asch Effect: The tendency for individuals in a small group to be swayed by the opinion of the majority.

Attitude: The disposition to behave in a way compatible with one's central beliefs and values.

Bargaining:
  – *National Advisory Level:* The discussion between TUC and CBI as well as perhaps government representatives to gain a gentlemen's agreement usually on broad economic issues.
  – *National Participative Level:* The top level of actual bargaining about practical issues between unions and the employers. Agreements in principle or to a minimum figure are often made. These can then be filled out at a local level.

Biases: Tendencies to emphasise certain aspects of information and de-emphasise others, leading to distortion.

Centralisation: In a dispersed organisation, the holding by the centre (HQ) of the key decisions and central responsibilities.

Closed Shop: The situation where all employees of a particular job function must be members of the established union if they are to work in that firm.

Collective Bargaining: Open-ended ('free') negotiation between disputing parties (usually labour and management) in settlement of differences (e.g. on pay claims, holiday provision).

Communication Nets: Pattern and direction of information flow among people in an organisation, especially as modelled by Alex Bavelas.

Conciliation: Bringing opponents in a dispute to a settlement which they both work out and accept, helped by a conciliator. *See* ACAS.

Confederation of British Industry (CBI): The employers' counterpart to the Trades Union Council representing the general management interests of firms (typically in discussion with Unions and Government departments).

Convenor: The senior shop steward in an organisation elected by his fellows to negotiate with management on their behalf. An employee of the firm rather than of the union. May speak on behalf of more than one union.

Decentralisation:

– *Federal:* Granting individual divisions or member firms within an organisation responsibility for a complete, or near complete, range of organisational functions (product development, production, budgeting, marketing and so on).

– *Functional:* Assigning responsibility for one function of a firm's operation to one division.

Decision Rules: The principles which guide the individual in choosing one course of action or another.

Decision Style: The way in which a person reaches decisions, e.g. by imposition of his own ideas or by consultation with subordinates. *See* Leadership.

Defence Mechanisms: Psychological 'self-protection' methods routinely brought into play when our prestige is threatened, or we are frustrated or cannot cope with basic demands of everyday life.

Delegation: Assigning initial responsibility for defined decisions (and therefore a degree of control) to subordinates.

Delphi Technique: An averaging method of decision making for reaching group consensus at a distance when members cannot physically meet.

Digit Span: Typical item in an intelligence test in which tester reads out a digit series of increasing length which the testee has to repeat back.

Economic Man: The ideal, completely informed and completely rational man who, it follows, will always make a riskless choice.

Equity Model: The notion that both employer and employee bring a contribution into the workplace, which both must perceive as equal, otherwise inequity and resultant corrective action must ensue.

Gambler's Fallacy: The decision rule that one ought to go for a particular choice because 'it's bound to be the right one this time' without assessing true probabilities.

Group:

– *Primary:* Any group of people small enough to allow regular, frequent and informal contact between members.

– *Secondary:* Larger group where person to person contact is rarer and also more formal when it does occur.

Groupthink: The insidious process identified by Janis by which individual members of a problem-solving group lull each other into in fact dubious courses of action.

Hawthorne Effect: After a famous study by Elton Mayo at the Hawthorne works of the General Electric Company showing that workers' motivation levels and not the changing physical environment was the best explanation for changes in production levels.

Heuristics: General guidelines by which problems can be solved, but without guarantee of success (cf. algorithms).

High Achievers: People who are very highly motivated to do well in life, especially in their careers.

Interpersonal Variables: Factors such as like/dislike; dominance/deference; which determine how effectively two people interact with each other.

Job Enrichment: Reducing the repetitive, tedious aspects of a job by increasing its size and scope (e.g. increasing responsibility for input methods and final quality).

Leadership:

– *Autocratic:* When the appointed leader takes decisions concerning the group without consultation with other members.

– *Democratic:* When the leader consults to varying degrees before deciding.

– *Laissez-faire:* When the leader for practical purposes opts out, whereupon group decision-making efficiency is seriously impaired.

Levels of Hierarchy: The number of steps in an organisation's management structure between shopfloor and boardroom.

Line: Those employees involved in the main activity of an organisation (e.g. the actual production or marketing).

Linear Networks: One form of communication net in which information has to be passed rigidly along a chain or line of personnel without direct communication between non-adjacent members in the line.

Maintenance Factors: Herzberg's characterisation of those factors which define the acceptability, to workers, of the work situation (e.g. security, pay and benefits, working conditions, social aspects, information and status); the absence of these are the main causes of job *dis*satisfaction, but when in good order allow *motivational factors* such as responsibility, approval, personal achievement and personal growth to operate.

Management by Objectives: Consultative setting of agreed, realistic targets for profit centres and for individuals so as to give coherence and direction to the whole enterprise.

Minimax: The decision rule which says always take the course of action which minimises your maximum losses.

Model: Representation of a decision situation, e.g. through computer simulation or perhaps testing a prototype, so as to bring out unanticipated factors which if ignored would have made the decision a poorer one.

– *Normative:* A set of rules for ideal (theoretical) decision making.

– *Descriptive:* A set of rules for decision making of the less than ideal kind that occurs in practice.

Non-verbal Communication: Conveying information through facial expression, voice, stance, etc. so as to reinforce or modify the verbal message itself.

Norms: The codes of practice that evolve in any group over a period of time concerning leadership, consensus, deference, what is permissible, and the like.

Overload: The condition in which the human processor has more information than he can process at one time, so giving rise to stress and suboptimal decisions.

Participation: Explicit involvement of those affected by decision consequences in developing the actual decision.

Perception: The taking in of information at the initial stage of the processing sequence.

Personality Factors: The components of a person's personality (i.e. temperament and character) which are the basis of differences among people.

Piece Work: Payment by each 'piece' or 'unit' of work produced.

Profit Centre: Any accountable person or group of persons constituting a functional group for which profit/loss may be ascertained within an organisation.

Projective Test: A set of ambiguous pictures or incomplete statements which allow the testee to 'project' his own needs into the interpretations given.

Random Sequence: A sequence in which all elements of a set have an equal chance of occurring on each occasion, e.g. for a fair coin, a head or tail will have an equal chance on each coin toss regardless of what has happened on previous tosses.

Rationality:

– *Objective:* Having decision criteria which reflect the true risks as they exist in the environment.

– *Subjective:* Having decision criteria which may be erratic to the observer and at odds with reality but which makes sense to the person concerned.

Risky Shift: The general finding that when groups take decisions they follow options offering smaller guarantees of success than do the same individuals deciding separately, i.e. groups show a 'shift' to risky decision-making relative to individual members.

Role: The part one is required to play in fulfilling some social function, e.g. the same person may be a father, teacher, a violinist, but each 'role' requires somewhat different behaviour.

Satisficing: The notion put forward by H. Simon that people do not try all the time to maximise utility so much as make a choice which is 'satisfactory' on the various criteria they may be employing.

Self Fulfilment: The need of the individual to achieve, express himself and become the kind of person he aspires to be.

Shareholder: The owner of 'shares' in a company which normally give rights to a proportion of any profits either as dividends or through adding to a company's reserves or net value.

Shop Steward: A trade union member, elected by fellow union workers to represent them in the workplace. The position is unpaid and is not within the formal structures of the unions. Employed by the company *not* the union.

Span of Control: The number of subordinates directly controlled by a given person in the management hierarchy.

Stressors: Any influence, either external (such as noise or heat) or internal (such as anxiety) which reduces the efficiency of information processing.

Trades Union Congress (TUC): The central organisation to which most unions belong. Like the CBI it is a pressure group and advisory body.

Transmission Loss: Information lost as the communication is passed from sender to receiver.

Uncertainty: The state that exists when one has incomplete, or indeed, no, information about outcomes that might result from particular decisions.

Unplanned Change: The unexpected, unanticipated, incidental, changes in the decision environment which often occur following a decision.

Utility: The subjective usefulness or value to the decision maker of a particular outcome: it is implied that different outcomes will have different utility values for different people depending on various aspects of their psychological make-up (individual constraints).

Wechsler Adult Intelligence Scale (WAIS): A well-regarded instrument for measuring adult abilities or intelligence.

Works' Council: A body set up in the workplace with members drawn from different sections. Their job is to consider issues that affect any parties in the workplace.

Index